# Marital Communication

Key Themes in Family Communication

Douglas L. Kelley, *Marital Communication*

Thomas J. Socha and Julie Yingling, *Families Communicating with Children*

# Marital Communication

*Douglas L. Kelley*

polity

First published in 2012 by Polity Press

Polity Press
65 Bridge Street
Cambridge CB2 1UR, UK

Polity Press
350 Main Street
Malden, MA 02148, USA

ISBN-13: 978-0-7456-4789-0
ISBN-13: 978-0-7456-4790-6(pb)

A catalogue record for this book is available from the British Library.

Typeset in 11 on 13 pt Sabon
by Servis Filmsetting Ltd, Stockport, Cheshire
Printed and bound in Great Britain by the MPG Books Group

The publisher has used its best endeavours to ensure that the URLs for external websites referred to in this book are correct and active at the time of going to press. However, the publisher has no responsibility for the websites and can make no guarantee that a site will remain live or that the content is or will remain appropriate.

Every effort has been made to trace all copyright holders, but if any have been inadvertently overlooked the publisher will be pleased to include any necessary credits in any subsequent reprint or edition.

For further information on Polity, visit our website: www.politybooks.com

# Contents

Preface                                                                                          vii

1   The Uniqueness of Marital Communication: Context,
    Mindlessness, Arousal                                                          1

2   Living and Working Together: Effective Daily
    Interaction                                                                         26

3   Closeness: Achieving Intimacy and Love in Marriage        60

4   Close Conflict                                                                    93

5   Couple Communication across the Life Cycle               128

6   Destructive and Restorative Marital Processes            161

References                                                                            198
Author index                                                                         231
Subject index                                                                        235

# Preface

*Marital Communication* is a labor of love. As you will find in Chapter 3, that means this book is the result of great commitment and emotional connection. But marital communication between couples is also a labor of love. Couples who marry typically begin with high hopes that the relationship will stay happy, close, and committed for the long term. Soon they find that daily communication, maintaining love and intimacy, and managing conflict become life-long negotiations. Some experience the dark side of marriage and, possibly, experience forgiveness and reconciliation. These experiences serve as the framework for *Marital Communication*.

*Marital Communication* synthesizes a large, interdisciplinary body of research that specifically focuses on communication in marriage. Some of the insights presented reflect my own research with married couples. Some come from my own counseling-related studies. The result is a book with a solid research foundation, presented in a manner to help researchers, practitioners, and couples think about "real" relationships.

It is important to note that while this book has focused on *heterosexual marital communication*, the principles offered may apply to a variety of relationship types. As noted in Chapter 1, I have tried to focus my review and thinking on long-term, publicly committed, romantic partners. Individuals interested in relationships that fit these criteria will find use in this book.

I want to thank several people for their extensive help with this project. Students of mine, Katie Chase, Carmen Goman, and Matt Nolan, helped research specific topics and gave editing advice. Thanks to the reviewers who provided early comments on chapters. In addition, the entire staff at Polity has been wonderful to work with. Specific thanks to Andrea, who was constantly positive and encouraging as she received frantic emails from me regarding various writing contingencies. I hope we can work together again.

Special thanks to Vince Waldron for a decade of research together. In the book, when you read, "My research . . .," this often references work that Vince and I have done together. I am a better scholar than I might be because of Vince.

Finally, there is no way to fully thank my wife, Ann, for her constant support. It is a testimony to our love for one another, and the strength of our marriage, that she could be completely honest with me as she edited early drafts of each chapter. Thanks for walking with me on this journey.

Doug
Phoenix, AZ
May 2011

# 1

## The Uniqueness of Marital Communication

### Context, Mindlessness, Arousal

*I think one of the big benefits is the joy of a special person who walks hand in hand with me and shares a lifetime of experiences. Someone that I know I can rely upon and trust. It's the joy of a shared life together and knowing that I'll be there for Diane and she will be there for me.*

Jeremy, married to Diane for 45 years

Clearly, marriage is a significant relationship type in Western culture. As Jeremy describes, when characterized by constructive behaviors, marriage has numerous positive outcomes – someone to walk with, to touch, to rely on, to trust. On the other hand, when marriage fails, the consequences are potentially serious (Gottman, 1994). Most of you reading this book have been in a serious romantic relationship, are in a serious romantic relationship, or will be at some time in your life. Serious dating partners must choose to continue or terminate their relationship. The choice to continue the relationship generally results in the decision to maintain the status quo, move in together, or eventually marry. Even those who choose to live together with a romantic partner may view cohabitation as a step toward marriage and will eventually marry.

Historically, virtually all societies have had some form of marriage. Currently, most Western societies are experiencing evolving perspectives toward marriage and much debate regarding the constitution of marriage (e.g., legal partnerships, civil unions, same-sex marriage, and covenant marriage). Understanding the nature of marriage is further muddied in that many "non-marriage" relationships that exist today may be considered *marriage-type* relationships; and, ironically, some of the legal marriages that exist today have little to do with how marriage is often viewed in modern, Western culture.

As such, I begin this chapter by identifying relational and social contexts of the marriage relationship, specifically as these contexts affect marital communication. Next, I look at the psychological and physical effects of these contexts on married partners. Finally, I examine two cognitive and physiological processes that, because of marriage's unique relational characteristics, affect

## Box 1.1: Changing Ideas of Marriage

Kristin and Rob were engaged in the spring and planning their wedding for the fall. Part of the wedding discussion turned to whether or not they would sign a marriage license, making the union "legal" in the state of Arizona. As Christians, they both wanted to be married before God, but, disillusioned with the current divorce rate and certain marriages they had witnessed, they wanted the longevity of their marriage to be based on a daily choice to say "I love you," rather than a legal bond. Certain family members were uncomfortable with omitting this legal step, but the question was resolved when Kristin's mom, Hope, began losing her battle with cancer well before the planned wedding date. As Hope was beginning to rapidly decline, Rob's mom, an ordained minister, asked if the couple were ready to marry. Kristin and Rob nodded, "Yes!" and they were married within the hour at Hope's bedside, creating one of the last memories Hope would take with her as she passed from this life. Later that night, Kristin and Rob, who had not lived together before, went back to Rob's place, now their "own home," married in the eyes of God, but without marriage documents from the state.

marital communication and couples' ability to make productive change in their communication. Without an understanding of these key elements, the rest of the book is interesting "food for thought," but lacks practicality in creating healthy marital relationships.

## Contexts and Effects

All communication takes place within a context. Two types of context play a significant role in shaping marital interaction. First, the couples' relationship itself forms a unique context for communication. Second, the broader social context (e.g., parents/in-laws and children) influences the *how* and *what* of couples' interaction. These unique relational contexts create a setting for the marital relationship that results in significant psychological and physical effects.

### Marriage as a Unique Relational Context

As a researcher of interpersonal communication processes, I am primarily interested in the relational dynamics of marriage. Within this context I choose to define marriage as *a relationship between long-term, publicly committed, romantic, partners*. Each of these characteristics makes marriage a unique relational context. Let's look at each of these *four marriage characteristics* in turn.

### Long-Term

Perhaps most representative of the long-term aspect of marital relationships is the phrase commonly heard in marriage vows: *'til death do us part*. This element of the marriage relationship creates a unique context for communication, because individuals respond differently in long-term relationships, or relationships that are intended to be long term, than in short-term encounters. For example, research on beginning romantic relationships shows that they are characterized by a variety of positive (e.g., warmth, anticipation, joy) and negative (e.g., anxiety, fear, envy) emotions.

Other studies show that deception detection may be more difficult for those in long-term relationships (Knapp, 2006). Most specifically, long-term relationships are unique in their development of expectations, interaction history, and relational culture.

*Expectations.* Communication in long-term relationships is unique in that relationship partners form expectations for future interaction. My own research has demonstrated that married couples' perceptions as to whether their relational expectations (e.g., intimacy and dominance) are fulfilled are strongly related to marital satisfaction (D. L. Kelley & Burgoon, 1991). Other research on role expectations (Jacob, Kornblith, Anderson, & Hartz, 1978), attributions and efficacy expectations (Fincham, Harold, & Gano-Philips, 2000), and standards (Wunderer & Schneewind, 2008) has demonstrated similar findings.

Weddings provide a clear example of expectations couples have for creating a positive, long-lasting relationship. Wedding vows commonly include statements of long-term commitment to one another ("'til death do us part"), through good times and bad (e.g., "in sickness and in health"). Marriage rituals, such as a ring exchange, symbolize the expectation of never-ending love (Chesser, 1980).

Expecting a relationship to be long term influences communication choices. Whereas in short-term relationships individuals can engage in strategies that achieve short-term goals with little regard for long-term relational consequences, long-term partners must consider the potential impact of their behavior on the partner and relationship over time. For example, studies indicate that individuals hold expectations for how long-term relationships should develop (Honeycutt, Cantrill, Kelly, & Lambkin, 1998). S. A. Lewis, Langan, and Hollander (1972) found that subjects were more likely to conform when making decisions if they believed there was the possibility of future interaction. Stamp's (1999) interpersonal communication model acknowledges that individuals in long-term relationships alter their patterns of communication (e.g., for example, emotional expression) (Aune, Buller, & Aune, 1996). The emphasis here is that when individuals anticipate a long-term relationship, communication is modified to facilitate positive interaction and achieve interpersonal goals over the expected span of the relationship.

*Interaction history.* The flip side of managing behavior to ensure positive future interaction is recognizing that interaction history affects present communication. In other words, a husband and wife's interaction when they come home after work is influenced, in part, by how they communicated in the morning before they went to work as well as the longer history of their interactions together. This historical influence is one of the elements that makes it difficult to understand how married partners assign meaning to particular behaviors in specific interactions. For example, a simple question, "Is dinner ready yet?" may provoke a negative response that is understandable only within the context of the relationship history. To address these issues, marriage researchers may use an insider objective perspective to conduct their research (Fitzpatrick, 1988; see Box 1.2). An example of this approach to research is to have couples view a video recording of their own interactions. Watching this recording gives couples a more objective understanding of their behavior rather than relying solely on memory of what they *think* happened. On the other hand, it gives the researcher the couple's own perspective on what was happening during an actual interaction – something that researchers are seldom privy to.

Interaction history creates patterns of communication behaviors – habits, if you will. These "habits" may work to couples' advantage or disadvantage as they develop constructive and destructive communication patterns. (I discuss this perspective further in the section on mindful and mindless communication.)

*Relational culture.* Related to interaction history is the development of subculture unique to each individual marriage relationship. Braithwaite and Baxter (1995), in their study of wedding vow renewal, argue that marriage vows serve to celebrate marriage as a "uniquely constructed culture of two" (p. 193). Functioning at their best, the patterns of behavior created by this

# Box 1.2: Approaches to Marital Communication Research

Marital communication is studied using four basic research approaches (Fitzpatrick, 1988): insider subjective, insider objective, outsider subjective, and outsider objective.

Insider approaches are based on couples' own perspectives. The *insider subjective* approach is used by many universities to conduct course evaluations each semester and is most familiar to students. Participants/students are asked to reflect on their experience and answer open-ended questions or rate their experience on scales (e.g., strongly disagree = 1, neutral = 3, strongly agree = 5).

The second approach is *insider objective*. As discussed in the text, this approach gives researchers the couples' perspective (insider), but is somewhat more objective because couples are responding to a video or audio recording of their own behavior, rather than responding based on memory.

Outsider approaches don't consider the couple's perspective, but rely on outside observers. *Outsider subjective* approaches provide insights from outside sources such as counselors engaged in marital therapy. This approach is considered subjective because, typically, insights are not gained using a structured, reproducible system of observation.

*Outsider objective* approaches are characterized by judgments made by trained researchers observing couple behavior. For example, researchers may record physiological measures during couples' conflict or may train coders to identify nonverbal behaviors while viewing video recordings of couple interaction.

Because of the difficulty of observing naturally occurring marital interaction, researchers use multiple approaches to give a more complete understanding of couple communication.

couple culture provide for predictability and efficiency of interaction between the married partners. Functioning at their worst, these same patterns lead couples mindlessly into a web of conflict before they are fully aware of the potential negative effects on their interaction.

Relational culture also provides a means of interpreting and creating meaning within the relationship. Leeds-Hurwitz (2002), in her study of intercultural weddings, tells us that, "Each choice [in designing the wedding] makes the ideas and assumptions, thus the identities claimed by the new couple, evident to all who attend" (p. 28). Further, she states:

> Weddings can appropriately be described as *performance narratives*, because each bride and groom is given an opportunity to create, and then display (perform) in public, their own story (narrative) of identity: Who they have come from, who they are now, and who they wish to be in the future. Like other types of stories people tell, weddings not only say what the tellers wish to be true, the telling itself actually makes the statements true, for it is through the display of identity that it becomes real. . . . (p. 129)

## Publicly Committed

Marriage relationships are unique because of the partners' public commitment to one another. Traditionally this commitment takes place during a formal marriage ceremony. The structure and composition of the wedding create a public sense of community, identity, and meaning (Leeds-Hurwitz, 2002). The ceremony may be short or long, include readings of poetry or sacred texts, and may feature special music. Ritual behaviors often associated with the wedding ceremony include setting the date, ring exchange, the kiss, lighting candles, use of flowers, and wearing a wedding gown (Chesser, 1980).

Public commitment is also demonstrated in that wedding licenses in the United States, to be legal, are to be signed by the two individuals getting married, the officiate, and one or two witnesses. Having someone witness the commitment between the two marriage partners is intended, in part, to validate the commitment and, thus, stabilize the relationship. The potential effect of public commitment has been one of the elements argued in favor of gay marriage (Shipman & Smart, 2007).

Other possible benefits of public commitment include a greater sense of security, greater follow-through on one's commitment, and community investment in the relationship.

## Romantic

Marriage in contemporary Western culture is typically considered a romantic relationship. All of us know marriages where we think the romance has died (and, for some of us, we are certain our parents were never romantic in any way!), but in modern Western cultures marriage relationships typically evolve out of romantic dating relationships. Exceptions to this may include individuals who marry due to health or financial concerns or for immigration-related reasons. Even in cultures that have arranged marriage, the marriage relationship is one where certain aspects of a romantic relationship are expected to evolve, such as having sex or developing a common bond (Xiaohe & Whyte, 1990).

By *romantic* I am referring to aspects of a relationship related to sex or behaviors associated with potential movement toward a sexual relationship. For example, a kiss can be considered a romantic or non-romantic behavior. When Aunt Alice kisses you, it is not a romantic behavior. There is no possibility of eventual sexual interaction. However, when you kiss a romantic partner, the potential for the behavior to be sexually arousing is present. Even if you believe in waiting until marriage to have sex, kissing in the dating relationship is a behavior that is likely part of your sexual trajectory.

Understanding marriage as romantic affects interpersonal interaction in terms of expectations and behaviors. Psychologists report sexual problems as some of the most common complaints couples have (Notarius & Markman, 1993). Specific problems may include performance issues, frequency, and inability to communicate about sex.

These findings are important to communication scholars, who tend to view sex as a communication act. Expectations regarding sex and actual sexual behavior are typically related to intimacy development and maintenance within the relationship. This sets romantic relationships apart from other close committed relationships, such as "best friends."

## Partners

Understanding married individuals as married *partners* emphasizes the interdependence of the couple. Married partners share common goals. Working together to achieve these goals makes marriage a unique personal relationship. More than most other personal relationships, marriage partners negotiate and pursue both instrumental goals, such as maintaining a mortgage and raising children, and relational goals, such as the need for intimacy and personal affirmation.

The term "partner" also presumes notions of equality. If you are under the age of 40 and were raised in the United States, you most likely expect your marriage partner to be a close, if not best, friend. Close friendships are based on notions of equality. In short, understanding marriage as a relationship between partners emphasizes goal orientation and equality, both of which affect *how* married couples interact with one another and *what* they interact about.

## The Social Context of Marital Interaction

All relationships exist within a social context, although researchers often neglect this aspect of couple life in favor of measuring individual and relational attributes (Schmeekle & Sprecher, 2004). Social context is especially important to marriage relationships. To return to our wedding example, couples who have a public wedding are making a commitment to one another within a specific social context. Typically this gathering includes family and friends, some of whom gain a new normative role status within the newly constituted marriage relationship. For example, parents, after the reciprocated *I dos*, become in-laws. If one or both partners bring children into the marriage union, parents also become grandparents, the children become stepchildren or stepsisters or stepbrothers. Additionally, friendship networks may merge, if they haven't already, or may change entirely as the couple begins to spend more time with other married couples.

Children, whether a result of the current marriage union or brought into the marriage by one or both partners, create a new social context within which the married partners must learn to communicate. It is generally accepted that, when children are in the home, it is a stressful time for the marriage (Gottman & Notarius, 2002). The additional stress, as well as the physical presence of children in the home, may affect the style of the couples' communication as well as their communication content. In terms of style, once couples have children, they may alter how they have conflict with one another or how freely they express intimacy. For instance, mere fatigue may lead to more arguments and less spontaneous intimate interaction. In addition, the birth of the first child cuts "couple time" in half (Huston & Holmes, 2004), and if there is difficulty with the child early on, couples either rally with collaborative partnership or the problems drive a wedge between the marital partners (McHale, Kavanaugh, & Berkman, 2003). These elements often make blending families difficult: for example, there is no childless married time for the new couple to establish basic patterns of communication. Braithwaite, McBride, and Schrodt (2003) found that couple interactions in stepfamilies are characteristically short, focused on the children, and most often via telephone.

Regarding communication content, parenting is often listed as one of the top issues over which couples have conflict. My interviews with married couples (see Waldron & Kelley, 2008) revealed differing parenting styles to be a common source of conflict. Additionally, the advent of the first child often brings with it a shift to more traditional division of labor, in spite of the fact that many expectant mothers expect household roles to be more egalitarian (Segrin & Flora, 2005).

In a review of literature examining social network influences on primary partnerships (e.g., marriage), Schmeeckle and Sprecher (2004) observe that network density (e.g., close-knit networks), network overlap, size of network, involvement with network, and network reactions all impact one's relationship. For example, involvement with extended family is related to levels of relationship satisfaction and stability. The presence of in-laws creates new opportunities for support and stress (McGoldrick, Heiman, & Carter, 1993). Couples who have positive relationships with their parents may experience psychological, emotional, and financial support, as well as practical help. However, perceived obligations to parents/in-laws, such as time spent together, amount and quality of information shared, and social expectations (e.g., holiday celebrations), create unique possibilities for conflict between married partners. Additionally, couples who are financially dependent on one or both sets of parents may experience stress, particularly when one considers that financial stress is listed in the top three issues with which couples have conflict (Notarius & Markman, 1993). Relationships with other family members (e.g., siblings and grandparents) and friends may produce similar opportunities for support or stress (Schmeeckle & Sprecher, 2004).

## Psychological and Physical Effects of Marriage

It has been well documented that *healthy* marriage relationships produce positive psychological and physiological benefits (Horwitz, White, & Howell-White, 1996; Kiecolt-Glaser & Newton, 2001, Waite & Gallagher, 2000). In general, these effects apply regardless of age, number of years married, or gender. Studies show that never-married persons report a higher prevalence of nonfatal diseases than do married persons (Pienta, Hayward, & Jenkins, 2000); young adults who get and stay married report higher levels of well-being than those who remain single (Horwitz, White, & Howell-White, 1996); mid-life couples who are not married rate themselves lower in health and higher in depressive symptoms than those who are married (McIlvane, Ajrouch, & Antonucci, 2007); and married couples moving toward retirement experience advantages compared to their non-married counterparts in terms of chronic diseases, impairment, functional problems, and disability (Pienta et al., 2000). While marriage clearly benefits partners' health, it is possible that these benefits are limited over time. Pienta et al. (2000) found that, when comparing individuals married various lengths of time, health benefits were most pronounced for partners married 20–29 years.

## Gender

Certain marriage benefits differ for husbands and wives: however, both experience marriage gains (Pienta et al., 2000; Umberson, Williams, Powers, Liu, & Needham, 2006). Studies have found that men who marry report less depression than those who do not and women who marry report fewer alcohol problems (Horwitz et al., 1996). While certain studies have found that men receive more social, emotional, and physical benefits from marriage (T. B. Anderson & McCulloch, 1993; Antonucci & Akiyama, 1987), others have argued that this effect is more a result of women's extensive social support networks, rather than actual marriage benefits (Pienta et al., 2000). Consistent with this thinking, for men in better-adjusted marriages, frequent spousal-only interaction is associated with less heart disease, while women's experience of less heart disease is more associated with total social interactions (interactions that include spouse and non-spouse) (Janicki, Kamarck, Shiffman, Sutton-Tyrrell, & Gwaltney, 2005). Similarly, Clements, Cordova, Markman, and Laurenceau (1997) found husbands' marital satisfaction to be primarily associated with happiness in marriage (e.g., no regrets, agreement on affection and sex), while wives' satisfaction was based on this "happiness" dimension, but also included happiness with how they interacted with other people (e.g., agreement as to proper behavior, in-law issues, friends).

Gender effects are also influenced by quality of marriage and divorce. While men's health seems to benefit from being married, women's health appears to be more related to the quality of the marriage. Women suffer most when the quality of the marriage is low (Janicki et al., 2005), but both men's and women's health decline with marital strain (Umberson et al., 2006). Other research indicates that marriage results in health benefits (lower levels of biological, lifestyle, and psychosocial risk factors) for women, but only when satisfaction is high (Gallo, Troxel, Matthews, & Kuller, 2003).

### Explanatory Frameworks

Possible reasons for the positive effects of marriage can be understood in two broad categories: selection and protection (Pienta et al., 2000). *Selection* suggests that men and women select mates who are psychologically and physically well. From this perspective, the marriage health effects are largely a result of marriages consisting of healthy individuals. *Protection* refers to the marriage relationship serving to set appropriate boundaries for potential high-risk behavior (Sherbourne & Hays, 1990), and provide positive elements that protect against negative effects (e.g., depression). Positive elements include such things as increased financial security and conjugal support (Ducharme, 1994). Social support may include health-related social control (communication that involves influence, regulation, and constraint of health-oriented behavior), which has been related to partners' health-enhancing behavioral responses (M. A. Lewis & Butterfield, 2007).

It is important to realize that positive elements may change over time as needs and challenges in the relationship change. For example, in their seven-year study of newly married couples, Horwitz et al. (1996) found that high marital quality was related to better mental health, while there was no effect for length of marriage, social support, economic well-being, and the presence of children. What seems certain is that, regardless of age and length of marriage, quality of the marriage relationship is key to positive psychological and physical health benefits.

# Cognitive and Physiological Processes That Make Marital Interaction Unique

A common tendency when studying marital communication is to focus solely on behaviors exhibited by marital couples, with little attention to how context influences those behaviors. We have just discussed elements of relational and social contexts, along with their resulting physical effects. I finish this chapter by introducing you to two processes, one cognitive and one physiological, that contribute to making marital communication unique. Both processes – mindlessness and arousal – are present to some degree in all social interaction. However, these phenomena play a unique and particularly important role in long-term, marital relationships.

## Mindful and Mindless Communication

Most people believe their lives are lived mindfully. They believe they are conscious of and purposeful in the actions they take each day (e.g., eating breakfast, driving to work, talking to their children). However, it may be more accurate that most of our human behavior is mindless (Langer, 1978, 1989). Motley (1992) addresses this issue regarding communication behavior, "In the interest of cognitive efficiency (though perhaps not necessarily in the interest of communication quality), most encoding decisions are made nonconsciously and automatically . . . except when unusual circumstances serve to make one or more of the decisions conscious" (p. 306). Mindless behavior plays a particularly important role in long-term relationships – like marriage – that are prone to develop patterns of behavior over time. Understanding the nature of mindlessness is particularly important to creating more mindful marital communication and changing unwanted communication patterns into effective, positive communication.

### The Nature of Mindful and Mindless Communication

Scholars have debated the exact nature of mindful and mindless communication (Burgoon & Langer, 1995). While there are possible conscious states that exist between mindless and mindful extremes, for the purpose of the current discussion (to better understand marital communication), I have chosen to classify our cognitive states, and resulting behaviors, as either mindful or mindless.

Langer (1989) understands the key qualities of mindful awareness as: creation of new categories, openness to new information, and awareness of more than one perspective. In essence, mindfulness is attention and response to one's environment based on *current* incoming information. As such, it involves active, fluid information-processing, the adaptation to context and multiple perspectives, and the ability to draw novel distinctions (Burgoon, Berger, & Waldron, 2000). Mindfulness is what most would commonly refer to as "thinking." When mindful, there is a certain degree of awareness of one's thought processes as one encounters the world and makes conscious choices to respond to the world.

Scholars long thought that this mindful model of the "thoughtful person" (Folkes, 1985) was the predominant way human beings operated in their environment. However, Langer and others have challenged this notion and argued that most human behavior is actually mindless: "Much of what we know and most of what we do – language, socialization, perception – happens unconsciously" (Kellermann, 1992, p. 293). Specific to communication, researchers have recognized that there is a "remarkable capacity for humans to disassociate thought and talk" (Burgoon et al., 2000, p. 105).

Mindlessness, in contrast to mindfulness, is based on past rather than present information (Burpee & Langer, 2005). Mindlessness is unconscious, automated behavior patterns often learned tacitly from past experience (Kellermann, 1992). Individuals develop patterns of behavior in response to their environment. These behavior patterns often *appear* mindful (Langer, Blank, & Chanowitz, 1978). Yet, mindless behavior is overlearned, stereotyped, automatic behavior (Bavelas & Coates, 1992) that can be performed without conscious thought; much like when you are listening to someone, nodding your head and looking straight at them, but are thinking about something else.

*Responsibility* If mindless behavior occurs without conscious choice, then are individuals free from responsibility for what they do mindlessly? I'm afraid not. To be free from responsibility, two conditions have to be present. First, it would have to be true that mindless behavior is without intent or purpose. Second, it would have to be equally true that mindless behaviors are uncontrollable.

Regarding mindlessness and intentionality, Kellermann (1992) argues that communication is mostly unconscious and automatic (mindless), yet very much intentional and strategic:

> Despite communicative choices being intentional (i.e., not involuntary or uncontrollable), they need not, indeed most often are not, consciously made. ... I reject wholeheartedly that purposeful behavior must occur within conscious awareness. ... I am arguing that strategic behavior in general, and communicative behavior specifically, must be uncoupled from assumptions of conscious acquisition and use. I am arguing that communication, as strategic behavior, occurs *primarily* automatically. (p. 293)

At first glance, the idea that behavior, and specifically communication behavior, can be unconscious yet intentional may seem paradoxical. Nonetheless, examples of unconscious-intentional behavior are more commonplace than might be expected. Two common examples of intentional mindless behavior are driving a standard transmission car or the typing that I am doing now as I am writing. Did I think about writing w-r-i-t-i-n-g?[1] No. Did I intend to write w-r-i-t-i-n-g? Yes. Driving to work today, did I think about shifting into third gear? No. Did I intend to shift into third gear? Yes.

Now let's expand the example and make it more communicative. When a young man first kisses his girlfriend, does he think about it? Yes! Is it intentional? Yes! But, after five years of marriage, when he rolls over before going to sleep and kisses her goodnight as his wife, does he think about it? Perhaps not. It is performed automatically. (In fact, it may have become so habitual that it is often difficult to remember if the behavior was performed – "Did I already kiss you goodnight?") But, does he intend it? Absolutely (or so we hope).

Uncontrollability, the second necessary condition to be released from responsibility for our communication, also is not present. Mindless communication behavior, though automatic and unconscious, is controllable because it can be brought into conscious

---

[1] I am using the word *thinking*, here, in the common way most of us experience it – thinking as being mindful – as opposed to thinking as cognitive processing.

awareness. For example, tone of voice is a communication channel that married partners use without much thought, unless one's partner is offended by a particular tone. Armed with the knowledge that one's spouse objects to a tone of voice, an individual can bring the questionable tone into conscious focus, and choose to work toward change. This represents a key difference between mindless behavior and subconscious behavior (or unconscious processes; Langer, 1989). We have direct, conscious access to our mindless behavior – once made aware of it. The subconscious is only accessible through dreams, therapy, hypnosis, and the like.

In sum, because mindless behavior can be understood to be intentional and changeable, married partners are responsible for their mindless actions. However, as I discuss later, *it takes mindful choices to change resistant mindless patterns.*

### Potential Benefits of Mindlessness

Language used to describe mindlessness can give the impression that it is a negative phenomenon. For example, in the following statement by Burpee and Langer (2005), "[mindlessness] results in insensitivity to context and perspective" (p. 43), insensitivity could be misconstrued to mean that mindlessness is negative (insensitive) and has no place in marital interactions. However, the reality is that a major portion of our behavior is mindless – we are mindless beings. And, it is mindlessness that allows us to be mindful about the elements in any given situation on which we want to focus (Kellermann, 1992). Let me illustrate, first, with a non-communicative example.

Dad is dishing up dinner. His two-year-old daughter wants to take her plate to the table "all by myself!" After failing to convince her otherwise, Dad lets his precocious two-year-old take on the daunting task. She carefully takes the plate of food and does extremely well headed to the table – until she has to step over the vacuum cleaner cord. As soon as her mental focus shifts to stepping over the cord, her plate tips and her food quickly slides to the carpet.

This scenario demonstrates the need for mindless behavior. The complex tasks of balancing a plate and walking over a cord are too much mindful activity for the young girl. However, thankfully, mindlessness allows more mature individuals to balance the plate, without "thinking," while shifting attention to stepping over the cord. In essence, certain aspects of any complex action, to be done well, must become mindless – that is, out of one's awareness – to be performed well.

For those who play sports, you know this only too well. As soon as you begin "thinking" about your golf swing, or your batting stance, or your free-throw shot, it is difficult to perform well. Each of these activities is too complex to keep all of their various components in one's consciousness. In fact, the words we use to describe athletes when they are performing well reflect our intuitive sense of mindlessness: "He's a machine," "She's unconscious," "He's in the zone." So, you can be mindful to keep your elbow up when you swing during batting practice, but once you're in the game, your batting needs to be mindless as your attention shifts to other aspects, such as watching the pitcher's delivery.

Each of the tasks described above is complex, but relatively simple when compared to language usage. Consider what speech would be like if you had to "think" about each of the various components of creating a sentence. For example, suppose you were able to be 100% mindful when asking your friend if she would like to go the store with you. Some of the things you would have to think about before you spoke would be: search your personal lexicon for the most effective words to use; filter those words for the ones that would make most sense to your friend whose first language is German; make certain that you have a subject and predicate in the sentence; make certain that adjectives come before the nouns they are modifying. Oh, and then you need to add in tone of voice, volume, inflection, and appropriate facial expressions. In other words, total mindfulness would paralyze us in our attempts to communicate with one another.

This simple example makes clear the need for the majority of our complex behavior to operate at a less than conscious level. *The key for positive marital communication is not to try to eliminate mindlessness from our experience, but rather to use mindfulness to establish positive mindless patterns of behavior.* Gottman (1994) suggests the need for overlearning so that positive marital interaction skills become less easily disrupted when the couple is highly aroused (see discussion below).

## Potential Costs of Mindlessness

I hope it is clear at this point that in a world of myriad stimuli and complex responses, mindlessness is necessary for efficient functioning. And, yet, this fantastic capacity has a number of potential downsides. To begin, mindless responses are often difficult to distinguish from mindful behavior (Burgoon & Langer, 1995). As such, married partners may misinterpret one another's mindless behavior. For example, Jan's mindless reaction to withdraw during conflict may be misinterpreted by Pat as disinterest.

Another potential downside to mindlessness is that mindless behaviors are resistant to change. The fact that individuals are typically unaware when learning a mindless behavior (Kellermann, 1992) makes the behavior difficult to alter. As I discuss below, this may be particularly true for married couples who build substantial patterns of behavior over time. In addition, some mindless behavior patterns are learned at such an early age of development that changing those behaviors is especially difficult. For example, human infants begin to learn vocalization patterns in the first year of life, well before they learn to use language (Burgoon, Buller, & Woodall, 1989).

Finally, highly negatively aroused (e.g., fear, anger) individuals often turn to what is known best – overlearned (mindless) patterns of behavior (Gottman, 1994). Thus, when individuals perceive a high threat level (e.g., negative conflict with one's spouse), the tendency is to rely on overlearned, mindless behavior. Instead of creative, *mindful* responses that provide the ability to adapt to new information, *mindless* responses often fall back on ineffective old habits.

## Mindlessness in Marriage

Marriage relationships are particularly vulnerable to negative mindless behaviors because of the amount of time spent together and the routine duties couples perform. Mindlessness leads to patterns of response based on past behavior, rather than current, active, information, and may result in "insensitivity to context and perspective" (Burpee & Langer, 2005, p. 43). In other words, rather than spouses responding to what a partner is actually saying during conversation, they may "unthinkingly" react with an automatic response. Research has consistently demonstrated that unhappy married couples exhibit rigid patterns of behavior, specifically regarding reciprocity of negativity (Gottman, 1994) and demand–withdraw patterns (Caughlin & Vangelisti, 2000; Heavey, Christensen, & Malamuth, 1995). This rigidity may largely be the result of mindless responses to behavior. For example, Gottman's (1994; 1999) work on couples' ability to be "flooded" by one's partner's negative affect suggests the occurrence of mindless patterned responses, such as limited ability to process information well and tendency to rely on past patterns of behavior. These elements reflect the forementioned insensitivity to context and perception. The importance of this is demonstrated as mindlessness, when compared to similarity (another important relationship variable), plays a much stronger role in predicting marital satisfaction (Burpee & Langer, 2005). These ideas will be developed more fully in Chapter 4, but clearly couples need to understand that negative mindless patterns will undercut their attempts to work toward positive change in their relationship.

Understanding mindlessness is also important to marriage because it can help married partners better learn how to avoid blaming behavior, and instead work toward a model of responsible communication. Blaming behavior, often associated with defensive patterns of communication, can be exchanged for collaborative strategies based on an understanding of how to change well-ingrained, overlearned, non-productive patterns (see Chapter 4).

Finally, understanding mindlessness can help couples understand why change is often hard or slow. For example, a husband who tends to take flight in the face of conflict may find it difficult to change a lifetime of "fleeing" behaviors; however, his wife may exhibit greater patience, as he tries to change, because of her understanding of mindless processes.

## Arousal and Mindlessness

Arousal is a physiological process that plays a significant role in making marriage communication unique. Arousal is a physiological state of activation; specifically, it is an alertness or orientation response (Burgoon, 1993; Burgoon, Kelley, Newton, & Keeley-Dyreson, 1989). It plays a central role in such psychological processes as the flight or fight response (Gottman, 1993), and has been identified as a key component of various interpersonal communication theories (e.g., Andersen, 1985; Burgoon, 1983, 1993; Cappella & Greene, 1982; M. L. Patterson, 1976, 1982).

Although the relationship between arousal and task performance is complex, in general, moderate to moderately high levels of arousal are associated with high levels of performance (Gottman, 1994; Yerkes & Dodson, 1908). For example, athletes who are "up" for the game are typically at this level of arousal. When at moderate to moderately high levels, arousal, as a focusing agent, helps individuals screen out extraneous stimuli and focus on what is most pertinent in a current situation. However, when arousal reaches high levels, the individual moves into "hyper-focus" (e.g., constricted focal attention/consciousness; Berscheid, 1983). At this point one is unable to perceive, adapt, and respond to the environment in optimal ways because one's focus has become too narrow for optimum processing. For example, an individual with high levels of public speaking anxiety experiences hyper-focus – that is, his conscious processing becomes primarily limited to his anxiety. As such, this state of restricted information processing often results in mindless behavior – that which is known and comfortable. Gottman (1994) comments on this process, specific to the marriage relationship: "This increased diffuse physiological arousal makes it unlikely that the couple will be able to process information very well, will have access to new learning, and more likely that they will rely on previously overlearned tactics . . ." (p. 412). Clearly, high levels of arousal work against productive communication when negative mindless patterns are engaged.

Besides Gottman's approach that helps us understand arousal

in couples' communication patterns, Interdependence Theory, as described by Fitzpatrick (1988), recognizes the role of arousal when couples experience unexpected change in expected sequences of behavior. Berscheid (1983) posits that couples' lives are intertwined into predictable patterns. When these patterns are disrupted, arousal is generated and labeled as either positive or negative. For example, couples often learn ways of telling stories together. After vacation, Susan and Brett build a pattern of telling their "vacation story." If, on occasion, Susan tells some of Brett's part, Brett is likely to experience increased *negative* arousal. On the other hand, if Brett is expecting to come home from work Friday night and watch videos and have pizza and, instead, Susan surprises him with two tickets to fly to San Diego, Brett is likely to experience increased *positive* arousal. As such, arousal has a significant impact as to how change is experienced and mindless or mindful behaviors are engaged.

## Choosing to Be Mindful

We've determined that mindlessness has both positive and negative consequences, and that negative consequences may be most pronounced during times of high arousal when one's ability to balance mindfulness and mindlessness is compromised. As such, married couples may seek to create a productive communication environment consisting of positive mindless patterns, moderate arousal levels, and increased mindfulnesss.

Mindfulness can be characterized by the practice of three basic principles: "Drawing novel distinctions and questioning automatic behavior, defying the limits of categories and premature cognitive commitments, and considering alternative perspectives" (Burpee & Langer, 2005, p. 45). These three principles work in contrast to mindless tendencies. For example, Burpee and Langer suggest that over time mindlessness in marriage discourages partners from making choices, recognizing alternatives, and attending to the uniqueness of any given situation. Each of the three mindful principles is useful in creating productive couple communication. Using these three principles, couples can work to avoid old patterns of observation and response, resist drawing conclusions from one's partner's "trigger" statements, and be open to seeing things in new ways.

Mindfulness is typically triggered by one of nine conditions (Burgoon et al., 2000; see Table 1.1). These nine conditions can be understood to represent four types of experience that encourage mindfulness. Couples can practice choosing mindfulness in these situations. First, *novelty*. Novelty requires mindful processing to be effective. Existing patterns of response can be reassessed to respond to new situations. Second, the *unexpected*. When situations don't proceed according to what one expects (i.e., a situation doesn't run according to our scripts or behaviors are discrepant with what we expect), one can choose to make mindful reassessments and adjustments. Third, *internal* (e.g., discrepant goals,

**Table 1.1** Elements that prompt people to become more thoughtful

| | |
|---|---|
| Novel situations | No script; or the script becomes more difficult due to new/greater demands |
| Novel communication formats | Computer-mediated; texting |
| Uninvolving situations | Low level of involvement allows one to disengage from mindless scripts |
| External interruptions | Interference with expected scripted actions |
| Conflict, competition, confusion | Interference in achieving message goals |
| Anticipating negative response | Forecasting a negative response to one's message |
| Time delay/processing difficulty | Nonroutine delay or difficulty between message formulation and transmission |
| Discrepant signs | Discrepant features of the modality, message, source, or situation (such as incongruence of verbal/nonverbal messages, working with an untrustworthy source, or implausibilities in a message) |
| Unexpected consequences | Positive or negative consequences that are highly discrepant from previous consequences |

*Source*: Adapted from Burgoon et al. (2000).

message encoding problems, heightened uncertainty/confusion) or *external* (e.g., interruptions) *difficulties* in enacting well-learned patterns. These pattern enactment difficulties require mindful responses in order to accomplish one's communicative goals. Fourth, *cognitive disturbance*, such as recognition of incongruence in the speaker, message, modality, or situation (e.g., verbal and nonverbal messages are incongruent), or anticipation of negative response to a message one plans on sending. Mindful response is necessary to manage the uncertainty created by cognitive disturbance or anticipation of negative response.

*Moderate arousal* can be considered alongside Burgoon et al.'s (2000) mindfulness list. While moderate arousal doesn't necessarily encourage mindfulness, it does limit high arousal levels that encourage mindless response. To maintain open and creative marriages, couples can strategically work to keep arousal at moderate levels (more on this in Chapter 4).

## Final Thoughts

In this chapter I have laid a foundation from which to examine marital interaction. Understanding the unique context in which marital communication takes place and the cognitive and physiological processes that influence the success of partners' communication with one another, it is possible to create more positive mindful and mindless communication patterns in long-term, publicly committed, romantic relationships.

## The Uniqueness of Marital Communication

### Basic Principles: The Family Context

1 Marriage is a unique *relational context* for communication.
The following make a communicative difference:
  (a) Marriage is intended to be long term.
  (b) Married couples make a public commitment.
  (c) Marriage relationships are romantic presently or in their history.
  (d) Married individuals are partners.
2 Marriage operates within a unique *social context*.
The following create a unique space for communication:
  (a) children;
  (b) in-laws;
  (c) social circles (e.g., friends).
3 Mindfulness/mindlessness and arousal are *cognitive and physiological* processes that play a unique role in marital communication.
Mindlessness can have both positive and negative consequences.
Negative consequences may be most pronounced during times of high arousal.
Optimal goals for productive communication include:
  (a) balancing mindfulness and mindlessness so that appropriate stimuli can be attended to mindfully;
  (b) creating positive mindless patterns;
  (c) keeping arousal levels in the moderate range;
  (d) choosing mindfulness in response to novelty, the unexpected, internal/external difficulties, and cognitive disturbance.

### Questions You Should Ask
*(as a Researcher or as a Relational Partner)*

1 How do the four characteristics of marriage (long-term, publicly committed, romantic, partners) affect specific marriage communication events, such as conflict interaction?
2 Why do some people in current U.S. culture choose to marry? How might their reasons relate to the four characteristics of marriage (long-term, publicly committed, romantic, partners)?
3 How does social context (e.g., children, in-laws, friends) affect specific communication events in marriage?
4 What are the potential positive and negative consequences of mindless behavior?
5 How effectively can couples be trained to maintain moderate levels of arousal?
6 How effectively can couples be trained to develop mindful communication patterns?
7 How effectively can couples be trained to develop positive mindless communication patterns?

# 2

Living and Working Together

Effective Daily Interaction

*Angie and Steve had been married six months. They experienced the normal ups and downs of a young couple adjusting to married life. Overall, they were excited about their new marriage – their lives were filled with learning to live together and manage their home, beginning their careers, and hanging out with friends. When asked what was most surprising about their first six months of marriage, Angie quickly answered, "He is always there."*

Angie's response betrays a truth that many young couples don't realize until they are in the midst of negotiating their new relationship – it is often the "small stuff" that makes a difference. Angie didn't mention that they were arguing more than she expected or that his parents were driving her crazy. No, it was the simple act of trying to coordinate their daily interaction, and balance their autonomy and togetherness, that was the surprise.

Daily interaction is the mortar between the bricks of marital communication. The remaining chapter topics of this book (e.g., intimacy and love, conflict, forgiveness) form the bricks of the relationship. They are the elements typically noticed when a relationship is going well or falling apart. They are what movies are made of. However, daily interaction is the mortar that holds the bricks together – it is the stuff of which successful marriages are made.

The bulk of married couples' lives is spent in relatively mundane, seemingly unmemorable interactions. Couples accomplish daily chores, such as grocery shopping, mowing the lawn, taking the kids to soccer practice, and paying the bills. They choose times and ways to relax, like watching television, walking the dogs, or sitting in the hot tub. They make the bed, pick colors to remodel the kitchen, and take one another to the airport. They play cards or tennis, or ski together. In essence, they connect, they plan, they coordinate their actions.

It is easy to pass over routine processes as significant to marital interaction; however, Duck (1988) points out the importance of daily interaction in personal relationships: "It is very clear, but often under-appreciated, that daily events are typically centered on and intertwined with our relationships in remarkable ways" (p. 6). He highlights the seemingly mundane as significant to how we relate to one another. Driver and Gottman (2004) suggest that "[t]he mundane and often fleeting moments that a couple experiences in their everyday lives may contribute to the health or deterioration of a relationship by serving as a foundation to major couple events such as conflict discussion and caring days" (p. 301).

Likewise, Victor Frankl (1963), in his classic book *Man's Search for Meaning*, demonstrates the importance of the little things. Here he discusses the memories of prisoners in Nazi concentration camps:

> When given free rein, his imagination played with past events, often not important ones, but minor happenings and trifling things. . . . In my mind I took bus rides, unlocked the front door of my apartment, answered my telephone, switched on the electric lights. Our thoughts often centered on such details, and these memories could move one to tears. (pp. 61–62)

Remarkable – the emotional power of memories that reflect the mundane, the daily. In a similar way, a student of mine who was researching this area found herself in conversation with an older man in a grocery store checkout line. She told him that she was researching love in long-term marriages. He looked at her and said:

Do you want to know what love is? I'll tell you what love is. Love is no longer being able to make toast in the morning, because your wife has died. Every morning I used to put the toast in the toaster and, when it popped up, she would butter it. Now, I can't make toast any longer.

Apparently, it is the seemingly insignificant that makes up the *stuff of life*. As such, in this chapter I examine how communication is related to the daily stuff. As Gottman (1999) has pointed out, "Every couple in their daily life together messes up communication . . ." (p. 7). As such, the chapter begins by examining behaviors associated with marital satisfaction. Then, recognizing that different approaches to daily living result in different interaction patterns, I describe the various means by which couples maintain their relationships and how they engage decision making. I finish the chapter by looking at specific issues, such as how couples organize their relationships and the ways they learn to live together.

# Communication and Marital Quality

The way marriage partners communicate with one another affects their sense of relational quality. To fully understand this dynamic we need first to examine what is meant by marital quality, then focus on how communication affects couples' relational experience.

## Marital Quality

Marital quality has typically been understood as individuals' subjective evaluations of their marital experience. Researchers have used various concepts to assess couples' experience in marriage, such as marital adjustment, satisfaction, quality, happiness, success, intimacy, and complaints (Fincham & Bradbury, 1987; Sabatelli, 1988). According to Sabatelli (1988), while marital adjustment, satisfaction, and quality have been most commonly used to assess marital relationships, there is considerable confusion between these terms. Marital adjustment has been conceptualized as a process whereby couples move along a continuum, being well adjusted or maladjusted. Spanier's (1976) Dyadic Adjustment Scale has been one of the most frequently used scales to assess adjustment. For Spanier, marriage (dyadic) adjustment consists of movement toward or away from dyadic satisfaction, dyadic cohesion, dyadic consensus, and consensual agreement. Within this framework, satisfaction is seen as one of four components comprising adjustment. Spanier's scale uses both behaviorally based items (e.g., "How often do you and your partner quarrel?") and subjective evaluations (e.g., "In general, how often do you think things between you and your partner are going well?").

Others have argued that quality should be measured using global evaluations rather than behavioral descriptions (Fincham & Bradbury, 1987; Norton, 1983). From this perspective, including descriptions of marital behavior in marital outcome measures may obscure the need to study the behavioral items (e.g., communication). In addition, behavioral items complicate the ability to study marital behavior because of built-in correlations between behaviorally based satisfaction scales and other behavioral measures. Norton (1983) suggests the following non-behavioral terms to assess positive evaluation of the marriage relationship: good, strong, stable, a team, happy, satisfied.

It is important to recognize that most research in this area does not distinguish whether communication behavior leads to increased couple satisfaction, or if being in a positive relationship leads to communicating in more positive ways. Likely, this is a reciprocal relationship – good communication leads to increased liking and positive affect, and feeling good about the relationship and one's spouse leads to increased positive communication.

## Marital Satisfaction across the Life Cycle

A considerable body of research has demonstrated a U-shaped relationship between satisfaction and time: that is, marital satisfaction is highest in early marriage, drops when children join the dyadic system, and then rises again (although not necessarily to original levels) once the children leave the household (S. A.

Anderson, Russell, & Schumm, 1983; Belsky, Lang, & Rovine, 1985; Patrick, Sells, Giordano, & Tollerud, 2007). In fact, Glenn (1990) posited that this relationship is one of the few certainties in social science research. Researchers have speculated that the transitory nature of satisfaction is due to the transition to parenthood, resulting changes in partners' roles, length of marriage and quality of long-term marriages, adaptation to changing beliefs, and intimacy and differentiation (Glenn, 1998; Patrick et al., 2007).

It should be noted that in spite of the prevalent finding that marital satisfaction is U-shaped over time, not all researchers have reached the same conclusion. Some have argued that the pattern is more one of a steady decline in satisfaction or an initial decline and then a leveling off (VanLaningham, Johnson, & Amato, 2001). Conversely, Gottman (1999) actually claims that "many couples followed the opposite pattern, growing closer over time" (p. 21).

Several elements must be taken into consideration when trying to understand the satisfaction-over-time effect. First, much of the research is cross-sectional in nature: that is, the researchers have examined couples in various stages of marriage rather than following the same couples over time. Second, the longitudinal research that has been done has typically only followed couples for relatively short periods of time. Third, certain effects, such as couples entering marriage with unrealistic relational expectations, may give a false sense of whether "real" satisfaction has actually deteriorated in the relationship. Some of the drop in satisfaction may represent a natural process of adjusting expectations. Fourth, changes in marital satisfaction over time may not indicate that marriage doesn't "work." For instance, VanLaningham et al. (2001), using a 35-point scale, found that on average satisfaction only dropped 4 points over time. When one considers that some of this drop may simply represent a realignment of unrealistic expectations, this amount of change may not be considered overly significant. Finally, even if marital satisfaction does diminish over time, it can't be inferred that, therefore, people would be happier if not married. For example, Bailey and Snyder (2007) found adults to have more hope if married than if separated, divorced, or widowed. On the other end of the marriage cycle, Stafford, Kline, and Rankin (2004) found few differences, in terms of relational satisfaction, between couples who entered directly into marriage, those who cohabitated then married, and those who cohabitated and never married.

## Aspects of Communication That Influence Marital Quality

So, marriages can be assessed as good, strong, stable, a team, happy, or satisfied. Of course, the next step is to determine behaviors that are associated with these evaluations. Communication behaviors related to marital quality have been examined in terms of daily interaction, expectations, relational maintenance, intimacy, and conflict.

### Daily Interaction and Satisfaction

A consistent finding is that negative partner interaction is associated with low relationship quality (Stanley, Markman, & Whitton, 2002). Gottman (1994) concludes that the interactions of unhappily married couples are more negative, less neutral, and less positive even when not in conflict. He also argues that reciprocity of negativity is even more important than simple increases in negativity. In short, reciprocity of negative behavior and affect may result in "the greater probability that negativity is an absorbing state" (p. 65). In other words, couples who are struggling in their marriages may find themselves so absorbed in negativity that it is difficult for them to interpret incoming messages positively or respond in positive ways. This can create a dangerous cycle of defensiveness.

Everyday communication differentiates "happy" couples from "counseling" couples. For example, Pasupathi, Carstensen, Levenson, and Gottman (1999) state that positive and responsive listening is characteristic of happy couples more so than unhappy couples. Two studies, by Yelsma (1984) and Navran (1967), emphasize seemingly mundane activity, such as talking over pleasant things from one's day, when examining behaviors related to marital satisfaction. Yelsma (1984) found that happily married partners, compared to individuals in marriage counseling, feel understood (e.g., "know what the other person is trying to say"), talk over pleasant things from their day, don't express emotions through sulking or pouting, talk about mutual interests, discuss things together before making important decisions, talk over unpleasant things that happened during the day, and have a propensity to talk over most things in their marriage. These findings are highly consistent with research by Navran (1967), who found happily married individuals differ from unhappy marrieds in that they more frequently talk over pleasant things from their day, feel more frequently understood by their spouse (e.g., "that their messages are getting across"), discuss shared interests, talk over most things together, and are more able to tell what kind of day their spouse has had without asking.

Similarly, daily shifts in marital satisfaction were examined in a study by Barnett and Nietzel (1979). They measured the relationship between daily engagement in instrumental behaviors (behaviors surrounding meals, children, and finances) and affective events (positive events, such as acceptance, affection, approval; negative events, such as disapproval or dislike). As would be expected, a decline in marital satisfaction (when measured daily) was correlated with increased frequency of displeasurable instrumental and affective behaviors.

### Expectations and Satisfaction

Perceived fulfillment of couples' expectations has been linked to marital satisfaction. Some of my early research demonstrated a positive relationship between satisfaction and relational expectation fulfillment (D. L. Kelley & Burgoon, 1991). We found married partners were more satisfied when they believed that expectations they held for relational behavior were fulfilled. Specifically, we discovered that perceived fulfillment for intimacy, dominance, equality/trust, distance, and noncomposure/arousal expectations was related to experience of satisfaction.

Previous research revealed similar findings for the relationship between marital role expectations and marital satisfaction. Bochner, Krueger, and Chmielewski (1982) argued that subjective evaluations of marriage (e.g., dis/satisfaction) are influenced by perceptions of expectancy fulfillment. They found marital adjustment related to perceptions of fulfillment of sexual affective roles (e.g., openly expressing affection) and outside task roles (e.g., maintaining the car). Likewise, Quick and Jacob (1973) and Jacob et al. (1978), using the Marital Role Questionnaire, found discrepancies between prescriptive expectations and perceived actual behavior to be higher in marriages in which partners were distressed or disturbed than in those classified as normal. In a similar vein, Veroff, Douvan, Orbuch, and Acitelli (1998) found fulfillment of gender-role expectations associated with increased marital satisfaction, and Perry-Jenkins and Crouter's (1990) research indicates that when married partners experience congruence between their role beliefs and role enactment (e.g., regarding household chores) they are more satisfied.

Based on these findings, we must be careful not to conclude that only perception matters. Rather, the reported findings on expectations and perception of fulfillment are significant in that perception is essential to determining behavioral response (Canary, Cupach, & Serpe, 2001). And, it must be emphasized that behaviors themselves constrain possible interpretations. That is, communication behavior occurs within a social context and, as such, has consensually recognizable interpretations (Burgoon, Buller, & Woodall, 1989). In other words, *how couples behave does matter; however, couples' perceptions of behavior is important, as well.*

### Relational Maintenance and Satisfaction
Couples engage in a variety of behaviors to maintain their marriages. A significant amount of research has found many of these maintenance behaviors related to marital satisfaction. Later in the chapter I explore each maintenance behavior in detail; for now, I briefly discuss how maintenance is related to satisfaction.

Canary and Stafford's (1992, 1993, 2001; Stafford & Canary, 1991, 2006) research program has identified five marital maintenance strategies (positivity, openness, assurances, social networks, and sharing tasks) and discovered significant associations between these strategies and such relational outcomes as satisfaction and equity (see Box 2.1). Research examining both husbands' and wives' perceptions has found all five maintenance strategies positively related to marital satisfaction (Stafford & Canary, 2006).

Importantly, use of these maintenance behaviors affects satisfaction *over time*. Weigel and Ballard-Reisch (2001) discovered that couples' use of maintenance behaviors affected marital satisfaction one year later. Most specifically, higher ratings of wives' positivity, assurances, and network and husbands' positivity and network were related to increased satisfaction by husbands and wives. Interestingly, lower ratings of husbands' tasks were related to both wives' and husbands' higher ratings of satisfaction. (Later in the chapter I discuss possible reasons for gender differences regarding maintenance behaviors.)

In a similar vein of research, Rusbult, Olsen, Davis, and Hannon (2001) describe six pro-relationship maintenance mechanisms that are positively related to couple well-being. These six mechanisms represent three behavioral mechanisms and three cognitive mechanisms, as follows: accommodation behavior (willingness to react constructively to a partner's destructive behavior); willingness to sacrifice for partner and relationship well-being; forgiveness of betrayal; cognitive interdependence (shift from individual-based self-conceptions to collective representation of self and partner); creation of positive illusions about one's relationship; and derogation of tempting relationship alternatives.

*Intimacy and Satisfaction*
Intimacy is closely related to marital satisfaction. In the following chapter we will explore models and definitions of intimacy; however, to simplify this current section on the relationship between marital satisfaction and intimacy I define intimacy simply as psychological closeness.

Marital satisfaction has been conceptually related to intimacy (Patrick et al., 2007; Schaefer & Olson, 1981). My own research (D. L. Kelley & Burgoon, 1991) found that married couples expect their marriage relationship to be very intimate, with almost no experience of distance and moderately high levels of

# Box 2.1: Theory Checkpoint: Maintenance, Satisfaction, and Equity

Canary and Stafford (1992; Stafford & Canary, 2006) propose that equity and satisfaction can be used to predict marital partners' use of relational maintenance behaviors. In short, marriages that are experienced as equitable should be more satisfying and, as such, partners should expend more energy maintaining them, as opposed to allowing them to deteriorate.

Equity theory (Adams, 1965; Hatfield, Traupmann, Sprecher, Utne, & Hay, 1985; Walster, Berscheid, & Walster, 1973) holds that individuals evaluate their relationships in terms of equity. Equitable relationships are those in which partners' ratios of rewards to costs are equal. In essence, the actual values of rewards and costs might vary between partners, as long as the ratio of rewards to costs is equal. Consider a relationship in which the husband puts in one unit of effort (cost) and receives five units of reward, while the wife puts in two units of effort and receives ten units of reward. Because the reward:cost ratio for both can be reduced to 5:1, this relationship could be said to be equitable. On the other hand, imagine a wife and husband who both get ten units of reward from the relationship; however, he puts in two units of effort (cost) while she only puts in one. This relationship is inequitable. Even though both partners receive the same amount of reward from the relationship, the wife's reward:cost ratio is 10:1, while the husband's is only 5:1. In this second scenario the wife is considered to be *overbenefited* and the husband *underbenefited*. Researchers have demonstrated that typically people find equitable relationships more rewarding than either *overbenefited* or *underbenefited* relationships (Sprecher, 1986; Stafford, 2003).

reciprocity and equality/trust. Consistent with this, couples' perceived fulfillment of intimacy expectations predicted higher levels of satisfaction. Likewise, Patrick et al. (2007) found that intimacy and spousal support successfully predict married couples' satisfaction.

Early work by Tolstedt and Stokes (1983) found verbal, affective, and physical intimacy all to be related to marital satisfaction, although the effect from physical intimacy appears mostly to be due to the relationship between physical intimacy and verbal and affective intimacy. Greeff and Malherbe (2001) explored the relationship between five aspects of intimacy (emotional, social, sexual, intellectual, recreational) and marital satisfaction. They found all five aspects of men's and women's experienced intimacy to be related to satisfaction, except social intimacy (the ability to share social networks) for women.

## Conflict and Satisfaction

Conflict management is considered by many researchers and scholars to be one of the most important skills necessary for a successful marriage (Gottman, 1994). Because conflict is examined in depth in Chapter 4, here I briefly highlight the preponderance of research linking conflict to marital satisfaction.

Segrin, Hanzal, and Domschke (2009) posit that conflict styles are strongly related to marital success. They found that in early marriage, hostility, negativity, and withdrawal are related to lower satisfaction, no matter who is the source or target of the behavior. This is consistent with research by Gottman (1993, 1994) that has identified five types of couples based largely on the way they manage conflict. Much of Gottman's research has focused on the potentially damaging effects of negative affect.

One specific conflict pattern, the demand–withdraw pattern, has received much attention from researchers and has been shown to be related to marital satisfaction (Caughlin, 2002; Caughlin & Vangelisti, 2006). For example, Weger (2005) found that the demand–withdraw pattern of conflict in marriage leads to both husbands and wives feeling less understood (self-verified) and, subsequently, that the feelings of being less understood are related to lower ratings of satisfaction.

On the darker side of marriage, a relationship between poor conflict management and depression has been demonstrated, such that husbands' and wives' dysphoria (e.g., depression) levels are related to negative expressions of conflict and a lack of positive strategies (Schudlich, Papp, & Cummings, 2004). Other findings suggest that any type of intimate partner violence is significantly related to relationship disruption and a reduction of relational quality (Johnson, 2006).

### Communication and Satisfaction Summary

It is evident that communication plays a key role in understanding marital satisfaction. The degree of positivity or negativity, perception of expectancy fulfillment, and employment of maintenance strategies are essential to everyday happiness in marriage. In addition, the successful development of intimacy and management of conflict are central to perceptions of marital quality.

# Relational Maintenance

Relationship maintenance is dependent on communication (Dindia, 2003). This is particularly evident in marriage relationships due to the necessary negotiation of various tasks, intimacy and other relational themes, and conflict. As reviewed previously in this chapter, it is evident that successful maintenance is necessary for happy relationships.

## What Is Relational Maintenance?

Relational maintenance can be understood as a process used to meet any of four relational goals (Dindia, 2003; Dindia & Canary, 1993). Framed within a marital context, the first maintenance goal is to keep one's marriage from ending (e.g., divorce). The second goal is to keep one's marriage in a particular state or condition (e.g., maintaining a particular level of trust or intimacy). A third maintenance goal is for the relationship to remain satisfactory. A fourth goal is to keep the marriage in good repair: that is, to keep the marriage running well. This may include the need to repair things when something has "broken" or "gone wrong" (Baxter & Dindia, 1990; Dindia & Baxter, 1987).

## How Do Couples Maintain Their Marriages?

Couples who are in satisfying relationships typically behave in ways to maintain those relationships. This maintenance behavior may be *strategic* or *routine* in nature (Dainton & Stafford, 1993; Dindia, 2003). Strategic behavior is associated with consciousness of action and intent to maintain the relationship. Routine behavior is characterized by lower levels of consciousness and is engaged without the direct intent to maintain the relationship (although the behavior may in fact function as maintenance behavior).

This distinction is similar to the mindful/mindless distinction discussed in Chapter 1, and is just as complex. As I argued there, mindless behavior may be understood to be strategic in the sense that it can be considered purposeful. Dan Canary (personal communication, August 2, 2001, as cited in Stafford, 2003) supports this position: "Strategic communication is implicitly learned and often mindlessly enacted." Essentially, maintenance behavior is either consciously thought out ("Ashley has had a hard day. I think I'll surprise her by cleaning the kitchen.") or routine (during a difficult extended family meeting, Ashley leans over to her husband and gives him an encouraging pat on the leg; later she doesn't remember doing it).

Several researchers have identified maintenance behaviors in intimate relationships. I begin with a review of three early studies on relationship maintenance and then conclude with Canary and Stafford's comprehensive program of research.

An instructive place to begin is Kaplan's (1975–1976) theory of maintenance in interpersonal relationships. He suggests that relationships are maintained through emotional expression (e.g., bottled-up negative emotion can damage the relationship), definition of the relationship (e.g., clarifying what is expected from one another), and preservation of some sense of order (e.g., partners must learn to coordinate their behaviors with one another). These three maintenance functions may be engaged through *expression*, which includes talking about one's feelings or observations about the relationship, or *suppression*, which is represented by less direct communication, such as joking or talking to a third party.

Davis (1973) discussed three types of preventative and corrective behaviors in intimate relationships. The first type is the creation of an external environment that will keep the couple psychologically close. They second type is "work-it-out" (e.g., directly discuss an issue) or "have-it-out" (e.g., have an argument about the issue). Interestingly, Davis speculates that some couples may "have it out" as a test of the relationship, but only because of optimism about the outcome. The third type is renew the relationships through *reintegration ceremonies*. Reintegration ceremonies may be formal (e.g., celebrate one's anniversary) or informal (e.g., recall a positive time in the relationship).

Dindia and Baxter's (1987; Baxter & Dindia, 1990) empirical examination of maintenance and repair behaviors was based on Davis's notion of preventative and corrective maintenance, although they found only minor differences in what couples did to maintain, as opposed to repair, their relationships. Dindia and Baxter's work explains relational maintenance in terms of dialectical tensions (see Box 2.2): "We conceptualize relationship maintenance as a complex process in which partners strive to sustain a dynamic equilibrium in their relationship in the face of many possible types of dialectical tension" (Baxter & Dindia, 1990, p. 203). For example, couples may experience the tension between too much autonomy (e.g., too many lone activities) and too much connection (e.g., feeling "smothered" by one's partner), or between too much openness (e.g., telling inappropriate details of past relationships) and too much closedness (e.g., sharing too few details about events that influence one's emotional state).

In discussing their findings, Baxter and Dindia (1990) suggest that couples maintain their relationships through managing these multiple dialectics. Couples recognize that there is a need to balance daily talk and other kinds of communication that should

## Box 2.2: Theory Checkpoint: Dialectical Tensions

Leslie Baxter (2004, 2006; Baxter & Montgomery, 1996) has offered *Relational Dialectics Theory* as one theoretical approach to understanding the dynamic nature of interpersonal relationships. Relational Dialectics Theory, based on work by Russian social theorist Mikhail Bakhtin (1981, 1984, 1986), views relationships in constant flux between various dialectical tensions. Baxter argues that rather than seeing closeness as good and distance as bad, relationship partners are in constant movement between the two. For example, during early marriage and career building, couples may experience pressure to focus on individual issues (e.g., advancing their careers) and struggle to find enough time together. They may manage this tension by building a date night into their week or going on regular vacations together.

The various dialectical tensions create a balance between partners fusing their perspectives and, yet, retaining parts of their individual viewpoints. This process creates a "dialogic dance . . . [that] organizes a given couple's meaning of their unique marriage" (Baxter, 2006, p. 133). This *dialogic dance* typically takes place around three categories of contradictions (opposites that exist in tension). The *dialectic of integration* represents autonomy, separation, and independence in tension with connectedness, integration, and interdependence. The *dialectic of uncertainty* represents the balance between stability, continuity, certainty, predictability, and routine, on the one hand, change, novelty, surprise, and newness, on the other. The *dialectic of expression* recognizes the pull between openness, disclosure and candor, and discretion, privacy, and secrecy.

Relational maintenance can be conceptualized as managing various dialectical tensions. For example, couples may choose to emphasize one option (e.g., predictability over novelty) at various times in their relationship (e.g., during financial hardship). Partners may also find themselves cycling within various tensions (e.g., openness and closedness): for example, the birth of a child may create sufficient uncertainty and fatigue that couples find themselves moving rapidly between times to talk and times to sleep. Couples may also use the dialectical tensions as diagnostic devices to improve their relationships (e.g., "We've been so busy we've hardly seen each other. Let's create a once-a-week date night.")

happen less frequently (e.g., discussing relationship problems or partner faults, compliments, calling in the middle of the day to say "hi"). Also, finding the right tension between togetherness (e.g., spending more time together) and autonomy (e.g., time for individual prayer or being alone), and novelty (e.g. surprises) and predictability (e.g., reassurances of fidelity) was perceived as constructive.

Canary and Stafford's (1992, 1993; Stafford & Canary, 1991, 2006) research program has identified five central couple maintenance strategies: positivity, openness, assurances, social networks, and sharing tasks. *Positivity* represents cheerful, supportive communication. It includes such behaviors as asking how one's day has been, being patient, romantic, fun, polite, cooperative, and forgiving. In addition, it involves building up one another's self-esteem, giving compliments, and avoiding criticism. The importance of positivity has been demonstrated by Gottman and Levenson (1992), who reported that a 5:1 ratio of positive-to-negative behaviors is necessary for couples' satisfaction.

*Openness* refers to talking about one's thoughts and feelings with one's partner. Most specifically it focuses on having relationship talks and discussing what each partner wants in the relationship and assessing the relationship's quality. Openness can also include reminding each other of past decisions as they take into account each partner's desire for the relationship's future.

*Assurances* represents four central ideas: first, affirmation of one's commitment to the relationship; second, future-oriented communication regarding the relationship; third, demonstration of one's "faithfulness" in the relationship; and, fourth, acts of love that show one's commitment to the relationship. As will be developed more fully in the next chapter, commitment and love are concepts that are closely linked.

*Social networks* refers to how joint involvement in a social network helps maintain a relationship. For example, having common friends and spending time with them helps maintain one's marriage. Typically this outcome isn't a consciously strategic goal, but some friends do make explicit commitments to one another in order to help maintain the relationships (e.g., "Let's always be there to support our marriages.") Network strategies may also include a willingness to spend time with one another's families.

*Sharing tasks* involves two elements. The first is sharing household tasks that need to be accomplished. Gottman (1994) has suggested that husbands' participation in household tasks is related to more involvement in the marriage and less illness, over time, for the husband. The second element is joint responsibility. Partners don't simply "help" one another, but share the relationship's responsibilities. For example, when working on my counseling degree, it was pointed out to me that many husbands "help" their wives in the kitchen: that is, they see their wives as primarily responsible for the kitchen, and they (husbands) are glad to help. Likewise, more traditional wives (see later discussion, this chapter, regarding Fitzpatrick's couple types) may be willing to work to "help" financially, but in actuality see providing financially as primarily their husband's responsibility. This is not to say that healthy couples don't differentiate various tasks ("I take care of the outside; you take care of the inside."). Rather, as discussed previously in this chapter, the important element is that each marriage partner sees the relationship as equitable or fair (Stafford & Canary, 2006).

Common to these maintenance-focused studies is an emphasis on direct and indirect communication. At times, couples are directly open, emotionally expressive, and make positive relationship statements, including direct statements of commitment.

Other influences are less direct as couples construct rituals and relationship routines and participate in an external environment that presses them to stay connected (e.g., involvement in couple-friendship networks). It is important, as well, to recognize that maintenance is not static. Rather it is a dynamic process of negotiating dialectical tensions that helps maintain the relationship definition and emotional health of the relationship.

## Gender and Maintenance

I typically ask students in my relationship courses to raise their hand if they think women and men are different in the way they communicate. As you might guess, virtually every hand in the room goes up (excepting those who have previously taken other relationship courses or think that the question is so painfully obvious that it must be a trick question). And, yet, research has demonstrated many similarities in the way men and women communicate, and differences that have been found tend to account only for small relationship or interaction effects (Dindia, 2006).

Similarly, gender differences regarding maintenance have been discovered, but it should be emphasized that men and women have significant similarities as to how they maintain their relationships and the effect that these behaviors have on relational outcomes such as satisfaction. For example, Baxter and Dindia (1990) found husbands and wives view maintenance strategies similarly, and Weigel and Ballard-Reisch (2001, 2008) discovered that both wives' and husbands' satisfaction ratings were related to perceptions of their own use and their partner's use of maintenance behaviors.

While Stafford and Canary (1991) found only a weak relationship between gender and perception of maintenance strategies, certain research has identified gender differences that provide grounds for interesting speculation regarding gender roles in marriage. Stafford (2003) summarizes her work and that of others by stating that women may use maintenance strategies more than men. For example, Ragsdale (1996) asked couples to keep diary logs over a two-week period and concluded that wives invariably

*43*

reported using more of each of the five maintenance strategies. He argues that women's greater use of openness and network strategies is due to their relationship orientation. Largest differences were found in that wives used more sharing task strategies than their husbands. Regarding task sharing, Weigel and Ballard-Reisch (2001) found that husbands' reports of performing tasks and chores was related to less satisfaction one year later, while wives' reports regarding tasks had no relationship with their satisfaction. Weigel and Ballard-Reisch speculate that partners' fulfillment of what they consider to be their gendered task roles may lead to satisfaction. Women may also place higher importance on the relational messages associated with tasks: that is, they may be more concerned with the overall sense of relational equity and intimacy than if their spouse accomplishes a task.

Regarding equity, Stafford and Canary (2006) found that wives' satisfaction, more so than husbands', is related to the extent that they are underbenefited in the relationship (see Box 2.1). Also, married women's assessment of equity is a better predictor of maintenance behaviors than men's. Interestingly, women's reports of equity and satisfaction have additive effects such that, together, they better predict self-reported maintenance use than either concept alone. Stafford and Canary, and others (e.g., Fincham & Linfield, 1997; Gottman, 1994; Michaels, Edwards, & Acock, 1984), argue that these differences illustrate that women are typically more sensitive to relational events and judgments of equity within the relationship.

## Decision Making

One of the most common forms of daily communication is decision making. The nature of the couple partnership (e.g., long-term, committed) demands coordination of daily tasks and determination and achievement of long-term goals. As such, couples are engaged in decision making, from the mundane (e.g., "Shall we get pizza?") to the extraordinary (e.g., "Should we consider the job offer in Beijing?"), and from that which is primarily reason-based (e.g., "Would it benefit us financially to increase our end-of-the-year giving?") to that which is emotionally laden (e.g., "Do we need to send John to a treatment facility?"). Following, I focus on certain process elements of decision making, highlight decision making across the life cycle, and finish by suggesting the *how* of decision making that can be used to draw couples together or pull them apart.

## Elements of the Decision-Making Process

Much of the research and thinking about decision making has focused on formalized decision-making processes (Sillars & Kalbfleisch, 1989). However, while married couples may engage in somewhat formal, structured decision making (e.g., a planned meeting to discuss the year's financial budget), much of a couples' decision making occurs informally in the midst of other activities. For example, a 16-year-old comes home from school and tells his parents he needs $100 by five o'clock to secure his place on the band tour. The couple's response to their son's late request occurs with little opportunity for planning and while the dad is under the car changing the oil.

Sillars and Kalbfleisch (1989) identify two decision-making styles used by couples: implicit and explicit. These styles are each represented by seven contrasting characteristics (explicit characteristics listed first in the following list). The first, explicit agreements vs. silent arrangements, recognizes that some decisions are verbally stated whereas others are implicit without verbal assent. Second, prospective vs. retrospective arrangements contrasts interaction in which both partners are aware they are making a decision with those wherein couples only recognize the decision-making aspect of the interaction after the fact. Third, proactive planning vs. incrementalism highlights the distinction between rational problem solving before a decision and "muddling" through or impulse-based decisions. Incremental decisions may actually be the result of small decisions accumulating with such force that a larger decision is somewhat predetermined. Fourth, syntactic vs. pragmatic code usage reflects the difference between nontraditional relationships in which there are fewer shared expectations and traditional relationships in which partners share numerous verbal shortcuts. Fifth, explicit vs. implicit process management notes the difference between couples who are more aware of *how* they make decisions and thus engage in direct metacommunication about their decision making and those who more or less "feel their way" through. Sixth, conflict engagement vs. conflict avoidance highlights the basic tendency for couples to engage (e.g., conciliation or confrontation) or avoid (e.g., denial or equivocation) issues in the relationship. Finally, mastery orientation vs. stoicism represents the tendency to attack a problem (requiring more communication to coordinate a response) in contrast to accepting the problem (less communication to accept things "as is"). Sillars and Kalbfleisch (1989) suggest that implicit characteristics are the baseline responses for couples because they require the least effort and are a common response when couples are overloaded in terms of expertise, time, and energy (p. 197). When implicit decision making becomes difficult, couples may turn to managing the process explicitly.

C. P. Cowan and Cowan (1992) identified four patterns of how couples decide to make the transition to parenthood. Most of the couples in their study, when discussing whether to have children, used explicit approaches. The first decision-making type, *Planners,* explicitly discuss whether to have a child and eventually come to an agreement. *Ambivalent* partners also typically have explicit discussions. Both partners have pro and con feelings about having a child, although one is typically more pro and the other more con. They seem able to tolerate mixed, or even polarized, feelings, although this ambivalent state may reduce satisfaction. *Yes–No* couples are typified by strong unresolved conflict regarding pregnancy. Late in the pregnancy, and even after the child is born, these couples may be still struggling over the decision they have made. *Acceptance-of-Fate* couples take more of an implicit approach as they accept their "fate" when they find themselves pregnant. Most of these couples wanted children but were "pleasantly surprised" to find themselves pregnant.

## Decision Making across the Life Cycle

Married couple decision making becomes more complex with the addition of the first child (see Chapter 5 for more detail on couple communication across the life cycle). Decisions that may have been made by one spouse alone now may become grounds for extensive negotiation (C.P. Cowan & Cowan, 1992). For example, pre-conception, a career change may have been primarily an individual decision (e.g., "I'm tired of working in this industry.") However, after conception this same decision has broader impact on the family. Additionally, post-birth decisions may be more constrained by lack of couple resources (Fincham, 2004), such as time, energy, and finances. For example, after the addition of a child, many couples will find it difficult to find time or energy to make decisions about topics such as finances, community involvement, career, and household maintenance and repair. In addition, new child-related expenses may constrain other financial decisions (e.g., deciding to wait to replace the bathroom faucets). Sillars and Kalbfleisch (1989) note that the presence of children may also increase the complexity of decision making as the number of competing interests increases and couples find themselves needing to make decisions about issues for which they have little knowledge (e.g., child-related issues such as depression, drugs, or self-destructive behaviors such as cutting).

Certain research suggests that couples' communication may actually improve in later stages of the life cycle due to the acquisition of positive relationship skills through the child-rearing years (Blacker, 2005). Fingerman, Nussbaum, and Birditt (2004) believe that psychological development of middle-aged adults results in perspective taking and the ability to manage emotion that can facilitate more positive communication. Similarly, Sillars and Kalbfleisch (1989) suggest that younger couples' expressivity is related to more explicit relationship negotiation, while older couples (middle-aged and older) rely more on implicit consensus based on their long relational history. However, couples whose children no longer live at home are not free from difficult decisions. Adult children wanting to move back home ("boomerang kids"), health, and financial decisions may prove to be formidable foes as couples try to make productive decisions (Waldron & Kelley, 2009).

Remarried couples encounter significant decision-making challenges (see Chapter 5 for more detail). For example, couples blending family systems have relatively short decision-making histories compared to parent–child relationships, and must manage a wide range of emotionally laden topics (e.g., establishing a new family identity, establishing relationship boundaries with stepchildren, financial decisions involving each partner's biological children or ex-spouses; McGoldrick & Carter, 2005). A relatively short courtship and lack of a "honeymoon" period may lead remarried couples to favor explicit negotiation (M. Coleman, Ganong, & Fine, 2004; Sillars & Kalbfleisch, 1989).

### Factors That Affect Decision Making

Because implicit decision making is the path of least resistance (Sillars & Kalbfleisch, 1989), it is important to identify factors that may affect the decision-making process. Poole and Billingsley (1989) identify dominance, affiliation, and task orientation as three dimensions of relationships that affect decision making. They argue that the nature of the relationship influences who is in control of the decision-making process, the degree of openness during decision making, and the likelihood that the relationship will distort dyadic reasoning. For example, C. P. Cowan and Cowan's (1992) four types of decision-making couples (discussed previously) each vary in terms of dominance, affiliation, and task orientation.

Another distinguishing characteristic of marital decision making is that emotional expression is often more acceptable within this personal context than in other social contexts. In addition, as we have seen, many of the topics couples discuss are emotionally laden: for example, making day-care decisions for the couples' first child. Interestingly, Cowan and Cowan's (1992) work with couples transitioning to parenthood discovered that partners' feelings about their marriage was more related to how they felt about the process of talking about any given problem, as opposed to whether the problem was resolved. This effect may be due, in part, to emotional flooding. Gottman (1994) describes emotional flooding as a condition in which partners filter incoming information through their emotions (typically negative) to such an extent that it hampers normal cognitive processing. This influences the partners' ability to interpret and respond to one another in a positive manner. When emotional regulation is not managed well, couples may not feel heard and so repeat their message louder and more forcefully (C. P. Cowan & Cowan, 1992). In addition, this highly aroused state may lead the couple to respond in mindless (habitual) patterns that precipitate (hasten or give rise to) inefficient decision making, defensiveness, and even irrational behavior (Guerrero & La Valley, 2006).

I close this section on decision making by admitting that as a researcher of communication in intimate relationships, I have often underestimated what is common knowledge regarding couple communication. As such, I offer the following quotation regarding the importance of communication and problem solving to central relationship outcomes, such as intimacy and satisfaction:

> Most couples, we have learned, do not know that some conflict and tension are inevitable in any intimate relationship. Nor do they realize that the key to a satisfying marriage is not whether a couple has challenging problems or whether they always resolve them, but *how they talk to each other* about them. (C. P. Cowan & Cowan, 1992, p. 185)

In C. P. Cowan and Cowan's (1992) examination of couples' transition to parenthood, they specifically noted that effective problem solving regarding key issues (e.g., whether to have a baby) was associated with satisfaction over the following two years. Their research indicates that problem-solving interactions that feel productive and satisfying for both partners generate partner well-being as well as warmer, more positive family relationships. Likewise, Cohan and Bradbury (1997) found that problem solving moderates the potential negative effects of life events. Their research emphasizes the importance of identifying the functions of various communication behaviors. For example, wives' expression of anger (presumably without whining or contempt) is related to increased marital satisfaction, possibly because it signals high distress and engages the male partner (Fincham, 2004). This is consistent with work by Gottman and Krokoff (1989) that found that anger and disagreement may improve marital satisfaction over time. The key seems to be that marital distress results from behaviors that are unlikely to resolve problems and possibly even make them worse (Roloff & Miller, 2006).

Overall, it appears that couples who rely on more positive problem–solving techniques and use fewer complaints and criticisms (Roloff & Miller, 2006) benefit their relationships. These responses may signal positive relational messages between partners. For example, Poole and Billingsley's (1989) identification of dominance and affiliation as relational dimensions affecting the decision-making process has implications for relational outcomes. My own research (D. L. Kelley & Burgoon, 1991) has identified perceived fulfillment of dominance and intimacy expectations as related to marital satisfaction. As such, balanced control and appropriate openness during decision making are likely to lead to higher levels of marital satisfaction and sense of closeness. And cooperative decision making, overall, may send important messages regarding the couples' perception of themselves as a team working together.

# Other Daily Communication

## Couple Types

Daily communication is also influenced by the manner in which couples negotiate their relationships and the ensuing roles each partner plays in the marriage. As such, I conclude this chapter with a discussion of couple type, roles, and special contingencies for dual-income couples.

It is obvious to state that not all married couples are alike. Researchers have identified a variety of ways to understand these differences. One approach is to identify various couple types. I focus here on the program of research established by Fitzpatrick (1988). In Chapter 4 I develop Gottman's (1994) typology based on conflict styles.

Based in part on work by Kantor and Lehr (1975), Fitzpatrick (1988) generated a research program designed to identify how couples vary in terms of ideology, interdependence/autonomy, and communication. Ideology represents how the couple values traditionalism and uncertainty. Interdependence/autonomy is determined by the couple's perspective on sharing, autonomy, undifferentiated space, and temporal regularity. Communication is represented by conflict avoidance and assertiveness.

Based on these three dimensions, Fitzpatrick's (1988) work has identified three main couple types: traditional, independent, and separate. Traditional couples are characterized by conventional ideology about marriage. They tend to emphasize traditional customs, such as the woman taking the man's last name. They value stability over spontaneity and uncertainty. There is a great deal of interdependence in these marriages, characterized by a high degree of self-disclosure and spending time together. The high level of interdependence encourages more regular time schedules and shared household spaces. They tend not to be assertive with one another, but deal with conflict when needed.

In contrast, independent couples hold nonconventional values about marriage and family and are more open to uncertainty in their relationships. Like traditionals, they value sharing and companionship, but they also emphasize individual autonomy, possibly through keeping separate physical spaces and less predictable time schedules. They are somewhat assertive with one another and somewhat freely deal with conflict and differences.

Interestingly, separates hold on to both the ideology of traditionalism and uncertainty. This is achieved by maintaining traditional values but, also, highly valuing autonomy. Separate couples tend to maintain more psychological distance from one another, but may have predictable schedules. They tend to avoid conflict.

Mixed couples can have any combination of the three couple types, although separate/traditional (husband separate/wife traditional) is most common (Fitzpatrick, 1988). Mixed couples (separate/traditional in particular) tend to value affection and be competitive during conflict. They are not likely to compromise and will energetically try to persuade one another.

Specific to communication skills, couple types vary in their expression of affect and conflict (Fitzpatrick, 1988). Traditionals tend to express more positive nonverbal cues than other couples and give more positive self-disclosure. Independents exhibit fewest positive nonverbal cues. This may be due in part to their tendency to self-disclose both positive and negative feelings at high rates (Fitzpatrick, 1987; Segrin & Fitzpatrick, 1992). Separates demonstrate lower levels of cohesion and affection, and tend to avoid conflict more than other couple types.

Research has typically shown traditional couples to be most satisfied, followed by mixed (traditional/separate), independents, and then separates (who also are more likely to experience depression); although it should be noted that all couple types can maintain satisfactory relationships. In the late 1990s (D. L. Kelley, 1999) I examined relational expectations within couple type in an effort to understand why traditional couples tended to be happiest. Results from this research demonstrated that most couples held traditional expectations about their marriages, although only traditionals acted in traditional ways. As such, violation of one's expectations regarding one's own and partner's behavior may drive a portion of the reduced satisfaction for independents and separates. A more recent study demonstrated a relationship between satisfaction and commitment for both independent and separate couples (Givertz, Segrin, & Hanzal, 2009).

## Roles

One developmental task of married couples is to develop and clarify roles. I'll have more to say on this in Chapter 5, specifically as it relates to parenting; however, two other areas of responsibility demand clear development of roles: household tasks and careers.

### Household Tasks

Household labor has been defined as "unpaid work that contributes to the well-being of family members and the maintenance of their home" (Y. S. Lee, 2005, p. 230). As such, completion of household tasks is important on two levels: pragmatic and relational. At a pragmatic level, necessary tasks (e.g., paying bills, taking children to school) must be accomplished to keep the family functioning and to facilitate individual development. At the relational level, married partners' involvement in household tasks and parenting is one reflection of equity (as demonstrated by engagement and involvement) in the marriage (Gottman, 1994). For example, Gottman (1994) found husbands' participation in household chores to demonstrate an investment in the emotional life of the family. Gottman also reports that emotional availability of both partners has been related to perceptions of equity in one's marriage.

Equity has been consistently related to marital quality (Canary & Stafford, 1992; Stafford, 2003). For example, Vanfossen (1981) found that when employed women perceived inequity with their spouse (especially those who experience role overload), they were more likely to experience depression (this effect did not hold true for men). Similarly, over half the wives in Silberstein's (1992) study reported inequity in household chores and childcare was the major way their husbands hurt their careers. Specifically, wives reported making career compromises because of the husband's "not being as involved as he might be" (p. 61). On the flip side, Gottman (1994) demonstrated that husbands who participate in housework have less illness four years later, perhaps as a result of the strong relationship between fewer chores and avoiding conflict in the relationship. Likewise, Stafford and Canary (1991) found couples who share tasks to demonstrate more mutual control and relationship satisfaction.

Certain studies examining relational quality posit that household and childcare inequities especially affect wives' levels of marital satisfaction and their evaluations of their husbands (Gottman, 1994; Staines & Libby, 1986). Yet, other researchers raise issues regarding how to determine what is actually considered "fair" by husbands and wives (Huston & Holmes; 2004; Perry-Jenkins, Pierce, & Goldberg, 2004).

Specific to communication, in a study of "liberated" men (those who believe their wives' careers to be of equal importance to their own), not one of the 50 participants had discussed with their wives how to manage household chores (Gilbert, 1985). Other research has discovered that spouses have similar perceptions of the amount of time the wife contributes to household chores, while they differ in their perceptions of husbands' contributions (Y. S. Lee, 2005). Y. S. Lee (2005) suggests that the five-hour discrepancy (men estimate they contribute 18 hours a week to household chores, and women estimate their husbands contribute 13 hours) is due to men's overestimation, although it appears that both men and women overestimate their actual contributions. Perry-Jenkins et al.'s (2004) work provides means of framing "family work" communication. They suggest that communication focused on family work involves frequency of division of work negotiations, whether negotiations are direct or indirect, and who initiates family work discussions. In addition, they note that family work negotiations are likely to include discussion of fairness or equity.

### Dual-Income Couples

Today, it is commonplace to find marriages in which husband and wife work. These marriages experience unique challenges compared to marriages where the husband is the sole provider. For example, dual-career couples may have special needs to learn values clarification, communication, time and stress management, renegotiating roles and responsibilities, meeting emotional needs, dealing with competition, and sharing control and power (Avis, 1986; Jordan, Cobb, & McCully, 1989). Nielsen (2005) suggests that couples who are able to spend 90 minutes a day alone together (or 10.5 hours a week) are more likely to be satisfied than those who spend less than one hour a day. However, many couples struggling to manage work, family, and community obligations are likely to see this as an unrealistic goal.

The changing nature of women's and men's roles, and continuing changes in Western culture, have created ever-changing characteristics of dual-income marriage. For example, in the late 1980s some research failed to find differences between single- and dual-income marriages regarding perceived power and uses of influence strategies (C. S. Sexton & Perlman, 1989), while other studies found differences based on sex-role attitudes (Nicola & Hawkes, 1986). Silberstein (1992) states that "an expectation of two careers is not synonymous with an expectation of two equal careers" (p. 40). As such, expectations for careers are in continual need of negotiation by the couple.

Silberstein (1992), based on extensive interviews with 20 married couples, found that dual-career couples talk about their careers, including giving advice about career and office politics. Three-quarters of her participants believed that their marriage was helped by the self-fulfillment and stimulation each spouse gained from his or her career. Interestingly, however, Silberstein found that couples who openly struggled and experienced gradual change regarding commitment to job versus commitment to family were more satisfied than those who seemed resigned to their situation. In other words, satisfaction may be associated with continual communication that signals one's commitment to the relationship and interdependence with one's partner.

In addition, a majority of men and women in Silberstein's (1992) study reported that their spouse facilitated their careers by offering emotional support. On the other hand, over three-quarters of her couples indicated that work negatively affected their sexual relationship due to fatigue, emotional withdrawal, depression, or anxiety. Gender differences became evident such that wives were more likely to talk about work and socioemotional issues, and husbands more likely to give advice.

The spillover effect, also, has been well documented. That is, there is evidence that individuals' feelings at work may spill over to the home environment (H. Sexton, 2005). Studies have consistently demonstrated that as job satisfaction increases, work–family conflict decreases, and husbands are more likely than wives to transfer their dissatisfaction at work to their spouse (H. Sexton, 2005). In general, more satisfied husbands and wives are less likely to come home from work angry than less satisfied spouses (Nielsen, 2005).

It is important to recognize that not all dual-earner couples are alike. The distinction can be made between dual-career and dual-worker couples (Perry-Jenkins & Crouter, 1990). Dual-worker marriages are marriages wherein both husband and wife hold non-professional jobs. By contrast, in dual-career marriages, both partners hold professional jobs and consider their jobs part of their career trajectory.

Dual-earner couples can also be classified as coproviders, main/secondary providers, and ambivalent providers (Perry-Jenkins & Crouter, 1990). Coproviders see themselves as having equal responsibility in providing economically for the family. Main/secondary providers believe that one partner, typically the husband, is the main provider for the family – even if the spouses have comparable earnings. Ambivalent providers have mixed feelings about partners' roles in providing for the family.

Various perspectives on provision make negotiation of household chores, for working couples, an important task. For example, main/secondary provider husbands are typically less involved in traditional household chores than either coproviders or ambivalent providers (Perry-Jenkins & Crouter, 1990); also, Gottman (1994) found that husbands of women who work don't typically do more household chores. Such findings prompted Klein, Izquierdo, and Bradbury (2007) to propose that there is a premium on negotiating and enacting division of labor within the home for dual-career couples. Likewise, Steffy and Ashbaugh (1986) discovered female married professionals view dual-career planning and spouse support as positively related to effective problem solving and negatively related to interrole conflict; interrole conflict was also negatively associated with marital satisfaction.

Partner differences regarding division of labor and problem solving, may be due to individual identity issues. Silberstein (1992) found important gender differences regarding dual-career couples, such that most husbands in her study described career as highly important and central to personal identity. By contrast, wives also described career as highly important, but quickly qualified that they would adapt if they didn't have a career or were not successful. This distinction is important in that *career jobs* may have more influence on couples' decision making, especially when they are central to an individual's personal identity. For example, a spouse may be more likely to sacrifice family time for a career-oriented job than for a job that serves only to secure income, especially if the career-oriented job fits his or her self-perception.

## Final Thoughts

As noted at the beginning of this chapter, daily interaction is the mortar between the proverbial bricks of marriage. Clearly, daily interaction affects couples' experience of marital quality and facilitates maintenance of the marriage relationship. In particular we have seen that daily communication is experienced through positivity/negativity, relational expectancy fulfillment, intimacy, conflict management, and the engagement of various maintenance strategies. In addition, we have noted various ways to enact marriage, and highlighted the importance of negotiating roles concerning household tasks and careers. But this is just the beginning. As we will see in the next two chapters, daily communication forms the stuff of intimacy and love, and lays the foundation for productive conflict.

# Living and Working Together

## Basic Principles: Daily Interaction

1 Everyday communication is the mortar between the bricks of the marriage relationship.
2 Everyday communication is associated with marital satisfaction.
   (a) Negativity becomes an "absorbing state" for unhappy couples, and results in more negative and less positive communication throughout the day.
   (b) Happy couples listen more, talk over positive things from their day, and feel more understood by each other.
3 Marital satisfaction is also associated with perceived fulfillment of relational (e.g., intimacy, equality) expectations, relational maintenance, intimacy, and productive conflict management.
4 Couples maintain their relationships by balancing dialectical tensions such as connection–autonomy, openness–closedness, and novelty–predictability.
5 Couples use at least five strategies to maintain their relationships: positivity, openness, assurances, social networks, and sharing tasks.
6 Couples' perception of equity in the relationship is related to marital quality and how the relationship is maintained.
7 Decision making is a ubiquitous process for couples.
8 Couple decision making can be implicit or explicit, and primarily based on reason or emotion.
9 Couples manage their relationships in a variety of ways. Couples can be understood as traditional, independent, separate, or a mixture of any two of these.
10 Management of roles related to household tasks and career is a necessary and important task for today's married couples.

## Questions You Should Ask
### (as a Researcher or as a Relational Partner)

1 How aware are couples of daily communication patterns?
2 Are daily interactions of various couple types characterized by negative or positive communication?
3 How do couples talk about the small things (e.g., the weather, local sports, the neighborhood, school)?
4 How do expectations, maintenance, intimacy, and conflict interact to affect couples' satisfaction level?
5 What dialectical tensions are most prominent during non-conflictual marriage interaction (e.g., connection–autonomy, openness–closedness, and novelty–predictability)? How do couples negotiate dialectical tensions in their relationships during times of transition?

6  How can couples increase the use of underused maintenance strategies (e.g., positivity, openness, assurances, social networks, and sharing tasks)?
7  How do couples evaluate their sense of equality (balance, equity) in their relationship?
8  Are couples able to identify themselves as traditional, independent, or separate? If so, how might these self-assessments influence marriage outcomes?
9  How can partners effectively negotiate couple roles? Are couples aware of underlying relational themes (e.g., equality) that affect role expectations and satisfaction?

# 3

## Closeness

### Achieving Intimacy and Love in Marriage

*In order for us to have any time, I would stay up and wait for him to come home [from work] as tired as I'd be. I'd iron or I'd do chores while waiting for him, so that I could have a cup of coffee with him when he came home, otherwise we didn't touch base. We always felt strongly that we needed to do that because, we said, we could get lost. With these eight children and him working all the time, we could end up saying, "Who are you?" We always made a point to find some time, no matter when it was.*

Emily and Rick, married 48 years

Emily and Rick express what most married couples intuitively know – maintaining a degree of closeness is essential to a happy, stable marriage (Moss & Schwebel, 1993). Listen to Emily's statement again, as she describes why she would stay up late just so she and Rick could *touch base*: "[W]e needed to do that because . . . [w]ith these eight children and him working all the time, we could end up saying, 'Who are you?'" Researchers agree that intimacy and love have a profound effect on the marriage relationship, yet there is much confusion among relationship experts regarding the nature of these two concepts. Couples from my research seem equally confounded and talk about the difficulty of maintaining intimacy and love through the ups and downs of long-term marriage. Without a proper understanding and development of these important relationship characteristics, as Emily points out, couples and researchers alike can "get lost."

Early work that I conducted in this area discovered that individuals had little conceptual clarity between intimacy and love. For example, intimacy is often primarily associated with sex, and love with positive feelings. These common ideas are not necessarily wrong; they are simply anemic conceptualizations of two very rich concepts. The potential danger of this lay-couple perspective is that anemic understanding can lead to anemic (weak and fragile) relationships.

On the other end of the scale, researchers have had their own problems determining the nature of and relationship between intimacy and love (Moss & Schwebel, 1993). For example, certain researchers have conceptualized love as a component of intimacy (e.g., R. A. Lewis, 1978; Walster, Walster, & Berscheid, 1978), while others have conceptualized intimacy as a component of love (e.g., Sternberg, 1986). The danger, from a research perspective, is that lack of conceptual clarity leads to under- or overemphasis of certain concepts by researchers and, subsequently, by couples and practitioners. As I will present later in the chapter, failure to understand the interrelationship between love and intimacy can leave one particularly vulnerable in close relationships.

Therefore, in this chapter I develop conceptualizations of intimacy and love that I believe are useful to understanding and categorizing the research in this area of study, and that provide workable models for use by couples, researchers and practitioners. I begin by reviewing a sample of current intimacy models. I then overview the nature of privacy, which, when it is between two people (e.g., confidentiality in a relationship), can increase elements of intimacy. Based on this privacy perspective, I build a framework from which to understand how intimacy can be expressed behaviorally, with specific emphasis on self-disclosure, emotional expression and affection, and sex-related communication. Subsequently, the chapter turns toward love. I make an important distinction between intimacy as a relational (bilateral) process and love as unilateral, and offer several models of love and its behavioral and decisional correlates. I finish the chapter by examining the relationship overlap of love and intimacy in marriage.

## Intimacy

Intimacy can generally be understood as a feeling of closeness and connectedness between communication partners (C. Hendrick & Hendrick, 1983; Laurenceau, Barrett, & Rovine, 2005). Perlman and Fehr (1987) review intimacy definitions and summarize their findings in terms of three common themes: partner closeness and interdependence, extent of self-disclosure, and warmth of affection. Perlman and Fehr also identify unique elements of intimacy definitions. They describe some conceptualizations of intimacy as based on behavior and interdependence, while others focus on cognitive evaluations; others, still, represent intimacy in terms of motivation or capacity. Similarly, Petronio (2002) suggests that intimacy is the "feeling or state of knowing someone deeply in physical, psychological, emotional, and behavioral ways because that person is significant in one's life" (p. 6).

The interpersonal process model of intimacy (Laurenceau et al., 2005; Reis & Patrick, 1996; Reis & Shaver, 1988) provides a dyadic, communicative perspective on the intimacy process. In this model, intimacy is conceptualized as an experiential relational outcome that may be momentary. This intimacy experience is the result of two intimacy processes: self-revealing disclosure and partner responsiveness. The process begins when one shares revealing and relevant information with one's partner. The partner must then respond in a relevant way that contributes to perceptions and feelings of understanding, validation, and care. Essentially, the higher one's perception of a partner's responsiveness, the higher one's experience of intimacy – that is, the more one feels understood, validated, and cared for by one's partner, the more one experiences intimacy. Due to the transactional nature of the communication process (e.g., speaker–listener roles in constant flux), this process often leads to the experience of mutual intimacy (Laurenceau et al., 2005).

Prager's (1995) review of intimacy research and theory manages the great variety of perspectives by conceptualizing intimacy across two major categories: intimate interaction and intimate relationships.

# Closeness

*Intimate interaction* is composed of intimate behaviors and intimate experience. Intimate behavior includes verbal elements, such as self-disclosure and emotional expressiveness, and nonverbal elements, particularly those that are shared in some way (whether reciprocal or in a complementary manner), such as squeezing hands, sexuality, or laughing together.

Intimate experience, the second element of intimate interaction, is the cognitive/perceptual and affective components of intimacy. The cognitive/perceptual component constitutes partners' experience of feeling understood. Affective experience includes positive involvement, interest, or feelings regarding one's self, one's partner, or the relationship. Prager's view of affective experience has marked similiarities to Burgoon and Hale's (1984) description of relationship messages. Burgoon and Hale describe relational messages as representing how one sees one's self and one's partner within the context of the relationship, and how one sees the relationship itself. Burgoon and Hale's (1984, 1987) research in this area consistently identifies intimacy as a central relational theme. Specific to marriage, my own research (D. L. Kelley & Burgoon, 1991), built on Burgoon and Hale's relational schema, identifies satisfying intimacy expectations as central to predicting marital satisfaction.

Prager's (1995) second basic intimacy category, *intimate relationships*, represents those relationships characterized by intimate interactions or what can be termed *relational intimacy*. Relational intimacy takes place when there is a history of repeated intimacy behaviors and experience, and an expectation for the same in the future. In addition, Prager argues that intimate relationships may also be understood in terms of their by-products, such as affection and cohesion; or by elements that are necessary to maintain intimacy, such as trust.

It should be recognized that intimate relationships can also be understood as those defined by cultural norms. For example, in Western nations, marriage is typically considered to be an intimate *relationship* (Laurenceau et al., 2005); although marriage relationships are not always characterized by intimate *interactions*. Consistent with this thinking, H. H. Kelley et al. (1983)

argue that close relationships are not necessarily characterized by frequent intimate behavior or feelings. For example, most of us know couples who are married, but demonstrate few of the typical behaviors associated with intimate relationships, such as showing affection.

To summarize, intimacy is a term that can be used to describe a type of relationship or kind of interaction. Intimate relationships may be defined by culture or a prevalence of intimate interactions. Intimate interactions are characterized by certain verbal (e.g., self-disclosure and partner responsiveness) and nonverbal (e.g., physical affection, sexual behavior, tone of voice) behaviors, and the positive experience (e.g., having feelings and thoughts) of closeness and being understood. Next, privacy models help to further refine these ideas.

## Privacy

Petronio and Caughlin (2006) argue that privacy exists in dialectical tension with disclosure. As such, understanding privacy contributes to understanding disclosure (i.e., intimacy), and vice versa. As discussed in Chapter 2, dialectical theory posits that relationships are in constant flux around somewhat competing poles or dialectical contradictions. One of the most common contradictions regards the tension surrounding expression (Baxter, 2006). Couples constantly negotiate expression by moving toward self-disclosure and openness or privacy and discretion. Or, to use terminology that I will reintroduce later in the chapter, relationships move through periods of accessibility and inaccessibility (Altman, Vinsel, & Brown, 1981). Neither side of this continuum is better than the other (e.g., it is not better to always be open, expressive, accessible), but rather the competing poles represent discursive choices dependent on relational or contextual contingencies (Baxter, 2006).

Petronio's theory of Communication Privacy Management (CPM; Petronio, 2002 – see Box 3.1) presents private information as something that someone owns (e.g., the extent to which someone can make autonomous decisions about handling

# Box 3.1: *Theory Checkpoint: The Theory of Communication Privacy Management*

Marriage relationships require constant maintenance of a balance between public and private existence. The theory of Communication Privacy Management (CPM) (Petronio, 2002), as applied within a marital context, provides a framework to study how this balance between one's private life and one's relational life is achieved. Basic assumptions about privacy management include recognizing the dialectical nature of private disclosure, that people choose to reveal or conceal based on salient criteria and conditions, and that ownership and right to regulate access are central components to managing one's personal information. Most relevant to marriage relationships, choices to reveal or conceal are not solely individual choices, but are influenced by one's relational partner.

CPM proposes five suppositions to understand communication privacy management. First, it focuses on private information and disclosure, emphasizing the content of the disclosure as well as the process. Second, it recognizes the development and use of boundaries to manage the tension between public and private dimensions of one's life. Third, the concepts of control and ownership recognize individuals' perceptions of owning or co-owning private information and, subsequently, managing vulnerability by controlling others' access to private information. Fourth, it is recognized that boundaries are managed by rule-based systems: for example, private disclosure begins the process of boundary negotiation because of implicit expectations as to how the information "should" be handled. Fifth, CPM recognizes the dialectical nature of privacy–disclosure.

particular information). Individuals have personal boundaries for information they solely own, but can create collective boundaries for information they share. This process can create a sense of intimacy between spouses (Petronio, 2002). When someone shares private information with a partner, the partner becomes a shareholder (part owner) of the information and the collective boundary is maintained, in part, through confidentiality (Petronio & Reierson, 2009). Intimacy, then, may increase by creating a shared set of private information wherein partners share mutual responsibility (Petronio, 2002).

Consistent with dialectical theory, individuals experience a tension between keeping certain information to one's self or disclosing with one's partner (Petronio, 2002). This tension is regulated, in part, by rules that guide the following: who receives private information; the extent to which each partner owns the information; and the level of information that can be revealed to the partner or that the partner can reveal to third parties. The negotiation of these rules, which typically takes place through trial and error (Petronio, 2002), can promote closeness in the relationship (Burgoon, Parrott, et al., 1989). For instance, a long line of research has demonstrated a primarily positive relationship between sharing private information and liking, particularly in ongoing relationships (Caughlin & Petronio, 2004; Petronio, 2002).

Burgoon (1982; Burgoon, Parrott, et al., 1989) conceptualized privacy as the ability to control or limit access to the informational, physical, interactional (social), and psychological dimensions of one's self. She and her colleagues argue that privacy is as important to relational development as are intimacy-related constructs such as openness. For instance, privacy may create a balance to openness by keeping levels of risk in acceptable ranges, as well as by helping to manage uncertainty, emotional overload, conflict, and levels of dependency.

According to Burgoon (1982; Burgoon, Parrott, et al., 1989), there are four types of privacy that are negotiated verbally and nonverbally: informational, physical, social, and psychological. Information privacy is the ability to regulate the information one shares. As such, informational privacy in marriage can range from reading a partner's email to keeping information about an affair to one's self. Physical privacy involves freedom from intrusion or surveillance of one's personal space or territory by physical presence, touch, sights, sounds, or odors of others. Therefore, something as common as snoring could be viewed as an invasion of privacy by married partners. Social privacy regulates encounters with others – with whom one interacts, for how long, and when and where interactions take place. Married couples across the life cycle continually negotiate the amount and type of time they spend together. Finally, psychological privacy regulates access to one's thoughts, feelings, attitudes, and values. It allows for autonomy and self-identity as one is freed from the persuasive attempts of others. Like other types of privacy, married partners manage their psychological privacy by balancing what they share and what they keep private and by assessing the timing of disclosure if it is to occur.

Although couples negotiate how to enact each of the four types of privacy, they also have to manage relationship dynamics when privacy expectations are violated. Interestingly, Burgoon, Parrott, et al. (1989) found that, overall, individuals are somewhat timid to try to restore privacy once it has been violated, and that privacy violations from intimate partners require a somewhat delicate response that doesn't signal reduced involvement in the relationship. In other words, couples may desire to maintain a sense of personal privacy, without diminishing the sense of relational intimacy.

Taking into account both Petronio's (2002) and Burgoon's (1982; Burgoon, Parrott et al., 1989) perspectives, it is interesting to examine how each type of privacy overlaps as couples develop intimacy. For example, when a couple create a collective boundary for sexual intimacy, each partner may express some openness physically, informationally, socially, and psychologically with the spouse, while limiting the same access to those outside the relationship. As such, a privacy-based perspective provides a view of intimacy that is communication-focused and serves to organize current marital intimacy research. Elsewhere I have discussed this perspective as the Access and Affect Model of Intimacy (D. L. Kelley, 2008).

## The Access and Affect Model of Intimacy

A basic tenet of dialectical theory is that each side within a given contradiction can be better understood in light of its competing discourse. That is, autonomy can be better understood in light of connection, stability becomes clearer as one experiences change, and, regarding our current discussion, openness (intimacy) can be best understood in light of closedness (privacy).

As such, the Access and Affect Model of Intimacy (D. L. Kelley, 2008) was developed based on notions of privacy, offered by Burgoon (1982; Burgoon, Parrott, et al., 1989) and Petronio (1991, 2002), to further understand the various communicative elements of intimacy and to distinguish it from and identify its relationship with related constructs (specifically, love). In the next few paragraphs I briefly describe the model and then use it as a framework to examine communication-focused, intimacy-related research on marriage.

As described previously, Burgoon's (1982; Burgoon, Parrott, et al., 1989) privacy model focuses on accessibility or nonaccessibility (Altman et al., 1981) across four dimensions: information, social, physical, and psychological. Perlman and Fehr (1987) remind us that the word "intimacy," itself, comes from the Latin term *intimus*, meaning "inner" or "inmost" (p. 15), and Petronio (2002) extends this idea by specifying that intimacy is "one possible outcome of *revealing the self* [emphasis added] to others" (p. 5). In other words, intimacy involves revealing, or giving access to, the inmost part of the self.

Within a collective boundary (Petronio, 2002), in our case within the marriage relationship, accessibility to one's partner creates openness and closeness, both of which are foundational elements of intimacy. Prager (1995) emphasizes this aspect when describing intimacy as a "positively cathected psychological relation between two or more people in which partners share that which is *private* [emphasis added] and personal with one another" (p. 67). In essence, at the most elemental level, intimacy involves giving access to one's self informationally, socially, physically, and psychologically. It is this aspect of the access–affect model that places unique emphasis on communication – one gains access to one's partner through communication behavior. However, access alone does not create an intimate experience.

Intimacy is also related to positive affect. Warmth and affection represent one of the intimacy themes discovered in Perlman and Fehr's (1987) review of intimacy definitions. Prager (1995) argues specifically that "intimate interactions by definition involve partners having warm feelings toward one another" (p. 24). As we saw in Chapter 2, Gottman (1994) suggests balanced couples maintain a 5:1 ratio of positivity to negativity. Essentially, relational partners will experience their relationship and interactions as more intimate when accompanied by high levels of access and positive feelings.

This bi-dimensional model of intimacy (access and affect; see Figure 3.1) allows for complex understandings of how intimacy changes as relationships change. For example, it would be tempting to view a happy newlywed couple as high in intimacy, and a couple who are recently separated after seven years of difficult marriage as low in intimacy. However, such judgments often primarily rest on perceptions of the partners' experience of affect (positive

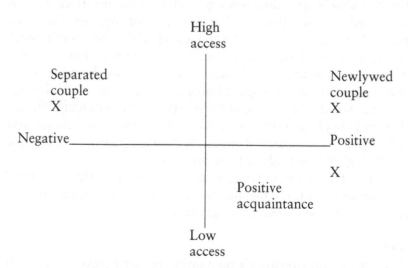

**Figure 3.1** The Access and Affect Model of Intimacy

or negative). In reality, a happy newlywed couple experiencing positive affect may be only experiencing moderate to moderately high access informationally and psychologically, and perhaps high access physically and socially; while the recently separated couple experiencing negative affect may be quite high in informational and psychological access, and low in social and physical access. The differences between the couples become evident during conflict. The newlyweds are being somewhat careful with one another and trying to learn how to do conflict well (because they don't know each other well enough yet within their new married context), while, based on historically high informational and psychological access, the separated couple know how to deeply hurt one another during conflict.

Understanding intimacy as access and affect also helps address problems with what has been termed the reversal hypothesis (Baxter, 1985; Duck, 1982). The reversal hypothesis proposes that intimacy diminishes in the same way that it develops. In other words, as a relationship develops, certain behaviors, such as self-disclosure and time spent together, increase; as the relationship begins to deteriorate, these behaviors decrease. At a basic level this thinking is appealing – when a relationship deteriorates there is typically less self-disclosure and time spent together. However, reversal of certain intimacy components is slow and doesn't match the regression of other expressions of intimacy. For example, while self-disclosure may lessen in frequency as the relationship deteriorates, the psychological knowledge that was gained through previous self-disclosure doesn't dissipate nearly as quickly. Thus, a divorced couple who have minimal contact with one another may still "fight like intimates" because of their deep informational and psychological knowledge of one another.

In the following sections I discuss intimacy-related marital research as it relates to the dimensions of access and affect, and the resulting interdependence they generate.

## Access

As discussed previously, giving another person access to one's self forms the basis of relational intimacy. Expression of relational intimacy includes granting informational, physical, social, and psychological access to another. The following review focuses on communication elements that are central to developing intimacy.

*Informational access* Married couples have access to information about one another through self-disclosure and observation. I will deal with self-disclosure more fully when I examine psychological access, but here I emphasize that daily disclosures contribute to individuals' stockpile of partner information. Altman and Taylor (1973) proposed a social penetration metaphor to understand how relationships move toward increased closeness. Social penetration occurs through informational access at two levels: breadth (e.g., number of topics available to discuss) and depth (e.g., amount of information revealed on any given topic). Similarly, Petronio (2002) emphasizes the importance of examining the public and private nature of information that couples share. It is important to recognize that each partner has his or her own perception as to how private or personal each piece of information is. For example, "I've gained three pounds," "My wisdom tooth started hurting last week," "I have a new supervisor at work," and "I was hurt last week when you were talking about your past girlfriends" vary for each individual in terms of how readily this information might be shared with the spouse.

Spouses living interdependently also gain information about each other from observation – a husband notices a suspicious mole on his wife's back; a wife sees her husband's speeding ticket when bringing in the mail; a husband notices his wife's anxiety as she prepares for an office presentation; a wife is surprised by her husband's anger when he is talking to his father on the phone. Fitzpatrick's (1988) research on couple types examines how couples variously negotiate interdependence. Interdependence is based on sharing, but also organization of household space. The more interdependent a couple, the more they organize their space to create a sense of togetherness. This includes use or creation of shared work and living space, structuring time together, and even such elements as opening each other's mail. This sense of interdependence, which is typically higher in traditional and independent couples than in separates, influences the ability to observe and gain information about one another.

*Social access*   One of the central components of social access is time. Time spent together has been considered a part of marital quality (Xu, Hudspeth, & Estes, 1997) and related to marital disagreements (Hatch & Bulcroft, 2004). Levenson, Carstensen, and Gottman (1993) explored the relationship between marital quality and time spent together and found middle-aged and older couples reported "things done together recently" as a source of pleasure, while dissatisfied couples experienced less pleasure in recent joint activities. Stafford, Dainton, and Haas (2000) reported that spending time with shared friends enhances marital relationships.

Doing things together is one way of building companionship. Fitzpatrick (1988) noted that couples' interdependence is negotiated, in part, by creating a sense of companionship, and her research on couple types identified differences in how couples structure their lives to find time together. Differences in how time is perceived may also be gender-based. McAllister, Mansfield, and Dormor (1991) reported that the meaning of togetherness for husbands was thought of as sharing space, whereas the meaning of togetherness for wives was represented by shared experience.

Another way of considering social access is through gifts. Parkman (2004) argues that when married (as opposed to when single), one increases access to certain commodities. A gift occurs when spouses use their time or income to offer a commodity that is of primary value to the partner. Gifts can be tangible, such as flowers or jewelry, or intangible, such as empathy, affection, and understanding. Parkman's findings suggest that women are more likely than men to seek divorce due, in part, to insufficient access to intangible gifts such as affection and understanding.

Social access can also be understood in terms of creating relationship rituals. Relationship rituals can be thought of as relational symbols and used in the creation and maintenance of intimacy (Baxter, 1987; Bruess & Pearson, 1997). Using questionnaires and interviews with married couples, Bruess and Pearson (1997) identified seven major types of marriage rituals: couple-time

72

rituals; idiosyncratic/symbolic rituals; daily routines and tasks; intimacy expressions; communication rituals; patterns/habits, mannerisms; and spiritual rituals. The most frequently reported ritual category, *couple-time*, consisted of three sub-categories: enjoyable activities, togetherness rituals, and escape episodes. Enjoyable activities consist of leisure activities and/or recreation, such as sports, hobbies, movies, and socializing. Togetherness rituals differ from enjoyable activities in that they are not activity-oriented, but may be spending time in the morning reading the paper together. Escape episodes are unique in that couples get away from their "normal" context.

Idiosyncratic/symbolic rituals were the second most frequently reported ritual and are also clearly related to social access and intimacy (Bruess & Pearson, 1997). This category includes such rituals as: favorites (favorite restaurants, activities, gifts), private codes (jointly developed words, symbols, phrases that represent shared experiences), play (intimate fun such as teasing, kidding, silliness, humor and laughter, games and contests), and celebration (appropriate and expected understandings for celebrating special events such as birthdays and anniversaries).

Dual-career couples may find social access a challenge in marriage. Silberstein (1992) reports that almost all dual-career spouses experience time as a central problem in their relationship. When asked about the disadvantages of dual-career marriage or what they would most like to change, most spouses responded "time." Nielsen (2005) suggests that time is a primary resource couples need to set aside for their marriage. His findings indicate that couples who spend 90 minutes a day alone together are more satisfied than those who spend less than an hour a day alone together. Likely, as Nielsen points out, time mediates other relational factors such as time to talk, managing conflict, and enjoying one another on a more intimate level.

*Physical access* Communicating affection plays a central role in the formation, maintenance, and quality of human relationships; specific to marriage, affection is significantly related to relational quality and satisfaction (Floyd, 2006). Direct nonverbal expressions of affection can be classified in terms of facial behaviors, vocalic behaviors, and postural/kinesic behaviors (Guerrero & Floyd, 2006). Facial behaviors include such elements as smiling, eye contact, and expressiveness. Vocalically expressed affection is marked by pitch (frequency), variance (range of pitches vs. monotone), and loudness. An interesting vocalic phenomenon that many romantic partners use is baby talk (Zebrowitz, Brownlow, & Olson, 1992). Floyd (2006) suggests that baby talk is used to communicate romantic affection because of its nurturant tones. Postural/kinesic behaviors are represented by space-oriented behaviors (e.g., posture and proximity), movement, and haptics (use of touch to communicate). Of course, most salient in this category is touch.

Touch is the communication channel that is most directly and immediately tied to intimacy escalation (Thayer, 1986). Affectionate touching includes such behaviors as hugging, kissing, caressing someone's face, holding hands, and sexual intercourse (Guerrero & Floyd, 2006), with myriad variations of how each of these behaviors can be expressed. For example, Guerrero and Floyd (2006) describe kisses as ranging from a peck on the cheek to prolonged mouth-to-mouth encounter, from closed mouth to open mouth, from dry to wet. And I'm happy to report that more recent work by Floyd (Floyd et al., 2009) suggests that increases in romantic kissing lead to improvements in perceived stress, relationship satisfaction, and total serum cholesterol.

Sexual intercourse is an important form of touch in marriage. Floyd (2006), in an overview of the physiology of affectionate communication, notes that the human body's chemical response during sex (during both sexual arousal and climax) contributes to relational bonding and attachment. Consistent with this perspective, most scholars believe that sexual satisfaction is a predictor of marital satisfaction (Christopher & Kisler, 2004), even in long-term marriage (Hinchliff & Gott, 2004). Similarly, Cramer (1998) posits that sexuality is associated with relationship compatibility, such that there is a moderately strong correlation between relationship satisfaction and sexual satisfaction with one's partner, and evidence that sex therapy may bring about improved relationship satisfaction. McCarthy (2003) suggests that sex in marriage functions to deepen intimacy, bring shared pleasure, and reduce the stresses of life and marriage. Central to this process is giving and receiving pleasure-oriented touch, and thinking, talking, and acting as an intimate team.

Communication is an important element in determining sexual satisfaction (Cupach & Comstock, 1990). Cupach and Comstock (1990) argue that satisfaction in sexual communication leads to sexual satisfaction, which then affects marital adjustment. They conclude that quality communication about sex is necessary, but an insufficient determinant of marital and sexual satisfaction. Sprecher and Cate's (2004) summary of the scant research on sexual communication indicates that the quality of a couple's sexual communication and the amount they talk about sex are positively related to satisfaction with sexual and nonsexual aspects of their relationship.

Finally, it is important to note that understanding the role of sexual communication is complex due to the fact that much of this type of communication is nonverbal in nature (Cupach & Metts, 1991). Work by Tolstedt and Stokes (1983) helps us take a somewhat integrated perspective by recognizing that much of physical intimacy's relational effect is due to corresponding verbal and affective components. Their research revealed verbal, affective, and physical intimacy all to be related to marital satisfaction and, importantly, that the impact of physical intimacy primarily appears to be due to the relationship between physical intimacy and verbal and affective intimacy.

*Psychological access*  Psychological access between partners is largely a function of self-disclosure, emotional expression/connection, and understanding. The most recognizable element of psychological access, self-disclosure, is the variable most often associated with intimacy (possibly other than sexuality). Specific to marriage, self-disclosure plays a significant role in developing intimacy (Derlega, Metts, Petronio, & Margulis, 1993) and is consistently related to marital satisfaction (Fitzpatrick, 1987). For example, a number of researchers have found positive relationships between marital satisfaction and couples discussing, or debriefing, positive aspects of their days (Navran, 1967; Vangelisti & Banski, 1993; Yelsma, 1984). However, because much research does not fully take into account content or depth of communication, Petronio (2002) argues for use of the term *private disclosure* instead of the common usage of *self-disclosure*. It is in this deeper sense that self (private) disclosure is associated with psychological access.

Self-revealing disclosure (e.g., private disclosure) and responsiveness are characteristic of satisfied and adaptive marriages, particularly when the disclosure reveals emotions and the responsiveness moves the partners toward understanding (Laurenceau et al., 2005). Using a daily-diary method with couples over 42 days, Laurenceau et al. (2005) found self-disclosure, partner disclosure, and perceived partner responsiveness to predict feelings of intimacy. Interestingly, their findings suggest gender differences such that the association between perceived partner responsiveness and intimacy was stronger for wives, and the relationship between self-disclosure and intimacy was stronger for husbands. So it appears that wives' sense of intimacy is more related to the perception that their husbands are responsive, whereas husbands' sense of intimacy is more related to their ability to self-disclose to their wives. Disclosure and responsiveness are particularly related to psychological access as emotional expression/connection.

Regarding the relationship of emotional expressiveness and responsiveness, Gottman (1994) reports that dissatisfied couples fail to validate expressed feelings and use fewer feeling probes and metacommunication sequences. In a work written for couples therapists, Gottman (1999) emphasizes the overall importance of emotional connection for couples. Likewise, Prager (2000) argues that emotional expressiveness defines a relationship as close. The importance of emotional expression may be due in part to its association with equity in the relationship (Guerrero & Andersen, 2000). Emotion is tied to equity in that positive emotions are considered important relationship benefits and predict relationship outcomes.

The final element of psychological access is understanding.

Psychological access is not simply increased knowledge of one's partner at emotional levels, but rather the perception of being known and understood by one's partner. For example, Sternberg (1988) conceptualizes intimacy as including mutual understanding between romantic partners. Gottman (1999) encourages couples and marital therapists to use a "love map" technique to assess the "amount of cognitive room partners have for the relationship – knowing one's partner's psychological world, and being known and feeling known as well" (p. 161). In essence, feeling understood is related to satisfaction for most married couples. It has even been suggested that understanding is the essence of quality communication (B. M. Montgomery, 1981).

## Affect

Intimate interactions are characterized by warm feelings that may develop into more enduring affection over time (Prager, 1995). The centrality of warmth of affection to intimacy has been identified by multiple researchers (Perlman & Fehr, 1987). In fact, research has consistently found dissatisfied couples to express greater negativity and less positivity during conflict (Gottman, 1994). Specifically, dissatisfied couples demonstrate enhanced levels of negative affect, lower levels of humor and laughter, and greater reciprocity of negativity. Interesting research by Sanford (2007) indicates that hard emotions (e.g., feeling angry and aggravated) are associated with power assertion, self-centered goals, and negative communication. Sanford also suggests that flat emotion is highly detrimental to relationships and is associated with withdrawal in marriage. Summarizing research on affectional expression, Fincham (2004) concludes that affectional expression between spouses actually moderates the effect of negative spouse behavior (e.g., disengagement and demand–withdraw patterns) on marital satisfaction.

## Interdependence

Emotional expression and connectedness and increased access to one another create interdependence between partners. Perlman and Fehr (1987) identified closeness and interdependence as one of the themes in common to both lay and researcher intimacy definitions. Wieselquist, Rusbult, Foster, and Agnew (1999) argue that, in relationships characterized by strong interdependence, partners have experiences that are "inextricably linked" (p. 960). Specific to communication, Petronio (2002) argues that as individuals give access to one another and share private information, they necessarily co-construct rules on how to manage shared information and future access to information. This process is so central to intimate relationships that disturbance of these co-constructed guidelines may lead to increased arousal in each partner. In fact, Wieselquist et al. (1999) state that intimate relationships develop "interdependence dilemmas." Interdependence dilemmas occur when partners experience tension between relationship and self-interest. Resolution of these dilemmas often requires significant effort and personal cost. As I discuss at the end of this chapter, love provides a context for safe resolution of such interdependence-based dilemmas.

## Love

Intimacy and love are intricately linked. Pose a simple question to friends about what it means to love someone and they will inevitably mention some of the components of intimacy presented in this text: sharing at a deep level, time together, and warm feelings. As mentioned earlier in this chapter, even social scientists have not always clearly distinguished these concepts – certain conceptualizations of intimacy include "loving persons" (Walster et al., 1978) and, as I present later, love models often include intimacy as a component of love (Sternberg, 1986). The focus of this section is to review existing love models developed by social scientists, with particular emphasis on Love Styles, Attachment Theory, Sternberg's Triangular Theory of Love, and Fehr's Prototype Approach to Love. As in my examination of intimacy research, I suggest a modified framework with which to organize and understand love research and the components of love.

# Closeness

## General Overview of Love Theory

S. S. Hendrick and Hendrick (1992) and Sternberg (2006) provide overviews of perspectives and approaches that have been used to examine love. For example, biological and evolutionary perspectives (Kenrick, 2006; Mellen, 1981) have examined love and emotion (Buck, 1989), affection (Floyd & Morman, 2002), and love acts (Buss, 1988, 2006), while sociological/philosophical perspectives (S. S. Hendrick & Hendrick, 1992; Solomon, 1981, 2006) have focused on notions of self, individualism, and society.

Certain research, generated primarily out of psychological studies, has been directed at identifying dimensions or types of love. Early work by Rubin (1973) discussed love in relation to attachment, caring, and intimacy. Berscheid and Walster (1978; and Walster & Walster, 1978) identified two types of love: passionate and companionate. Passionate love is characterized by sexual attraction, intense communication, and emotional turbulence, while companionate love reflects more of a quiet intimacy, predictability, and shared attitudes and values (S. S. Hendrick & Hendrick, 1992). Hatfield (1988) argues that it "takes some doing" to combine the "delights of passionate love with the security of companionate love" (p. 207). However, S. S. Hendrick and Hendrick (2006) note that it is common for young lovers to claim their partner is their best friend.

Noller (1996) also addresses the passion and companionship aspects of love and argues that feelings of both passion and companionship can continue throughout life. In addition, her theoretical work suggests that love has emotional, cognitive, and behavioral aspects that may be mature or immature. Immature love is characterized by such characteristics as limerence, infatuation, and love addiction. Mature love creates an environment where both partners can grow and develop.

Yela's (2006) examination of how love has been measured by researchers suggests a focus on passion, intimacy, caring (for the other), and attachment. These elements, and Noller's recognition that love may be mature or immature and has emotional, cognitive, and behavioral components, set the stage for discussing four prominent theories of love.

## Love Styles

J. A. Lee's research has identified love styles that can be understood as attitude/belief systems with an emotional core; yet, as "style" indicates, the styles are also somewhat related to actual romantic behavior (S. S. Hendrick & Hendrick, 2006; J. A. Lee, 1988). Described in brief, the six styles can be understood as follows: eros (passionate, erotic, focus on physical appearance); ludus (game-playing, uncommitted, can be deceptive/non-disclosive); storge (friendship, companionate, quiet); pragma (practical, calculating, lists of desired attributes); agape (altruistic, giving, sacrificial); and mania (obsessional, intense, alternating emotion). While much love style research has focused on non-married samples, Grote and Frieze (1994) found that passionate and friendship loves were positively associated with satisfaction, whereas game-playing love was negatively associated with satisfaction. M. J. Montgomery and Sorell (1998) found that married couples throughout the life cycle espoused love styles representing passion, romance, friendship, and self-giving love.

## Love as Attachment

S. S. Hendrick and Hendrick (1992) credit Rubin (1970, 1973) with beginning the surge of modern love research. Rubin's work was quite sophisticated, conceptualizing love as having the individualistic aspects of attachment and caring, and the dyadic aspect of intimacy. The first half of this chapter has focused on intimacy issues, so I focus here on attachment and, later, address the issue of caring.

From an attachment perspective, love is seen as multidimensional, composed of healthy and unhealthy aspects, and developmental (S. S. Hendrick & Hendrick, 1992). Essentially, based on early work by Bowlby (1982, 1988) and Ainsworth, Blehar, Waters, and Wall (1978), attachment theory posits that an infant's attachment with the primary caregiver (mothers have been the primary target of research) influences eventual adult romantic relationships (Trees, 2006). Trees (2006) reports that closeness, interdependence, and anxiety regarding potential abandonment create three basic attachment types as adults: secure, avoidant, and anxious-ambivalent (Hazan & Shaver, 1987). At the most basic level, secure attachment manifests itself as adults who are comfortable with intimacy, comfortable with interdependence in relationships, and have few abandonment fears. Their love experience is happy, friendly, and trusting. Avoidant individuals have a fear of intimacy and have difficulty depending on others. They express low acceptance of partners. Anxious-ambivalent individuals desire closeness, but fear abandonment, and experience emotional highs and lows and jealousy (Feeney, Noller, & Roberts, 2000; Hazan & Shaver, 1987; S. S. Hendrick & Hendrick, 1992).

Shaver and Hazan (1988) argued that J. A. Lee's (1973, 1988) love styles can be reduced to the three attachment styles. Research by Levy and Davis (1988) and Feeney and Noller (1990) largely supports these findings (Feeney et al., 2000) as follows: secure attachment (eros, agape), avoidant attachment (ludus), and anxious-ambivalent attachment (mania). However, it should be noted that others have argued that "romantic love is not attachment" (C. Hendrick & Hendrick, 2006, p. 162) but the two are related adulthood systems.

In a review of attachment research focused on marriage, Trees (2006) suggests that secure individuals report fewer arguments and negative communication behaviors, such as verbal aggression and defensiveness, and more validation and negotiation. In contrast, insecurely attached spouses report more negative behaviors such as anxiety, hostility, and anger, with avoidant men being less supportive and warm. In addition, marriage partners tend to engage in more positive and constructive communication when their spouse has a secure attachment, and exhibit less positive and more avoidant behavior when the spouse has an insecure attachment. For example, individuals tend to disclose less to avoidant spouses and to moderate the intimacy of disclosure, while increasing negativity, to anxious spouses. Secure wives are listened to more by their husbands, whereas husbands exhibit more rejecting behavior (during problem solving) with their insecure wives. On the flip side, wives tend to avoid conflict with anxious husbands. Overall, when both husbands and wives are securely attached, there is greater intimacy and less aggression and withdrawal.

## Sternberg's Triangular Theory of Love

Sternberg (1986, 1988, 1997) has proposed a triangular theory of love based on three components: intimacy, passion, and decision/commitment. In this model, intimacy references feelings of closeness, connectedness, and bondedness. It is the warmth of a loving relationship and is characterized as the emotional investment of the relationship. Between marriage partners it may include elements such as promoting one another's welfare, experiencing happiness, sharing emotional support and mutual understanding, helping one another, and valuing each other.

Passion is composed of the romantic drives, such as physical attraction and sexual consummation. Passion can be considered the motivational aspect of romantic love and includes elements of arousal. In marriage, passion includes sexual fulfillment, but also may be characterized by the pursuit of need fulfillment in areas such as self-esteem, nurturance, affiliation, dominance, submission, and self-actualization.

Decision/commitment is the cognitive decision-making aspect of love. It is the choice to love the other (decision) and maintain the love (commitment). While these elements often coincide, individuals can choose to love without committing to maintain that love, or may maintain the relationship itself while letting love die. Decision/commitment is the component of love that helps couples make it through the hard times. To some extent, it regulates the other love components. For example, a married partner may feel passion for someone not her husband but, nonetheless, choose to love and stay committed to her husband.

Sternberg (1986) suggests that intimacy be viewed as the warm aspects of the relationship, passion as the hot aspects, and commitment the cold. Likewise, the emotion of intimacy and the cognitive component of decision/commitment are typically more stable and less in a person's awareness than the arousal-based component, passion. Especially relevant to marriage, intimacy and decision/commitment are most important to close, long-term relationships, although clearly the three dimensions covary in other ways (e.g., sexual passion and commitment are often related to emotional intimacy). In addition, Sternberg suggests that over time in successful relationships, latent experiences of intimacy should continue to increase, while more public manifestations of intimacy may trail off. In other words, in a successful marriage the couple will continue to grow close, although there may be fewer public expressions (e.g., less kissing in public). Failed relationships differ in the sense that even latent intimacy begins to diminish over time.

In order to better understand the overlapping nature of the three components of love, Sternberg (1986) suggests various types of love (see Table 3.1 for more detail). The various types of love are anchored by non-love at one extreme (none of the love components are present) and consummate love at the other extreme (all three of the components of love are present). The model is useful for couples to evaluate the experience of love in their relationship. For example, a couple experiencing companionate love (intimacy and commitment) may decide to work on their relationship by further developing the passion component. Overall, couples, when rating their relational experience, tend to be happier when

**Table 3.1**  Sternberg's kinds of love

| | |
|---|---|
| Non-love | Absence of all three components |
| Friendship | Intimacy |
| Infatuated love | Passion |
| Empty love | Commitment |
| Romantic love | Intimacy, passion |
| Companionate love | Intimacy, commitment |
| Fatuous love | Passion, commitment |
| Consummate love | Intimacy, passion, commitment |

*Source*: Sternberg, 2006

partners' ratings of the amounts of love (sizes of the triangles) and the types of love (shapes of the triangles) overlap (Sternberg, 2006).

## Fehr's Prototype Approach to Love

As Sternberg (1986) developed his thinking on the triangular nature of love, he suggested that love is prototypically organized. A prototype approach identifies features typically associated with a particular construct and notes the centrality of those features (Prager, 1995). Typical prototypes can be considered as clusters of features that vary between individuals, but exhibit considerable overlap (Fehr, 1988, 2006). Fehr (1988) addressed the challenge of studying love and commitment from a prototype perspective by conducting six studies that focused on everyday use of natural language concepts. Study participants listed features of love and/or commitment, rated the centrality of features to love and/or commitment, and were tested in a variety of other ways to confirm the centrality of features' ratings for each concept (love, commitment).

Overall, Fehr (1988) found love and commitment to be somewhat interdependent, overlapping concepts. The resultant prototype framework for love consists of several feature groupings. One large grouping represents positive affect, such as happiness, caring, commitment, and affection. Another grouping represents more of the dark side of romantic relationships, for example when they are experienced as scary and uncertain. Another cluster that focuses on behavior is represented by elements such as helping, laughing, and gazing at the other; the flip side, cognitive aspects, includes ruminating (thinking about the other often) and positive distortion (only seeing one's partner's positive traits). Other clusters that represent love are expectations that the relationship will endure, lack of inhibition when with one's loved one, social support (e.g., empathy), and altruism (e.g., self-sacrifice).

The prototype framework for commitment is less complex. The largest cluster representing commitment is making a decision and following through with it. Likewise, commitment behaviors include hard work, and giving one's best effort. Cognitive features are mostly represented by levelheadedness and rationality (e.g., decision, promise, mutual agreement), although there is also an irrational component wherein one thinks about one's partner all the time. Possible negatively valenced features include feeling trapped and obligation. Social support and altruism are emphasized, but are tempered by notions of equity (e.g., give and take).

## A Model of "Full" Love

In 2008, I suggested that love be understood as emotional bonding, commitment, and other-centeredness (D. L. Kelley, 2008). My intent was to provide a framework to organize love research and provide a way to understand the relationship between individuals' experience of love and intimacy.

Emotional bonding represents a blending of Sternberg's (1986) passion component with more companionate (Berscheid & Walster, 1978) elements. In essence, emotional bonding is the underlying theme running through both of these aspects of love. As discussed previously, Sternberg (1986) claims that passion goes beyond sexual fulfillment, for example meeting the needs of self-esteem, nurturance, affiliation, dominance, submission, and self-actualization. Emotional bonding captures the larger nature of this dimension and recognizes the various expressions of passion. For instance, an elderly couple who, for health reasons, are no longer sexually active may nonetheless experience a deep passion for one another.

Commitment is the cognitive choice component of love, much as Sternberg (1986) and Fehr (1988) discuss it. For married couples who have made a relational covenant (Hargrave, 1994) with one another, commitment is both the decision to love and the choice to maintain that love. This dimension represents promise, maintaining the relationship, long-term relationship expectations, and working through the hard times (Sternberg, 1986).

Finally, I suggest that as love develops (e.g., one becomes more committed and emotionally bonded to one's partner), there is a significant perspective change – one becomes other-centered. In this same vein, Stanley, Whitton, Sadberry, Clements, and Markman

(2006) suggest that true commitment leads to genuine giving (e.g., healthy self-sacrifice) between partners. As healthy self-sacrifice creates space for individual growth and development, it moves the relationship to a mature love, as noted by Noller (1996). Other-centeredness is also related to the notions of altruism and self-sacrifice, as Fehr (1988) found in her prototype work on love. Components such as helping behavior, giving emotional support, and increasing the other's self-esteem also represent this dimension. Others have referred to this aspect of love as agape or unconditional love (S. S. Hendrick & Hendrick, 1992; J. A. Lee, 1988).

Using this framework to understand love is consistent with Fehr's (1988) conceptualization in that the dimensions are loosely connected with behavioral overlap. For example, providing emotional support for one's spouse can result from one's commitment, maintaining a deep emotional connectedness, and being other-centered. Others have also noted that emotion is related to commitment (Burke & Stets, 1999). Clearly, the framework has significant overlap with Sternberg's conceptualization (e.g., commitment and passion are represented in the current model). However, most strikingly, it removes elements of intimacy (as discussed earlier in the chapter) described by Sternberg (1986) and Fehr (1988) and emphasizes other-centeredness.

## The Interplay of Intimacy and Love

As I argue earlier in this chapter, there is conceptual confusion regarding intimacy as a component of love and love as a component of intimacy. What should be clear by now is that love and intimacy are typically viewed in relationship to one another. Here, I would like to highlight three important issues regarding the relationship between intimacy and love. First, while laypersons and researchers may be hard pressed to make distinctions between love and intimacy, relational turning points often call for conceptual clarity (Baxter & Erbert, 1999; Conville, 1991). Consider a situation wherein a young couple have been sexually intimate and, after some time, one of them finally says, "I love you" – suddenly the differences between love and intimacy seem critical. Similarly, when a wife tells her husband, "I am leaving you," she has created a complex situation. As we described intimacy earlier, the relationship will diminish in certain access dimensions (e.g., physical and social access), while others will remain at fairly high levels due to past history (e.g., informational and psychological access stay high for long periods of time). The affect dimension of intimacy will be complicated as feelings shift from somewhat positive feelings to a mix of anger, frustration, disappointment, betrayal, and most likely lingering feelings of liking (based on their long history of joint positive experiences). At the same time, love may be slow to shift if the husband wants to try to "work it out": he is still committed to her and the marriage, still emotionally tied to her (in fact one could argue that the change from positive to negative affect in intimacy is largely due to the fact that he is still emotionally connected to her – we hurt most over those we care about), and still wants the best for her (other-centered; in his view "the best" is to stay and work on the marriage).

Second, the previous example makes clear that intimacy is bilateral (relational) in nature; love is unilateral. In other words, you can love someone without having that love reciprocated. In this case, commitment, emotional bonding, and other-centeredness may remain high in spite of the lack of reciprocation. Intimacy, however, is dependent on the other's response – as in the previous example, one partner can singlehandedly deescalate a relationship. This distinction is especially relevant in marriage, where one's commitment is, or was at one time, very public and may be maintained in spite of low intimacy levels.

Finally, because intimacy by its very nature makes one vulnerable in the relationship (Petronio, 2002; Prager, 1995), it is important to determine how to develop relationships that are "safe," and to know how to deal with relationship hurt when it comes. We will deal with relational hurt in Chapter 6, but the conceptualization of love I offer in this chapter provides a means to think about creating a relationship safe for intimacy.

Intimacy is allowing another person informational, physical, social, and psychological access to one's self (D. L. Kelley,

2008). This access makes one dependent on, and vulnerable to, others (Holmes & Rempel, 1989; Petronio, 2002). Relationally, there is no way to ensure increased access will not be misused by one's partner from time to time. Thus, as Stanley, Markman, and Whitton (2002) suggest, safety and security are fundamental to marital success. And the development of trust becomes critical to maintaining intimate interaction (Reis & Rusbult; 2004; Prager, 1995).

Full love (emotional bonding, commitment, other-centeredness) creates the relational conditions for trust. First, commitment has the potential to create trust through promise: the cognitive decision to respect and love one's partner. Wieselquist et al.'s (1999) findings show a positive relationship between commitment and trust. Second, emotional bonding creates trust through motivation (e.g., Sternberg discussed passion as a motivational element to treat one's partner in a loving manner). Third, other-centeredness leads to trust through altruistic acts and a willingness to self-sacrifice. Whitton, Stanley, and Markman (2007) suggest that commitment shapes motivation and, subsequently, precipitates prorelationship behavior. Blending their findings with Wieselquist et al.'s (1999) longitudinal work, Whitton et al. (2007) describe the mutual influence between these elements as follows:

> Willingness to sacrifice for a relationship tends to increase partner trust, which then increases partner commitment and willingness to sacrifice in turn for the good of the relationship, which then increases the individual's trust and commitment, and so on in a mutually enhancing cycle. (p. 85)

This "mutually enhancing cycle" echoes Noller's view of mature love. Noller (1996) suggests that mature love is that in which lovers, and those who depend on them (e.g., children), are free and able to grow and develop. This perspective is consistent with the implied nature of sacrifice and commitment: that is, the belief that what benefits one's spouse and the relationship benefits one's self as well (Whitton et al., 2007). Holmes and Rempel (1989) state that "trust grows in an upward spiral, anchored by perceptions of a balanced reciprocation process" (p. 193).

Practical applications of this love and intimacy framework can also be found in the therapeutic literature. For example, cognitive-behavioral approaches to therapy have emphasized interaction processes associated with happy marriages (Walsh, 2003). These approaches tend to emphasize the couples' choice to maintain the relationship by modifying negative behavior patterns. In contrast, recent trends have focused on emotional response and attachment (Gottman, 1994). Emotionally focused therapy (EFT; Greenberg & Johnson, 1988) emphasizes the recognition of one's feelings/emotions as part of restructuring couples' interaction. Finally, the surge in positive psychology research has emphasized prosocial behavior, such as altruistic behavior, as a component of healthy marriage relationships. For example, Pickering (2008) examines the relationship between love and therapy and suggests altruism (caring for the other beyond one's self) and alterity (e.g., empathy and the recognition of otherness) are components of true love. Stanley et al. (2006) found that satisfaction with sacrifice (the degree to which an individual finds sacrifice, for partner or relationship, rewarding) was related to positive marital outcomes. They suggest that therapists can teach clients "to give unselfishly (in healthy ways) to their partners" (p. 302).

## Final Thoughts

This chapter has focused on intimacy and love as central processes to maintaining healthy marriage relationships. Intimacy is a reciprocal process whereby partners share mutual access and develop positive affect and substantive interdependence on one another. Intimacy in marriage is characterized by private disclosure, emotional expression, partner responsiveness, and physical/sexual connection. Love creates a safe context for the vulnerability that is an inevitable outcome of intimacy. Full, or mature, love is characterized by a deep commitment and emotional bond that leads to healthy self-sacrifice, such that the relationship becomes a place wherein partners grow and develop.

I end this chapter with a final thought to remind us that the theory and research we have been discussing is rooted in "real" relationships. Most of us do not express our relational experiences using social science terms, such as access or emotional bonding. Rather, we describe them in the same way we would tell a good story. When we talk about our relationships, we describe them holistically, as narrative. Sternberg (1998, 2006) addresses this issue by suggesting we view love as story. He believes that, based on our personal attributes and environment, we create love stories that we seek to fulfill; and his data suggest that couples who have somewhat similar story profiles tend to be happier. In essence, as students of marital relationships, we must remember that the theories presented in this chapter represent couples in real relationships – each living their own unique story of intimacy and love.

## Basic Principles: Intimacy and Love

1 Intimacy is used to describe a relationship or kind of interaction.
  (a) Intimate relationships can be defined by culture (e.g., marriage), or regularity of intimate interaction.
  (b) Intimate interactions are characterized by:
    (i) verbal behaviors (e.g., self-disclosure and partner responsiveness);
    (ii) nonverbal behaviors (e.g., physical affection, sexual behavior, tone of voice);
    (iii) positive experience (e.g., having feelings and thoughts) of closeness and being understood.
2 Privacy is related to intimacy.
  (a) Marriage partners experience a dialectical tension between openness and closedness; understanding closedness (privacy) helps to understand openness (intimacy).
  (b) Marital partners develop collective boundaries. Within these boundaries couples privately disclose with one another, creating a sense of intimacy in the relationship.
  (c) Privacy, and therefore intimacy, contains informational, social, physical, and psychological elements.
3 Intimacy is experienced in marriage when partners give one another informational, social, physical, and psychological access.
4 Intimacy is experienced when the marriage is characterized by positive affect (e.g., warm and caring feelings).
5 Marital intimacy is typically communicated through private disclosure, emotional expression, partner responsiveness, and physical/sexual connection.
6 The reciprocal and vulnerable nature of intimacy creates interdependence between partners.
7 Love can be characterized as passionate, companionate, caring, attachment, mature or immature, and as having cognitive, emotion, and behavioral components.
8 Individuals vary regarding how they express love.
9 Full, or mature, love is characterized by a deep commitment and emotional bond that leads to other-centeredness and creates a space where individuals can grow and develop.
10 Full love creates a safe environment for intimacy.

## Questions You Should Ask
*(as a Researcher or as a Relational Partner)*

1 How might the view of intimacy presented in this chapter be used to help couples assess their relationships more effectively?

2 How do happy married couples evaluate their relationships in terms of access (informational, social, physical, psychological)?

3 How do higher and lower rating of each access component affect marital quality?

4 How do partners' responsiveness ratings affect individuals' perception of intimacy?

5 How do couples who experience intimacy negotiate interdependence?

6 Considering the picture of full (mature) love presented in this chapter, how would couple ratings of each dimension (commitment, emotional bonding, other-centeredness) be related to relational quality?

7 At the end of the chapter I suggest that love creates a "safe" place for intimacy. How might each love component be empirically related to each intimacy component?

8 Since intimacy creates vulnerability, how do couples protect themselves from being hurt in intimate relationships?

9 Do couples with high ratings of full love feel less vulnerable in intimate relationships?

# 4

## Close Conflict

*Jack just made me mad. Whatever difficulties he had had that day at work, he brought them home and I was cooking and I was happy. Then he said something that upset me and I just ... I had a knife in my hand and I just turned and threw it at him! He looked at the knife, then at me, then went out the door, went to the store, came back in, put his beer in the refrigerator and we sat down for dinner. We didn't say very much. Then we went to bed and the next morning we got up and he says, "I'm sorry." And I says, "Okay." And that was it.*

Jessica, married 42 years

As the interview continued, Jessica revealed, "Jack realized he shouldn't have said what he said, and it made me upset. Then, we just started again. It was just the fact of knowing that we loved each other. It was just an incident."

It may have been "just an incident" as Jessica looks back, but this was not a one-time event. Throughout their marriage, Jessica and Jack *learned to do conflict together* in a manner that was neither productive ... nor safe! Their conflict interactions were often characterized by habitual responses fueled by high arousal levels. Both Jessica and Jack developed their own unique conflict style that, now, "feels natural" to them and that they use to *balance* the relationship. Jessica's style is typically shoot then aim; Jack's is classic retreat.

Conflict has become a central focus for marital researchers. As Cahn (1992) states, "Because conflict often brings out the worst in people, partners who find it difficult to deal effectively with their differences tend to be more unhappy and dissatisfied than partners who are better equipped for dealing with them" (p. 1). Most scholars conceptualize conflict as involving interdependent parties expressing struggle over perceived incompatibilities (Putnam, 2006). Marital conflict typically involves differences in partners' perspectives (Sillars, Roberts, Leonard, & Dun, 2000) that precipitate use of communication to work toward understanding, resolution of "practical" issues ("So, are we going to get a new car or not?"), and realignment of the relationship. Specifically, partners express, recognize, and manage conflict through communication (Canary et al., 2001).

As such, the focus of this chapter is to examine how communication contributes to constructive and destructive conflict processes. I begin by exploring why couples fight. Then I examine couple approaches to conflict, focusing on styles of conflict, sequences of conflict behaviors, and variations in conflict behavior based on couple type. This is followed by a discussion of factors that influence the conflict process, such as perception, mindlessness, arousal/emotion, and religiosity. The chapter finishes with suggestions for how to change couple conflict patterns for the better.

## Why Couples Fight

Managing conflict has become an increasingly important marriage skill due to the fairly dramatic change in marital roles in the last half-century. Today's couples must negotiate virtually every action in the marriage (at least until relational norms are set). For example, there are no longer clear societal guidelines as to who will be the primary provider in the family, who will be the primary caregiver, or who will take care of the cars. In my research with long-term married couples, we asked couples to describe how they worked through negative times in their relationships. Some of our couples, who had been married 40-plus years, responded, "Well, I'm sure we must have talked about it, but the fact was – he needed a job, so we moved." In other words, the more established the roles, the less conflict in decision making. The fewer established roles, the greater the need for direct communication and the greater potential for conflict.

Another cause of conflict is the mutual dependence of partners in a marriage relationship. Essentially, interdependence leads to conflict (Canary et al., 2001). While there are many benefits to interdependence, mutual dependency also creates the potential for conflict regarding the distribution and coordination of resources. Marital resources may include tangible items such as money, houses, and furniture or more affective elements such as physical affection and affirmation. Negotiating equitable distribution or use of these resources may result in conflict between partners (e.g., "Should we buy a new 65-inch plasma television?"; "I wish you would be more affectionate.") And, importantly, equity is a key determinant in maintaining relationship quality (Canary & Stafford, 1992; see extended discussion in Chapter 2).

Caughlin and Vangelisti (2006) offer five accounts to explain conflict: skill deficiency; gender differences regarding conflict expression; individual differences regarding characteristics such as attachment style; stressful circumstances; and perceived incompatible goals. Likewise, Spitzberg et al. (1994) propose a competency-based model of conflict that emphasizes incompatible goals (see Box 4.1). This model posits that behavior enacted during a conflict episode is assessed in terms of competence performance criteria. Conflict episodes are characterized as typically consisting of perceptions of incompatible goals. Under such conditions, meeting one's partner's expectations, as well as securing one's own goals, becomes a formidable challenge (Canary et al., 2001). Apart from perceptions of incompatible goals, certain topics, types of problems, and content/relationship issues influence the conflict process.

---

## Box 4.1: Theory Checkpoint: The Competence-Based Model of Interpersonal Conflict

The Competence-Based Model of Interpersonal Conflict (Canary & Spitzberg, 1989; Spitzberg et al., 1994) rests on the assumption that communicators evaluate communication behavior during conflict in terms of subjective standards of competent performance (Canary et al., 2001). As such, each interaction is evaluated in terms of appropriateness, effectiveness, and satisfaction. Appropriateness occurs when communication fits contextual and relational expectations. Effectiveness is essentially perceived goal attainment. Satisfaction is an affective response when competent communication between partners takes place.

This approach to assessing conflict episodes highlights three challenges to competent communication during marital conflict:

1 *Effectiveness*: It is difficult for relational partners to accomplish interactional goals during heightened conflict.
2 *Appropriateness*: During conflict, normative behavior is not always interpreted in a normative manner: for example, a typically benign statement may carry negative connotations within the context of a conflict episode (or, conversely, a behavior normatively interpreted as negative may have little or no negative effect).
3 *Satisfaction*: Conflict episodes are complex and difficult to interpret.

---

## What Couples Fight About

Couples fight about topics ranging from finances to children, the color of the bathroom to car repairs. However, identifying a topic is only one means of framing conflict interaction. During communication about specific topics, couples are also influenced by perceptions of whether the conflict is solvable, and what underlying relationship messages may be present in the interaction.

## Conflict Topics

Money is often listed as a central topic of marital conflict (Papp, Cummings, & Goeke-Morey, 2009). In a study focusing on trauma and recovery strategies, Harvey (2004) noted that money was the most frequently reported transgression by couples. Money issues are significant in marriage because financial decision making is often stressful decision making. As discussed previously, conflict over money represents the struggle to coordinate and distribute shared resources. Also, money issues often reveal other relational concerns such as power, control, and role fulfillment. Spouses have rated money issues as more intense and significant compared to other topics, and more pervasive, problematic, recurrent, and difficult to resolve (Papp et al., 2009).

Notarius and Markman (1993) report that married couples struggle most with money, followed by communication and sex. Communication and sex represent aspects of intimacy that have to be renegotiated as the married couple begin to shift focus from their relationship to such issues as career building, home buying, and having children (see Chapter 5). According to Notarius and Markman, issues related to children and in-laws are mid-level problems that couples are often able to work through. In addition, conflict topics may shift across the life of the marriage. Storaasli and Markman (1990) note that certain topics may decrease over time (e.g., friends, religion, and jealousy) while others increase (e.g., sex, communication, and recreation).

Fincham and Beach (1999) argue that more attention should be paid to couples' areas of conflict because certain topics may be more difficult to discuss effectively and are associated with divorce (e.g., extramarital sex and substance abuse). Interestingly, Sanford (2003) found a relationship between topic difficulty and relationship satisfaction and, subsequently, between satisfaction and communication behavior. In particular, at the distal level (i.e., global issues pertaining to the overall relationship and affecting communication across contexts) a person's high score on topic difficulty was associated with more negative behavior such as criticism and contempt when speaking, defensiveness when listening, and, for husbands alone, poor listening. The implications appear to be that when a relationship is stressed by a salient, unresolved area of conflict, couples experience a drop in satisfaction and negative communication increases (Sanford, 2003).

Evolutionary psychologists suggest other possible causes of conflict. The theory of evolution by selection suggests that human attributes have evolved to their current state because they benefit reproduction and the species' proliferation (Wilson & Daly, 2001). From this perspective, monogamy can be partially explained as the result of human infants requiring long-term care for survival (S. S. Hendrick & Hendrick, 1992). According to Wilson and Daly (2001), threats to a monogamous relationship are likely to create conflict. These threats may include: temptations to abandon the present partner for another; free-riding on the partner's investment in the couple's joint project; in-laws showing favoritism; dependent children from prior relationships; and extramarital affairs.

It is important to recognize that the topic of conflict is only one element of understanding the conflict process, and likely not the most significant (Sillars, Canary, & Tafoya, 2004). However, perceptions as to how solvable the problem is, and whether it is a content or relationship issue, play an essential role in the process.

## Solvable and Perpetual Problems

Research by Gottman and colleagues (Driver, Tabares, Shapiro, Nahm, & Gottman, 2003; Gottman, 1994) has identified two central types of problems couples encounter: solvable and unsolvable. Solvable problems can be resolved, like whether to keep a checking account at the credit union or bank. Perpetual problems seem unsolvable to the couple. They often result from differences in personality, needs, or culture: for example, one partner may be energized by being with people, while the other needs "down time" to reenergize. Happy couples learn to accept and understand their differences, and manage to handle them with positive affect and amusement. In contrast, unhappy couples become gridlocked in their positions, feeling overwhelmed and hopeless about finding a compromise or some sense of peace regarding the issue. Similarly, in my long-term marriage research, couples reported *accepting* one's partner as an important strategy in managing partner differences (Waldron & Kelley, 2008).

## Content and Relationship Levels of Meaning

Another way to view conflict is to examine levels of meaning that occur during marital interaction. In their classic work, *Pragmatics of Human Communication*, Watzlawick, Beavin, and Jackson (1967), based on work by Bateson, identify content and relationship levels of meaning. Content levels of meaning can be understood as the topic of conversation. The content is typically verbal and explicit in nature. In contrast, relationship levels of meaning convey a message about the relationship that is often implicit, though it can be explicit, and often nonverbal, though it can be verbal as well. In the same vein, Burgoon and Hale (1984) define relational messages as those that focus on some aspect of the relationship (e.g., dominance, intimacy, equality), how one sees one's self in the relationship, or how one sees one's partner in the relationship.

Levels of meaning are particularly related to conflict interaction because of couples' tendency to keep their verbal discussion at the content level while simultaneously (and often implicitly) working nonverbally on relational issues. Sillars et al. (2000) describe this process, "Thus, individuals may differentially attend to the literal substance of messages vs. the implicit relational implications and communicative acts and the broader contexts" (p. 496). Take note of the content and relationship levels of meaning in the following conversation between Katie and Sam (*with commentary*):

> Sam: I wish you would do a better job keeping the checkbook balanced. *(Sam makes a direct statement about something that he thinks is Katie's responsibility.)*

Katie: Sorry, I've been very busy lately. *(Katie hears Sam's comment as an attack and immediately responds defensively by saying "Sorry" with a little attitude, and by speaking louder with key words emphasized.)*
Sam: Sure, like busy shopping with your sister all day? *(Sam reciprocates the defensiveness through sarcasm and by rolling his eyes and using a belittling tone of voice.)*
Katie: I'm doing the best I can. If you need to have everything perfectly under your thumb, balance it yourself. *(Katie's voice sounds angry as she reciprocates the sarcasm; she attacks what she perceives as his need to control.)*
Sam: I just thought *you* liked knowing our finances are secure. We can't know that if we don't balance the checkbook. *(Sam, with a vocal tone that sounds disrespectful, reciprocates the perceived attack, by implying that Katie is being inconsistent.)*
Katie: Look, I'm not your Mom, and I'm not going to be. I'm not going to handle every little detail for you like she did! *(Katie feels that Sam compares her unfavorably to his mother and that he expects her to handle all the details of their relationship, like his mother did.)*
*(Each leaves the situation by going to separate rooms.)*

In the beginning, Katie and Sam sound like they are just talking about an explicit, verbal, content issue – balancing the checkbook. However, underlying relational issues escalate the conflict. Sam is disappointed in Katie because she does not meet his expectations, and at the end of the argument he feels personally attacked. Katie is defensive because she feels Sam begins the conversation by attacking her; in addition, she feels misunderstood. Note that Katie's last statement is an attempt to address the relational issue explicitly, but by this time the conflict has escalated to such an extent that the couple are unable to handle the discussion productively.

Interestingly, Sillars et al. (2000) found gender differences similar to Katie and Sam's experience, although the researchers state that these differences are not inherently gender-based. In their study, wives focused less than husbands on the content level of messages and their own intentions and behavior, and more on their partner's intentions and behavior. Both husbands and wives viewed their own conflict behavior and intentions more positively (constructive engagement) than the behavior and intentions of their spouse (confrontation).

## Couple Approaches to Conflict

Couple approaches to conflict can be viewed in terms of specific styles, sequences of behaviors, and couple types. I present each in order.

### Conflict Styles

Sillars et al. (2004) suggest, based on work by Van de Vliert and Euwema (1994), that marital and family conflict can be conceptualized along two continua: directness vs. indirectness and cooperation vs. competition. As such, communication acts during conflict can be understood in terms of four global strategies: negotiation – direct and cooperative; direct fighting – direct and competitive; nonconfrontation – indirect and cooperative; and indirect fighting – indirect and competitive.[1]

*Negotiation: direct and cooperative.* This category of conflict behaviors represents communication tactics such as agreement, communication talk (e.g., communication about communication), validation, positive mindreading (e.g., statements about one's partner's beliefs or motivations given with positive or neutral affect), and conciliatory remarks (e.g., supportive remarks, concessions, and acceptance of responsibility). In addition are problem-solving behaviors such as description of the problem, analytic remarks, expressing feelings about a problem, summarizing, and problem solving/information exchange (e.g., offering a possible solution). Other negotiation behaviors include appealing acts (e.g., appeals to fairness, appeals to other's motives, pleading), cognitive acts (e.g., seeking/giving information, giving reasons,

---

[1] See Sillars et al. (2004) for a complete list of citations for sample behaviors representing the four conflict styles.

exploring consequences), and reconciling acts (e.g., addressing blame, attempts to make up).

*Direct fighting: direct and competitive.* This style is also direct, but competitive rather than cooperative. Direct fighting includes confrontative remarks, disagreements, and coercive acts. It also includes more personal responses such as invalidation (e.g., deny responsibility, excuse, noncompliance, nonverbal behaviors that show disgust or disapproval), blame (e.g., criticize, threat, negative vocal tone), personal attacks, negative mindreading (e.g., statements about one's partner's beliefs or motivations, given with negative affect), and rejecting acts (e.g., giving up, leaving the field, rejecting one's partner).

*Nonconfrontation: indirect and cooperative.* The third style utilizes indirect tactics that are cooperative. These conflict tactics tend to focus on process and creating positive or neutral affect. Typical process behaviors include facilitation (e.g., assent, metacommunication, question, paraphrase/reflection), resolving acts (e.g., accept one's partner's plans or feelings, offer to collaborate), noncommittal remarks, and topic management. Positive or neutral management is created by use of friendly joking, positive physical contact, and positive mindreading (e.g., implying favorable qualities in one's partner).

*Indirect fighting: indirect and competitive.* This final style is also indirect, but also competitive. Most characteristic of this style is denial that a conflict exists or use of evasive remarks to neither confirm nor deny that a conflict exists (e.g., equivocation). Withdrawal is common and can involve moving the conversation off topic or actually withdrawing from the conversation. Not listed by Sillars et al. (2004), but also appropriate to this category, is using passive–aggressive tactics. Passive–aggressive acts appear passive, but have an aggressive effect (e.g., guiltmaking). A final communication act in this category is dysphoric affect (e.g., depressed or sad affect, self-complaint, whiny voice).

A final note about individual styles. As with any communication behavior, one has to consider from whose perspective one is interpreting the behavior. Sillars et al. (2000) found that when watching videotapes of their own couple discussions, partners differed in their interpretations of the interaction. Individuals tended to rate their partner's behavior less favorably (e.g., less cooperative and more confrontational) than their own behavior. Dissatisfied couples in high conflict situations focused less on conflict issues and had more blaming, angry, and pessimistic thoughts. Additionally, the more intense the conflict, the less agreement between spouse ratings and trained observer ratings. As will be discussed more fully later, these results are consistent with the effects of high arousal and mindless processing.

These findings are consistent with other work that indicates that perception of conflict behaviors or styles is important to relational quality. Segrin, Hanzal, and Domschke (2009) found support for the benevolent perception model, such that positively toned perceptions were associated with marital satisfaction. Likewise, Burleson and Denton (1997) found that communication skills were positively related to satisfaction for satisfied couples, but not for dissatisfied couples. They speculated that the difference was due to perceptions of negative intention.

## Sequences of Conflict Behavior

Individuals' use of conflict styles occurs within an interactional context. Behavior choice and use is affected by one's partner's behavior. This interplay of conflict styles and tactics is less predictable in satisfied couples than in dissatisfied couples. Possibly as a result of increased arousal levels and subsequent reliance on mindless behavior patterns, unhappy couples tend to fall into rigid (e.g., predictable) patterns of behavior (Fincham, 2004). Two common patterns are demand–withdraw and negative reciprocity.

### Demand–Withdraw
The *demand–withdraw* pattern of couple conflict has generated a tremendous amount of research and discussion (Caughlin &

Vangelisti, 1999, 2000; Christensen & Shenk, 1991). It is one expression of the most basic choice in conflict communication: to engage or avoid (Caughlin & Vangelisti, 2006). Demand–withdraw patterns are characterized by one partner pursuing the interaction via demands, complaints, or criticisms, while the other partner seeks asylum through defensiveness and passive inaction (Fincham, 2004). Typically the demanding party is dissatisfied about some issue and seeking change, and the withdrawer is seeking to minimize discussion or maintain the current behavior (Sillars et al., 2004).

Often the demand–withdraw pattern manifests itself through female demands and male withdrawal (Christensen & Heavey, 1990; Fincham, 2004), although certain evidence suggests that this pattern may not always hold (Sillars et al., 2004). Who demands may be dependent on whether the wife or husband is seeking change (Caughlin & Vangelisti, 1999; Heavey et al., 1995; Klinetob & Smith, 1996).

It is clear that the wife-demand/husband-withdraw pattern is associated with lower relational satisfaction (Caughlin & Vangelisti 2006; Heavey, Layne, & Christensen, 1993) and is a stronger predictor of marital satisfaction levels than negativity alone (Caughlin & Huston, 2002). Both husbands and wives feel less verification (less understanding) from their partner when the partner withdraws (Weger, 2005). Interestingly, this effect is not due to the couples' disagreement over an issue but, rather, it is perceived indifference that works against self-confirmation.

## Negative Reciprocity

A distinguishing characteristic of unhappy couples is their tendency to express negativity and reciprocate negative affect. Negativity has been operationalized as distributive conflict strategies and expressions of hostile and negative affect (Caughlin & Vangelisti, 2006). Specific communication behaviors that characterize this state include defensiveness, cross-complaining, lack of validation, and listener withdrawal (Gottman, 1994). Canary and Lakey (2006) also claim that dissatisfied couples increase their use of competitive tactics as conflict continues.

Negativity and negative reciprocity characterize dissatisfied couples' interactions and may lead to a decline in marital satisfaction over time (Caughlin & Vangelisti, 2006). Hanzal and Segrin (2009) describe negative affectivity as an enduring vulnerability (personality characteristic) associated with lower marital satisfaction. Gottman (1994) suggests that negativity becomes an absorbing state for dissatisfied couples. During conflict episodes, dissatisfied couples tend to focus on the expression of negative affect, resulting in somewhat rigid (predictable) patterns of negative behavior that are difficult to break. Particularly troubling about this pattern of negative reciprocity is the seeming inability of dissatisfied couples to shift their focus from negative affect to problem-solving skills, such as metacommunication, feeling probes and exploration, information sharing, use of appropriate humor, and appeals to basic philosophy and expectations in the marriage (Gottman, 1994, p. 63). Sillars et al. (2004) suggest that interactions by dissatisfied couples are characterized in the beginning by politeness, but then fall into patterns of increasing hostility.

Negative reciprocation may include symmetrical or asymmetrical patterns (Canary & Lakey, 2006). Negative symmetrical patterns may include complaint–countercomplaint, reciprocation of negative metacommunication, proposal–counterproposal (without recognition of the partner's initial position), and disagreement–disagreement (Canary & Lakey, 2006; Gottman, 1982). Assymetrical patterns may include demand–withdraw, withdrawal–hostility, and attack–defend (Canary & Lakey, 2006; Caughlin & Vangelisti, 2000; Roberts & Krokoff, 1990; Ting-Toomey, 1983).

## Couple Types and Conflict

Another means of examining how couples engage conflict is to examine behavior associated with various types of couples. Both Fitzpatrick (1988) and Gottman (1994) have well-developed programs of study that categorize couples by *type*. These couple types vary in their communication behavior; in particular, in their conflict behavior.

## Fitzpatrick's Couple Types

Fitzpatrick (1988) has identified three pure couple types (see Chapter 2 for general discussion of the types) that exhibit significant variability regarding conflict behavior (Fitzpatrick, Fey, Segrin, & Schiff, 1993). *Traditional* couples tend to engage in conflict over serious issues, but they tend to focus on content rather than relationship issues. They are conciliatory and cooperative with one another. *Independent* couples engage freely in conflict; they deal with both minor and serious issues. They are willing to disagree and negotiate with one another. Their high expressivity can lead to serious conflicts at times. *Separate* couples are conflict avoiders. They are characterized by interpersonal distance and have difficulty engaging in direct, open discussion. When a stressful conflict occurs, they tend to retreat. *Mixed* couples, most frequently characterized by a separate husband and traditional wife, are much like traditionals in that they deal with conflict when they have to. Typically it is the traditional wife who tries to raise and deal with issues.

Fitzpatrick (1988) has also examined the presence of complementary and symmetrical interactions for each couple type. Competitive symmetry is characterized by both spouses making control (one-up) moves during an interaction. Complementary interactions occur when one spouse takes the lead of the other (one-up followed by one-down). At a most basic level, a symmetrical interaction could look like, "Let's go out for pizza," "No, let's stay home," and a complementary interaction, "Let's go out for pizza," "Sure, I'd love to." Fitzpatrick demonstrated that independents use more competitive symmetry during conflict ("The house is a mess because you leave your stuff around." "No I don't. You're unorganized."), separates use relatively little, with traditionals in the middle.

In an earlier study, Fitzpatrick (1984) found that traditionals had shorter conflicts, used agreement less and information seeking more than other couples, used commands, and tended not to give up control. Independents were assertive and challenged one another while maintaining a sense of interdependence and mutual regard. Separates managed conflict by using avoidance behaviors such as speaking and interrupting less often, and talking for shorter periods.

## Gottman's Five Couple Types

As discussed briefly in Chapter 2, Gottman (1994) has identified three types of regulated couples and two types of unregulated couples. Regulated couples are stable: that is, they are not headed toward separation or divorce, and have found ways of achieving a functional balance of positive to negative behaviors in the relationship (5:1 – typically considered a ratio of five positive behaviors to one negative behavior). The first type of regulated couple, *conflict-avoiding* (also referred to as conflict-minimizing couples), are emotionally flat and distant and use few influence attempts with one another. They keep the relationship balanced with low levels of negative and positive exchange. *Volatile* couples are much more passionate, exhibiting a great deal of intimacy and autonomy, accompanied by frequent attempts to influence each other. They maintain balance just the opposite of conflict-avoiding couples – they fight often, but also express positive affect, such as humor, just as often. *Validating* couples take the middle road. They are emotionally close and highly interdependent; however, they find balance in their relationship by minimizing disagreement and the use of influence attempts.

As may be obvious, the three types of couples (conflict-avoiding, volatile, validating) discussed up to this point have significant parallels to Fitzpatrick's (1988) couple types (described in the previous paragraphs). This conceptual validation through two independent research programs should not be viewed lightly. Both researchers have found three couple types to be stable and satisfied. While these couples may vary in terms of their subjective experience of marriage, they all are able to regulate their conflict behaviors such that they maintain stable, happy marriages.

In contrast, Gottman's final two couple types are not stable. They are nonregulated in the sense that they are not able to maintain a productive balance of positive to negative behaviors in the relationship (5:1 for regulated couples compared to 1:1 for nonregulated). Practically this means that when conflict begins to escalate and negative affect is expressed, regulated couples are able to respond in ways that restore an appropriate positive:negative ratio, whereas nonregulated couples struggle to achieve a productive balance. As I discussed earlier, this may be due to less-satisfied couples experiencing emotional flooding and consequent patterns of negative reciprocity.

*Hostile* couples represent the first type of nonregulated couple. They are characterized by direct engagement (often attacking behavior), attentiveness, and defensiveness. A classic defensive interaction would include mindreading used with negative affect to attack the partner (e.g., "You never want to help me with the children."), followed by the partner's disagreement (e.g., "I do, too! You never give me a chance.").

The second type of nonregulated (unstable) couple is *hostile/detached*. Like hostile couples, hostile/detached attack one another and respond with defensiveness; however, they also exhibit emotional detachment. The detached state of these couples results in the expression of emotionally distancing behavior, such as the expression of contempt or disgust.

It is important to note that both regulated and nonregulated couples, at times, engage in destructive behavior patterns. However, characteristic of nonregulated couples is the inability to intervene in escalating conflict interactions and return to some sense of balance (e.g., 5:1, positive to negative). How couples can return escalating conflict to constructive, balanced interaction is dealt with in the following sections.

## Factors That Influence Conflict Processes

Having examined several approaches couples use to engage conflict, it is important to recognize factors that influence how these processes are performed. In order to improve couples' ability to manage conflict constructively, I turn our attention to how perception, mindlessness, and arousal affect couples' conflict.

## Perception

Conflict is in the eye of the beholder. No matter how hard you try to be reasonable, or possibly how hard you try to be nasty, the interaction will be influenced by your partner's perception of your behavior. You say something directly aimed at hurting your partner, but she deflects it by attributing your action to fatigue; or you do your best to support your partner, but he deflects it by attributing your action to hidden motives. The bottom line is that marriage partners must communicate in such a way to help create accurate perception and, conversely, must be aware that their perceptions may not always be accurate.

Unhappy couples tend to report lower levels of understanding and exhibit less congruence of perceptions than do happier couples (Sillars et al., 2000). Sillars et al. (2000) argue that selective perception is central to understanding these findings. As discussed previously, selective perception is the human need to manage the amount of information consciously processed. However, couples also focus on what they perceive to be pragmatic concerns during the interaction. For instance, the function of a partner's communication must be determined – is the partner apologizing, requesting information, or seeking compliance? Another component of the perception process is the dependence on mindless responses in order to "keep pace" in the interaction. Sillars et al. (2000) suggest that partners may reflect on the pragmatic inferences they make, but typically they do so between interactions when they do not have to process and respond so quickly. Due to the disorderly nature of serious conflict episodes, married partners are more likely during these times to selectively attend in order to make sense of the interaction. As Sillars et al. (2000) state, "Thus, relationship conflict presents a complex and confusing stimulus field, which increases the likelihood that individuals will attend to the interaction idiosyncratically and assign meaning based on a small set of cues that is personally salient or self-serving" (p. 483). Finally, it should be recognized that perception is affected by stress and high levels of arousal, both of which negatively impact one's ability to think complexly – specifically, one's ability to process multiple interpretations of partner behavior or assess possible self-responses is restricted.

## Attributions

Attributions in marriage are used by partners to establish the meaning of relationship-related behavior and are associated with relational outcomes. For example, attributions in marriage vary by partners' level of satisfaction. Happy couples tend to make attributions that enhance the relationship; unhappy couples make attributions that maintain relationship distress (Gottman, 1994). In happy marriages, when an individual exhibits positive behavior, his or her partner makes internal, stable, and global attributions regarding the cause. That is, it is assumed that the behavior stems from the partner's personality and so will continue and carry over into other areas of the relationship. Negative behaviors are seen in the reverse: the behavior does not reflect the partner's character, is not likely to occur again, and will not be generalized to other parts of the relationship. Unhappy couples see things just the opposite. When a positive behavior occurs they make external, unstable, specific attributions (i.e., the behavior is due to the situation, not the partner) and, vice versa, when they interpret something as going wrong they see the cause as internal, stable, and global (i.e., due to the partner's personality or disposition).

Other work regarding marital attributions has found that unhappy couples emphasize the impact of negativity and minimize the impact of positivity (Holtzworth-Munroe & Jacobson, 1985). For couples who are struggling in their marriage, this means the negative stands out. Likewise, unhappy couples attribute more selfish intentions to their partners than do happy couples (Fincham, Bradbury, & Scott, 1990). Gottman, Notarius, Markman, et al. (1976) found that distressed and nondistressed couples did not differ in terms of message intent: that is, in terms of how they wanted messages to be received by their spouses. However, distressed couples' messages were received by partners more negatively than intended.

A final observation. Attribution processes are especially important to understand in conflict processes because of their potential to extend positive and negative cycles of behavior. Couples who are already unhappy must realize they are more likely to make attributions that will continue negative conflict patterns (e.g., blaming); while happy couples are likely to make attributions that help them continue to practice cooperative approaches to conflict. Allred (2000) posits, "Once established, both the stressed and satisfied marital patterns are self-fulfilling and self-perpetuating" (p. 249).

## Power

Most conflicts concern power, whether directly or indirectly (P. T. Coleman, 2000). McDonald (1980) described power as the "ability to achieve desired goals or outcomes" (pp. 842–843). Important to wife–husband power, McDonald's conceptualization focused on power as an attribute of the system rather than the individual. In other words, in marriage, the power structure is determined by how the couple perceive and interact with one another. In this vein, researchers have focused on the importance of couples balancing power (P. T. Coleman, 2000; Gray-Little, Baucom, & Hamby, 1996; McDonald, 1980), and couples themselves have identified equality of power as a central function of talk (Honeycutt & Wiemann, 1999).

McDonald (1980) argued that power can be assessed in terms of three dimensions: bases, processes, and outcomes. Bases can be understood in terms of resources. For example, it has been suggested that men derive power from their role as provider (Spade, 1994). However, material resources are not the only contributor to partners' resources. Personal characteristics, such as gender, may play a large role in determining marital power (Komter, 1989). One interesting example of this is Tichenor's (1999) work that examined couples in which the wife made more money and had higher status than the husband; she found that gender roles continued to reinforce the husband's power. Interestingly, Kerber (1994) argues that marital therapy literature has taken a quid pro quo perspective of marital negotiations by examining marital conflict primarily as an exchange of resources.

The second dimension, processes, includes characteristics of the actual interactions – for our purposes, specific communication behaviors used to negotiate power during an interaction. For example, P. T. Coleman (2000) describes power as typically being understood in terms of competitive conflict strategies. He suggests that researchers put more focus on how parties (e.g., couples) can use cooperative and community approaches to using power. Another example of power process is Sanford's (2007) emotion research that discovered hard emotions, such as anger and aggravation, to be associated with power and attempts to achieve one's goals.

The outcomes dimension essentially represents who gets his or her way or who gets the final say. Research on gender differences in marriage has looked at outcome effects. For example, Noller (1993) proposes that husbands withdraw during conflict to maintain power and resist unwanted change demanded by the wife. Other research indicates that the partner who controls the checkbook, when financial resources are pooled, has considerable influence in the relationship (Tichenor, 1999)

The research on power is extensive; as such, my intent here has been simply to heighten awareness of this ubiquitous component of interpersonal relationships, and to highlight a small sample of power research related to marital conflict.

## Arousal

Another process that has the potential to affect long-term patterns of conflict is arousal. In Chapter 1, I discussed arousal as a physiological state of activation; a state of alertness or orientation (Burgoon, 1993). While moderate levels of arousal can benefit cognitive functioning, arousal extremes can inhibit one's ability to process information and consider possible responses. One trigger of this activated state is the perception of threat. And, since conflict often precipitates perceptions of threat, it is often experienced with significant levels of arousal (Gottman, 1994).

Besides breathing harder, feeling a knot in their stomach, or having sweaty palms, individuals who are highly aroused during a conflict interaction become "hyper-focused." In other words, as noted in Chapter 1, their heightened state of arousal restricts their ability to perceive, adapt, and respond to information. In essence, a highly aroused state inhibits one's ability to constructively respond to messages during a conflict episode. Guerrero and La Valley (2006) state that physiological reactions associated with high arousal lead to defensive and irrational behavior. Gottman (1994) suggests that this effect results when individuals experience a *flood* of negative emotions, especially when this becomes a chronic condition in the relationship. He points out that this highly aroused state (*flooding*) restricts one's ability to process information and increases the tendency to rely on "previously overlearned tactics" (p. 412). As such, high arousal during conflict situations results in a dependence on mindless communication ("previously overlearned tactics") during conflict interactions.

## Mindlessness and Arousal

The relationship between arousal and mindless patterns of behavior has significant implications for couples' patterns of conflict. Mindless communication is unconscious, automated behavior patterns that are used for or typically interpreted as communication behavior (Burgoon, Buller, & Woodall, 1989). As discussed in Chapter 1, mindless patterns of behavior are necessary to accomplish complicated tasks – specifically for our purposes, communication tasks. In particular, mindless communication behaviors are engaged during times of high arousal. As such, when in conflict, it is likely that couples will engage mindless communication behaviors that have become well learned as a couple. This results in two significant consequences. First, the combination of arousal and mindlessness often leads to conflict interaction "running away" with the participants. Second, the emotion component of conflict creates significant challenges to engage productive conflict process.

### Runaway Conflict
In spite of good intentions, many couples experience conflict interactions that seemingly take on a life of their own and end badly.

Like a runaway train, the couple feel out of control of their own interaction. This phenomenon is a result of high arousal, which limits one's ability to process varied interpretations of behavior and to evaluate various options to respond, culminating in reliance on well-learned mindless patterns that often are not productive. Gottman (1994) describes this process of emotional *flooding* as follows:

> The emotional state becomes disregulating in that a person can attend to or do little else when flooded. In this manner, flooding may be highly disruptive of organized behavior. Second I suggest that people in relationships that chronically generate negative affect blends that lead to flooding may become hypervigilant to potentially threatening and escalating interactions. They may become likely to misattribute threat potential to relatively neutral or positive acts. All of these processes have implications for the course of a conflictual marital interaction. (p. 76)

Gottman's (1994; Driver et al., 2003) *Four Horsemen of the Apocalypse* (see Box 4.2) represents four variables associated with runaway conflict. The variables do not necessarily follow a prescribed order, but often *complain/criticize* begins the process toward dissatisfaction and dissolution. Complaint is a behaviorally specific statement about something that is a problem or needs improvement ("It hurt my feelings when you told your father, 'yes,' without checking with me."). A problem arises when, over time, the complaint evolves into criticism – statements that make a stable and global attribution of the partner ("You are always so inconsiderate."). For example, Alberts (1988) reported that poorly adjusted couples focused complaints on personal characteristics of their partners. A second variable, *defensiveness*, tends to breed reciprocation of negative affect. Defensiveness often results in patterns of attack–counterattack, blaming, and communicating with a childish tone. A third horseman, *contempt*, often occurs when a partner exhibits a superior attitude toward the spouse. In essence, once labeled negatively ("You are so inconsiderate."), one's partner may engage in "put downs," be it with verbal or nonverbal behaviors such as sarcasm, mockery, or rolling the eyes. The

## Box 4.2: The Four Horsemen of the Apocalypse

Gottman's research on *the Four Horsemen of the Apocalypse* provides some of the most robust findings in marital research (Driver et al., 2003; Gottman, 1994, 1999). The Four Horsemen are so named because their presence signals the "end times." In fact, the presence of all four horsemen in a relationship is a strong predictor of relationship dissolution (Buehlman et al., 1992; Carrère et al., 2000; Driver et al., 2003; Gottman, 1994, 1999).

The first horseman, *criticism*, attacks one's character. "You always" and "you never" statements reflect the belief that there is something "wrong" with the partner and he or she is likely never to change. These statements are in contrast to *complaints*, which are behaviorally based ("It frustrates me when you don't fill the car with gas."). Criticism is often taken personally and, as such, often leads to defensiveness.

The second horseman, *defensiveness*, is a response to a perceived attack. Clearly, when one perceives one's partner to engage in character assassination (e.g., criticism), a natural response is to defend one's self. Gottman (1999) suggests that marital couples often respond to attack as an innocent victim, "You're too critical, I didn't do anything wrong." This response of countercomplaining, or counterattacking, typically increases arousal levels and the potential for runaway conflict.

The third horseman, *contempt*, has been characterized as the most damaging of all three horsemen (Driver et al., 2003). Contempt is any verbal or nonverbal behavior that places one's self above one's partner. Using a mocking tone of voice is typical of contempt. Gottman (1999) states that one of his favorite examples of contempt is when one partner corrects the other partner, grammatically, in the midst of an argument, "It's not, 'I could care less,' it's 'I couldn't care less.' At least get that right!" (p. 45). Contempt is particularly damaging because partners' disrespect signals emotional distancing and a lack of perceived equality – they are no longer partners (equals).

The fourth horseman, *stonewalling*, involves the withdrawal of the listener – communicatively, psychologically, or physically. Cues typically associated with listening – eye contact, head nodding, facial response, brief vocalization ("uh-huh") – are nonexistent with the stonewaller. Men are more likely to stonewall than women, yet women's stonewalling is highly predictive of divorce.

Gottman has found all horsemen, except contempt, to commonly show up in healthy marriages. The key is that healthy, regulated marriages find ways to repair after criticism, defensiveness, and stonewalling. On the other hand, Gottman finds the expression of contempt between partners to be so problematic that he actually recommends that therapists label contempt as psychological abuse.

final variable, *stonewalling*, is the somewhat natural response to withdraw from interaction after this sequence of potentially damaging behaviors. An overwhelmed spouse, typically the husband, may withdraw for the sake of self-preservation. Gottman and colleagues (Buehlman, Gottman, & Katz, 1992; Carrère, Buehlman, Gottman, Coan, & Ruckstuhl, 2000; Driver et al., 2003) have been able to predict divorce with 94% accuracy when all four of the horsemen are present in a couple's interactions.

The key element driving the four horsemen is emotional distance (Driver et al., 2003). In particular, contempt and criticism have distinct effects on the couple compared to anger and disagreement (Gottman, 1994). Contempt is the most corrosive of the horsemen as it tends to encourage reciprocal negativity, works against cooperative efforts, and shows disrespect (Driver et al., 2003). By contrast, emotions such as anger tend to be engaging rather than distancing, and may actually be a long-term resource for relational improvement over time (Gottman, 1994; Gottman

& Krokoff, 1989). Related to this, couples experiencing extreme levels of emotional disengagement may not demonstrate the four horsemen, but, rather, may look quite healthy on first glance (Driver et al., 2003). However, these couples may actually experience high levels of arousal during conflict and have a marked lack of positive affect.

As such, couples exhibiting the four horsemen interaction sequence and couples characterized by extreme levels of emotional disengagement are influenced by increased arousal levels. However, the arousal effect is considerably different for each of these couple types. Emotionally disengaged couples may experience high levels of arousal due to suppression of negative affect (Driver et al., 2003; Gross & Levenson, 1997). In contrast, couples engaged in the four horsemen are likely to engage in a destructive form of negative reciprocity, such that expressed negativity by one partner is responded to with increased negativity from the other partner. This pattern of negative escalation is associated with divorce (Gottman, 1998). Interestingly, couples who reciprocate negative affect without escalation (e.g., anger for anger or sadness for sadness) are at least risk of divorce (Driver et al., 2003).

Research has also shown that arousal has differential effects for husbands and wives. Husbands tend to become aroused more quickly and arousal dissipates more slowly than for wives (Gottman, 1994; Levenson & Gottman, 1983, 1985). A wife's emotional expressivity may be confused with her having a higher level of arousal, when actually her husband's higher level of arousal may be expressed through withdrawal or through an attack–withdraw pattern (e.g., a blowup followed by, "I don't want to talk about it any more."). Many husbands' discomfort with experiencing negative emotion leads to one of these two effects.

### Emotion and Conflict

Much of our discussion in this section has been related to the role of emotion in conflict interactions. Guerrero and La Valley (2006) propose five ideas that are central to understanding the relationship between emotion and conflict. First, emotions are generated during conflict when one perceives one's goals to be impeded. Second, most salient during this time is one's affect – the positive or negative valence of one's feelings. Third, emotional reactions are associated with physiological change. For example, level of arousal can be associated with how one experiences emotion as active or passive. Fourth, cognition is used to interpret one's emotional reactions. Work by Lazarus (1991) focusing on emotional experience suggests that cognition is used to label affective valence, assess whether an event is personally relevant, make attributions of blame, and consider possible coping strategies. Fifth, specific behavior patterns (e.g., action tendencies) are associated with specific emotions. For example, anger is associated with attack, fear with withdrawal from possible harm, and guilt with making amends (Lazarus, 1991).

Significant to marital functioning, dissatisfied couples frequently develop incongruent interpretations of emotional messages (Sillars et al., 2004). This effect is seemingly due to husbands' failure to clearly encode or decode messages with their spouses (Noller, 1980, 1981). Interestingly, this failure appears to be related to the relationship, rather than a skill deficit, as husbands can accurately decode messages from women who are not their wives (Noller, 1981; Sillars et al., 2004). This effect may be due in part to the effects of arousal and mindlessness in long-term marriages.

Research from various counseling perspectives (Dimidjian, Martell, & Christensen, 2002; Epstein & Baucom, 2002; Greenberg & Johnson, 1988) has focused on the experience and expression of hard and soft emotions. As noted previously, Sanford (2007) describes hard emotions as associated with anger, power, and control. Soft emotions reflect sadness, hurt, and other expressions of vulnerability. Sanford suggests that hard and soft emotions can be understood in light of Buck's (1999) developmental-interactionist theory of emotion. Viewed in this light, hard emotion is a "selfish" emotion associated with asserting power to pursue self-focused goals, regardless of relational consequences (Sanford, 2007). This includes blaming, competition, fighting and self-preservation behavior, as well as demanding in demand–withdrawal interaction. However, it should be noted that Noller

(1993) suggests withdrawal may be a way of getting one's way when a partner is demanding something that one is not ready to fulfill.

Soft emotion is "prosocial" and typically expressed in the context of a close relationship. Emotions such as sadness and hurt demonstrate attachment, cooperation, and an investment in a relationship. One does not typically feel sad or hurt in a relationship that does not hold long-term value or importance. Soft emotions during conflict often are expressed in conjunction with politeness and listening. Sanford (2007) also proposes that some emotions can be characterized as *flat*. Flat emotions are represented by boredom, apathy, and disinterest and may be expressed during conflict as avoidance, withdrawal, or stonewalling.

## Religiosity

In 2008, over 80% of the adult U.S. population identified themselves with some religious tradition and, interestingly, religious practice has been linked to conflict practice in marriage. For example, disparity of religious practices has been linked to more frequent disagreements (Curtis & Ellison, 2002), and increased risk of marital dissolution (Call & Heaton, 1997) and domestic violence (Ellison, Bartkowski, & Anderson, 1999). However, partner similarity on various religious variables, such as participation (Dudley & Kosinski, 1990) and couple prayer (Butler, Stout, & Gardner, 2002), has been reported to reduce marital conflict. Lambert and Dollahite (2006) sought to understand the mechanisms underlying the relationship between religiosity and marital conflict. Interviews with 57 married couples of the Abrahamic faiths (Judaism, Christianity, Islam) revealed that religiosity affected problem prevention, conflict resolution, and relationship reconciliation. Specifically, problems were prevented because couples shared a vision and purpose and valued relational virtues such as selflessness. Conflict resolution was impacted by use of Scriptural teachings as a standard from which to work, and by attending religious services together, and using couple prayer to help alleviate anger and create openness. Relationship reconciliation and repair were affected by couples' commitment to the relationship and willingness to forgive.

## Changing Couple Conflict Patterns

Arousal and mindlessness make conflict processes difficult to modify. Interestingly, certain research has demonstrated that married individuals who struggle to manage conflict productively with their spouses can manage conflict productively with others (e.g., Birchler, Weiss, & Vincent, 1975; Noller, 1981). Likely, during non-spousal conflict, emotional flooding is lessened due to lower arousal levels and fewer scripted (mindless) couple patterns. As such, managing conflict well is not necessarily a matter of learning new skills, although this is an important element to consider. Rather, it often is a matter of managing arousal and mindlessness.

### Managing Arousal

To manage arousal, Driver et al. (2003) recommend couples take a 20-minute break from the conflict. The purpose of this break is to allow arousal levels to drop. That may mean doing something soothing, such as walking outside or listening to music. As I will discuss further in Chapter 6, it is important not to use this break to ruminate over the problem. Because arousal is a physiological process, physical action can be used to reduce arousal. Walking, talking or venting with a friend, journaling, running or engaging in some other sports activity, and breathing exercises or yoga are all possible ways of dropping arousal levels over time. Couples may also choose to move their conversation to a new location, such as a favorite restaurant or outside patio to keep arousal levels low. In the early days of our marriage when we had no money, my wife and I used to have our budget meetings on an outdoor patio of a French restaurant. We had tea and croissants for three dollars and discussed our budget in a pleasant environment instead of in the kitchen of our small apartment.

## Managing Mindlessness

Changing unwanted mindless conflict behaviors can be accomplished through increased mindfulness (see Chapter 1). The goal is two-fold: first, become more mindful during conflict interaction; second, allow new mindful behaviors to eventually become positive mindless behaviors. As I emphasized in Chapter 1, mindlessness is not a negative phenomenon – it is necessary for complex human functioning. *The key is to build positive mindless behaviors that allow for the mental flexibility to be mindful about issues that demand conscious cognition.* In other words, to the extent that you create positive conflict habits, you are more able to be aware and think creatively regarding new or changing elements in the conflict interaction.

To be more mindful during conflict, couples can focus on four strategies. First, *novelty* can be used to encourage mindfulness during conflict interactions. As mentioned previously regarding arousal management, changing one's environment is one way to keep things feeling new. Attending a marriage workshop or going on a retreat are also ways to keep conflict fresh. Implementing new strategies can keep both partners mindfully involved until the new positive strategy becomes habitual. Second, *doing the unexpected* can increase mindfulness. This can include prosocial cooperative actions that avoid negative reciprocal affect or attack–attack or withdraw–withdraw patterns. Third, *recognizing internal and external difficulties* can lead to increased mindfulness. For example, acknowledging the struggle a partner experiences in overcoming habitual negative responses can lead one to put more cognitive effort into a response. Finally, *cognitive disturbance,* such as watching for incongruencies in partner verbal and nonverbal behaviors, can encourage a mindful response to determine meaning behind discrepant behavior. This requires questions, probes, or additional observation to keep one from reacting prematurely to any one aspect of the incongruent behavior.

## Prescriptive Approaches

Marriage enrichment programs typically involve some type of training in communication skills (Bowling, Hill, & Jencius, 2005) that focuses on active listening and validation of one another's perspectives (Cornelius, Alessi, & Shorey, 2007). There have been a variety of studies attempting to determine the effectiveness of various enrichment programs (Bowling et al., 2005). My intent in the following brief review is to highlight the communication dynamics of several programs that have demonstrated effectiveness in training married couples.

Mace and Mace (1975) developed the Association of Couples for Marriage Enrichment (ACME). ACME emphasizes couple strengths and long-term support within the context of community. Within the context of a safe and supportive environment, couples identify likes and dislikes in their marriage, learn communication, intimacy, and conflict skills, create a plan for growth, and make a recommitment to their marriage (Bowling et al., 2005; Williams, 2003).

Relationship Enhancement (RE) is a program for married or engaged couples, and can be used with distressed or nondistressed couples (Bowling et al., 2005; Williams, 2003). Essential skills taught include self-expression and empathetic listening to facilitate understanding. In addition, problem solving is emphasized with an emphasis on building trust and respect.

Similarly, early work by Gottman, Notarius, Gonso, and Markman (1976) suggested the following skills for couples:

- *listening and validation*: taking a nondefensive posture, and using feedback and paraphrasing to create greater understanding, and accepting (though not necessarily agreeing with) the partner's perspective;
- *leveling*: creating messages that are behaviorally focused and that deemphasize blaming, mindreading, and attacks;
- *editing*: making changes to one's initial reaction so that one's message can be more positively received;
- *negotiating agreements*: focusing on gripe time, agenda-building time, and problem solving; and

- *hidden agendas*: surfacing issues that have remained hidden – hopefully, increasing closeness.

ENRICH is a training program for married couples developed by Olson and colleagues (D. H. Olson, Fournier, & Druckman, 1986) that enables researchers to predict with 80–85% accuracy which premarriage couples will eventually divorce (Main, 1996). Research based on ENRICH and PREPARE (a premarital training program based on the same theoretical framework as ENRICH) demonstrates that communication and productive conflict management are key to happy marriages. In addition, happy couples tend to be egalitarian and exhibit a strong relationship between communication and sexuality. Regarding communication and conflict, ENRICH trains couples to listen and uses a 10-step conflict management model that includes such elements as defining the problem, discussing how the problem is perpetuated, and generating and selecting solutions (Bowling et al., 2005).

Training in Marriage Enrichment (TIME; Dinkmeyer & Carlson, 1984, 2003) covers similar topics to those discussed in previous models; however, this program focuses on goals that may help the marriage (e.g., teamwork and contributing) and those that may hinder (e.g., control and revenge) (Bowling et al., 2005). Communication skills include unconditional acceptance, listening, empathy, and congruent communication, which includes learning to express one's feelings with an awareness of one's partner's needs. Like other programs, conflict management is emphasized.

Prevention and Relationship Enhancement Program (PREP; Stanley, Blumberg, & Markman, 1999) focuses on communication, conflict management, problem solving, and commitment (Bowling et al., 2005). Stanley et al. (1999) outline four goals of PREP. First, teach couples to use the Speaker-Listener Technique to communicate and manage conflict (see Stanley, Markman, & Blumberg, 1997, for a good description of this technique). Second, focus on couples' negotiation of their expectations as a means of minimizing or working through conflict. Third, emphasize commitment to the current relationship, rather than focus on alternatives. Finally, encourage couples to have fun and to increase sensuality in their relationship.

While there has been considerable discussion as to the efficacy of couple communication training programs (Bowling et al., 2005), for newly learned behaviors to be effective, couples must keep arousal levels in the moderate range and learn constructive mindless patterns of behavior. To this end, Gottman (1994) suggests, "people do not have access to the learnings of therapy once they become physiologically aroused. Hence, I propose a soothing component to the therapy, and, second, that the minimal skills be overlearned" (p. 431). The minimal skills he is referring to are nondefensive listening and validating (discussed above). The soothing component reduces physiological arousal. Gottman (1994; Gottman, Notarius, Gonso, & Markman, 1976) suggests couples use "Stop Action" to reduce arousal. Stop Action is a technique whereby couples agree before conflict erupts that either partner may request an *adult time out* during conflict. Pre-agreement, at a non-conflict time, is important so that the Stop Action is not used as a power move in the interaction. In addition, a predetermined time length for Stop Action can help avoid using this technique as an avoidance strategy, rather than as a means of smoothing/arousal reduction. Likewise, Canary and Lakey (2006) suggest engaging in interactional control – becoming aware of the patterns of conflict – and, thus, not reacting impulsively, but rather mindfully. Mindfulness allows the communicator to avoid unwise reactions (often due to mindless reactions) and, instead, engage in verbal editing to respond in ways that are productive and helpful.

Guerrero and La Valley's (2006) six suggestions, intended to connect conflict theory to practice, provide a general framework form which to summarize the previously discussed programs. First, couples must realize that conflict is emotion-laden. Expecting some expression of negative affect may reduce nonproductive reaction to emotional expression. Second, as discussed previously, postponing intense, highly aroused discussion allows for more constructive responses. Third, couples should be aware of the Four Horseman of the Apocalypse, specifically learning to disrupt the process by complaining without making personal attack. Fourth, in light of Gottman's recommendation of maintaining a 5:1 positive-to-negative ratio, couples should keep mental track of this balance. Many prescriptive approaches emphasize increasing positive communication such as listening, validating, empathy, and expressing feelings. Fifth, focus on behaviors associated with communication competence, such as integrative communication, editing, leveling, and efficient problem solving, should help maintain the 5:1 ratio and break cycles of negative behavior. Finally, couples may do well to work on accurately decoding positive and neutral emotions, so that they are not mistakenly labeled as negative. Couples are encouraged to imagine their partner's thoughts and feelings and then verify those perceptions.

## Final Thoughts

Learning to manage conflict in marriage is critical to satisfaction and relationship longevity. While each couple have their own style of handling conflict, it is preeminent that couples learn to keep arousal levels in the moderate range and replace negative mindless behaviors with mindful or positive mindless behaviors. Then, as Canary and Lakey (2006) suggest, couples might be able to respond to one another with integrity.

# Close Conflict

## Basic Principles: Close Conflict

1 Productive conflict is one of the central characteristics of a healthy marriage.
2 Couples have conflict due to unclear roles, heightened interdependence, and incompatible goals.
3 Couples fight over various content issues (e.g., finances), although most significant conflict regards relationship issues (e.g., power, respect).
4 Individual conflict styles are important (direct or indirect, and cooperative or competitive); however, sequences of conflict behavior are closely related to marital satisfaction.
5 Unhappy couples tend to use predictable patterns of behavior (e.g., demand–withdraw; negative reciprocity).
6 Stable couples may be characterized by avoidance, volatility, or validation as long as they are able to maintain a 5:1 ratio of positive to negative behaviors.
7 Unstable couples (those headed to separation or divorce) are unable to maintain a 5:1 positive to negative ratio and are typically characterized as hostile or hostile/detached.
8 Healthy conflict is dependent on accurate perceptions and attributions.
9 Conflict interactions characterized by high levels of arousal and mindless processing are prone to:
  (a) runaway conflict;
  (b) reduced ability to process incoming information;
  (c) reduced ability to respond appropriately and creatively.
10 Healthy relationships avoid engaging in all Four Horsemen of the Apocalypse: criticism, defensiveness, contempt, and stonewalling.
11 Emotional distancing (e.g., fear, contempt) is a highly destructive emotional response in marriage.
12 Positive conflict processes are characterized by moderate arousal, mindfulness, desired mindless behaviors, and cooperative behaviors focused on understanding and problem solving.

## Questions You Should Ask
### (as a Researcher or as a Relational Partner)

1 How can couples learn to move from negative conflict patterns to positive?
2 How can couples identify underlying relationship issues during conflict?
3 Can couples effectively assess their own conflict styles?
4 Can couples effectively assess when they are caught in a demand–withdraw pattern?

126

5 In the same way that demand–withdraw and negative reciprocity patterns are destructive, are there particular patterns that are constructive?

6 How accurate are couples in discerning if they are maintaining a 5:1, positive to negative, ratio?

7 How effectively can couples assess their own arousal levels and make strategic choices to manage arousal? How can partners work together to keep arousal under control?

8 How might couples be trained to become more mindful during conflict interactions?

# 5

## Couple Communication across the Life Cycle

*I would say we've grown up together. I think we've gone from a real selfish relationship at first to learning to see each other's needs. I mean, when I first got married, I thought of my own needs totally, and how she could meet my needs. If we wanted to stay married, we couldn't stay that way.*

John, married 42 years

*Sam and I were talking about the challenges of managing our family, now that our child, Adrienne, was almost three years old. I finally said, "The business parties and going out on the boat, that's done." So he said, "That's part of your job." So I said, "Well, then, I guess I'd better look for another job." Which I did.*

Susan, married 47 years

*I trust him. And I think he trusts me. I know he's always there when I need him and when the kids need him. . . . He handled everything when I couldn't.*

Jan, married 38 years

Like everything else in life, marriage relationships change over time. The quote from John highlights what many couples find out when they get married – marriage challenges us to grow as individuals. In successful marriages, partners move from somewhat self-centered perspectives ("I thought of my own needs totally, and how she could meet my needs.") to focusing on their partners. Stanley et al. (2006) refer to this as healthy self-sacrifice.

128

Susan describes a different aspect of marriage across the life cycle. During the first few years of marriage she and her husband, Sam, primarily focused on building their careers. However, the increasing responsibilities of parenting changed her perspective on her career. Partying and "business" meetings on Lake Michigan began to pale in comparison to watching her child grow up. Susan's solution was to change careers to allow more time at home.

Finally, Jan talks about her relationship with Bill when she was fighting breast cancer. After 32 years of ups and downs, struggling to raise two children, and financial difficulties, Jan contracted breast cancer – and Bill was there for her. When asked, "Why stay married for the long term?" the couples I have interviewed consistently talk about the benefits of having a partner you can trust. Although the first three decades were not easy for Jan and Bill, they certainly learned to trust and love each other deeply during those times.

# Marriage across the Life Cycle

Marriages change as couples move through the life cycle and individuals move across the life span. As John recognizes, married partners "grow up" together. In fact, marriage facilitates personal development (Blanck & Blanck, 1968). While much marital research ignores the personal development of the adult partners, other research equally ignores the family context within which couples communicate. A life cycle perspective provides a view of marriage from within an ever-changing sociocultural context (McGoldrick & Carter, 2003). Although, most life cycle perspectives focus on the presence and absence of children within the family system, other factors such as individual growth, health, career, and retirement have a significant impact on communication within the system.

Carter and McGoldrick's (2005; McGoldrick & Carter, 2003) six family life cycle stages provide a concise framework from which to understand family transitions. From their perspective families/

couples typically experience the following: leaving home – single young adults; the joining of families through marriage – the new couple; families with young children; families with adolescents; launching children and moving on; families in later life. In light of this framework, in this chapter I emphasize elements particularly relevant to couple communication. As such, I begin by exploring the nature of transition. I then focus on couples with children in the home, followed by couples without children in the home (both those whose children are in the process of leaving or have left the home, and those who never had children). I finish the chapter by examining special issues that affect couples in blended families. Before we begin, a quick look at satisfaction across the life cycle and limitations of life cycle research.

## Satisfaction across the Life Cycle

There has been considerable debate regarding changes in marital satisfaction across the various life cycle stages. As we saw in Chapter 2, early research indicated that marital satisfaction was experienced in a curvilinear pattern across the life cycle. Couples began with high satisfaction, dropped in satisfaction with the emergence of the first child, experienced dips in satisfaction as children entered adolescence, and eventually experienced an increase in satisfaction as the children left the home (S. A. Anderson et al., 1983; Feeney, Peterson, & Noller, 1994; White & Edwards, 1990). Others believe that the curvilinear factor is an artifact of the way assessment over time is conducted, but still argue for an initial drop in satisfaction, with a leveling off over time (VanLaningham et al., 2001). A number of researchers have indicated that the drop in satisfaction, although statistically signif-icant, is somewhat moderate (Belsky et al., 1985; Doss, Rhoades, Stanley, & Markman, 2009). And, yet, others (Huston & Holmes, 2004) remain unconvinced that parenthood undermines marital satisfaction. Some researchers have demonstrated that satisfac-tion can actually increase over time (Gottman, 1999). Others report that relational satisfaction or love increases in the transi-tion to parenthood in one-third to one half of all couples (Doss et al., 2009) and that older couples (as compared to middle-aged couples) have reduced potential for conflict and greater potential for pleasure (Levenson et al., 1993).

Although results are mixed across studies, there is agreement that the transitions to marriage and in parenthood present significant challenges for the married couple. While others have argued that developmental issues (e.g., the young couple grows and matures together) may influence relationship quality over time (Adelmann, Chadwick, & Baerger, 1996), I have chosen to focus on life cycle transitions because of their potential to create unique communication challenges and opportunities for the married couple.

## Limitations of Life Cycle Research

It should be noted that life cycle research traditionally focused on white, two-parent families with children. However, this has changed in the last decade as life cycle researchers have explored culture, social class, sexual orientation, and gender (Carter & McGoldrick, 2005). In spite of these advances, McGoldrick and Carter (2003) recognize that life cycle research typically fails "to convey the considerable effects of culture, ethnicity, race, religion, and sexual orientation on all aspects of how, when, and in what way a family experiences various phases and transitions" (p. 395).

# Couple Transitions

Life cycle transitions are significant because they require implicit or explicit negotiation and precipitate an increase in couple communication (D. H. Olson & Gorall, 2003). These transitions may also lead to stress and account for many problems reported by couples (Miller, Yorgason, Sandberg, & White, 2003). For example, couples report an increase in problems related to sexual intimacy and communication as they transition to parenthood (Storaasli & Markman, 1990). Yet, transitions may also lead to increased quality of life associated with positive events (e.g., childbirth).

Life cycle transitions are often marked by rituals (e.g., the wedding) that reflect relationship patterns (Imber-Black, 2005). For example, Baxter and Braithwaite (2002; Braithwaite & Baxter, 1995) focus on renewal of wedding vows as family ritual. Creating and preparing for rituals is a significant developmental task for couples that presents opportunities to negotiate change in existing relationship patterns (Imber-Black, 2005; see also Box 5.1). Enactment of rituals involves three essential properties: transformation, communication, and stabilization (Baxter & Braithwaite, 2006; Wolin & Bennett, 1984). Transformation involves the suspension of daily family activity and places emphasis on family identity. Communication follows as the ritual is enacted and symbols produce a strong affective response. Finally, when the ritual is repeated, the family or couple experience stabilization as symbols link the past, present, and future.

Ritualizing varies across the life cycle (Baxter & Braithwaite, 2006). As children move out of infancy and become more aware of family identity and their surrounding cultural context, ritualizing increases (Fiese, Hooker, Kotary, & Schwagler, 1993). The increased social awareness of the child necessarily causes the married couple to discuss and define their current family identity. For example, as the child grows out of infancy, U.S. couples typically must decide if they will "trick or treat" at Halloween. Similarly, other work has shown that longer marriages have more rituals (Berg-Cross, Daniels, & Carr, 1992). And, of course, certain rituals are limited to a particular life cycle stage. For example, infant baptism occurs near the birth of a child, whereas vow renewal typically occurs later in the marriage.

Conville's (1991) five common elements to relational transition provide a framework with which to understand couples' experience as they transition across the life cycle. First, there is a time when partners are secure in their roles and share a mutual relationship definition. For example, the dating or premarital cohabiting couple have established roles and an understanding of their relationship. Yet, this will soon be disrupted as the couple renegotiate the relationship after the wedding. Second, there is a period of time wherein uncertainty increases and relational

# Box 5.1: *Ritual and Life Cycle Transitions*

Rituals are used to provide certainty and stability within families, as well as to create and maintain meaning (Baxter & Braithwaite, 2006). As such, rituals are linked to positive family outcomes and increased functioning during times of stress. Rituals in families serve a socializing function for children and help define the family in terms of attitudes, beliefs, and values (Pecchioni, Wright, & Nussbaum, 2005). According to Imber-Black (2005), life cycle rituals facilitate individual (e.g., from single to married adult), relational (e.g., from dating to married couple), system (e.g., adding or losing family members), and family-community change (e.g., retirement), and help reduce anxiety regarding these changes. Rituals are a powerful means of creating and maintaining couple/family identity, and reinforcing roles, boundaries, and rules (Baxter & Braithwaite, 2006; Fiese, 1992).

Bruess and Pearson (1997) state, "Rituals are relational enactments, as they manage inherent dialectical tensions and represent a type of relational cultural expression" (p. 25). In their research, they discovered numerous rituals used by married couples (see Chapter 3). Communication rituals, escape episodes, patterns/habits/mannerisms, enjoyable activities, and certain idiosyncratic/symbolic rituals (celebration rituals, favorites, and play rituals) were common to married couples and friends. Unique to married couples were couple-time rituals, spiritual rituals, establishment of daily routines and private codes (e.g., nicknames or unique communication shortcuts), and intimacy expressions.

Imber-Black (2005) argues that many contemporary transitions (e.g., bicultural marriage, gay or lesbian marriage, adoption, pregnancy loss, forced separation through hospitalization, end of non-married relationships, and relationships wherein one partner has an incapacitating illness) have certain characteristics in common. The couple have no familiar rituals or "maps" to manage the anticipated change.

They lack social support and find it difficult to achieve a balance of being like and unlike others. They often experience stigma from the wider community, have difficulty being involved with larger systems, and interrupt or abandon their own rituals (e.g., after the death of a family member, certain rituals may be abandoned because they are too painful to continue).

In response to these difficulties, Imber-Black (2005) suggests that designing and implementing rituals is a learnable skill that will enhance the successful management of idiosyncratic transitions. While designed for use in therapy, these suggestions can be adapted to help couples better understand how to develop rituals. To begin, new rituals can be created as part of a larger context of healing and a search for finding meaning in the event. As such, symbols and metaphors are chosen that can link the couple to the past as well as point toward growth in the future. The new ritual may occur in a specific space and a specific time, or occur over time. Also, the ritual may represent various dialectical tensions, such as holding on and letting go, or being open and closed. The couple should also allow imagination, humor, and playfulness to enter the process and possibly lead to creative problem solving. Some couples may want to alter existing rituals rather than create completely new rituals, and should feel free to take a break from the new ritual when necessary.

partners begin to question their relationship. For example, young couples after the wedding may struggle to reconcile their idealized marriage perceptions with the reality of the new relationship. Third, Conville describes a time of alienation in which partners may be prevented from taking on desired roles or pressured to stay in unwanted roles. This may lead to withdrawal, separation, or a sense of nonmutuality. For example, the transition to parenthood creates significant challenges for dual-earner couples as they negotiate household, childcare, and outside workloads (Huston

& Holmes, 2004; Silberstein, 1992). Fourth, resynthesis is the process of reformulating the relationship. This involves discovery, reduced uncertainty, confirmation seeking, possible redefinition of the relationship, and coping with dialectical oppositions. Finally, the relational partners settle back into security. They have renegotiated their roles and feel comfortable with how they are defining their relationship. For example, couples with small children experience resynthesis and security as they eventually establish stable marital and parental roles. In fact, research has demonstrated that drops in marital satisfaction frequently accelerate early in marriage relationships and then slow (VanLaningham et al., 2001). This effect may occur when couples successfully manage the transition to parenthood, but also likely involves adjustment of overly idealistic early-marriage expectations.

D. H. Olson's Circumplex Model (D. H. Olson, Russell, & Sprenkle, 1989) predicts similar changes when families experience stress (D. H. Olson & Gorall, 2003). The Circumplex Model focuses on couple and family cohesion, flexibility, and communication as key dimensions of family functioning. Balanced couples, those who are well adjusted in cohesion (e.g., from somewhat to very connected; as opposed to overly connected or disconnected) and flexibility (e.g., from somewhat to very flexible; as opposed to overly flexible or inflexible), tend to be more functional throughout the various life cycle stages. This model recognizes the importance of couple and family transition, and proposes five principles of stress-related change (D. H. Olson & Gorall, 2003). First, under stress, couples exhibit extreme behavior related to cohesion and adaptability. That is, they tend to move toward enmeshment and chaos. Second, communication typically increases during stressful events. Third, after the stressful event, couples tend to return to a similar (though not identical), pre-traumatic event, system. Fourth, it often takes six months to a year for couples to adjust to a major stressful event. And, fifth, balanced couples tend to become unbalanced during stress, but return to a relatively adapted and balanced system type. To summarize D. H. Olson (D. H. Olson, Russell, & Sprenkle, 1989; D. H. Olson & Gorall, 2003) and Conville (1991), relational systems that are able to adapt and survive begin with security (balance), move through stages of uncertainty and change, and return to a balanced (secure) system.

Keeping these central transition elements in mind, I now look at couples' transition to parenthood, then discuss couples without children in the home. The chapter finishes with an examination of couple communication during blended family transitions.

## Couples with Children in the Home

### Early Marriage

Early marriage encompasses three phases: engagement, the wedding, and the young couple. Engaged couples have special challenges to their relationship. They have not yet joined "officially" as a married couple, yet they are making decisions together that impact both family systems. For example, planning a wedding has the potential to create significant conflict and tension. Decisions regarding finances, details of the ceremony and reception, and family and friend involvement and attendance often bring a new level of pressure. As such, the young couple must begin to manage parental boundaries and learn to problem solve regarding potentially difficult issues. Interestingly, even with all of these new challenges, few couples go through premarital counseling before the ceremony (McGoldrick, 2005).

Weddings are significant family events (McGoldrick, 2005). A wedding provides the opportunity for romantic partners to use words and other symbols (e.g., rings) to make a public relationship commitment, to celebrate with family and friends, and to continue or create new family rituals (Leeds-Hurwitz, 2002). In addition, a wedding symbolizes more than a commitment of two individuals; it is a joining of two family systems (McGoldrick, 2005). In this sense, a wedding can function as a turning point in the realignment of family and friend relationships.

The early years of marriage present numerous challenges for many married couples. Newlyweds must negotiate new responsibilities, adjust high expectations to the reality of new marriage, and learn to manage conflict.

McGoldrick and Carter (2003) suggest that another important task for newly married couples is to establish their own relationship identity. Compared to previous generations, today's couples face a greater challenge defining the marriage relationship. Changing roles of women, increased diversity of partners, and increased distance of family members create considerable freedom for couples to create their own unique couple and family system. Central to establishing their own identity is creating new rituals unique to the family system (Leeds-Hurwitz, 2002), through which couples establish a unique relational culture (Bruess & Pearson, 1997). McGoldrick and Carter (2003) suggest that the establishment of rituals by the new couple can emphasize gender equality when the ritual symbolizes a move from parents to partner rather than primarily the wife moving from father to husband.

Moving from dreams and ideals that accompany the engagement and wedding to the reality of marriage is a second task of the new couple. Even though many couples today live together before marriage, failure to examine their own "myths" about marriage may lead to significant relationship problems (McGoldrick & Carter, 2003). Unexamined marriage myths likely result in unfulfilled expectations. As such, a central task for newly married partners is to renegotiate expectations, many of which are based on family and media (Segrin & Nabi, 2002; Starrels & Holm, 2000), with which they have entered marriage.

The final task confronting the young couple is negotiating relationships with extended family and friends. In-law issues that may confront the young couple include perceptions of intrusiveness, boundary setting, and managing feelings of guilt (McGoldrick, 2005). One or both partners may use the marriage to "escape" their family(s) of origin. In such cases, couples may cut off family relationships in order to gain independence or they may maintain contact, but minimize conflict and information sharing. McGoldrick (2005) suggests that the healthiest option is when both partners become independent from their families before the wedding, yet maintain close and caring ties. Likely, in this situation, the young couple and immediate family are able to talk openly and directly, and negotiate appropriate boundaries regarding such issues as time, responsibilities, and emotional connection.

Interestingly, the couple's initial experience of marriage may vary dependent on whether they lived together prior to marriage. A *cohabitation effect* appears to affect a variety of marital outcomes (Rhoades et al., 2009). For example, Rhoades et al. (2009) report that preengagement cohabitation results in lower marital satisfaction, dedication, and confidence, as well as more negative communication and a higher risk for divorce than those couples who did not cohabitate or did not cohabitate before engagement. Similarly, a review of literature regarding couples' premarital sexual history indicates that more sexual intercourse before marriage is associated with greater marital dissatisfaction and divorce (Larson & Homan, 1994). Stanley et al. (2006) suggest that these effects may be due in part to some couples marrying due to the social constraints associated with living together (e.g., financial dependence, social pressure). For example, after combining resources to live together it may seem "natural" to eventually marry. As such, part of the cohabitation–marriage effect may be due to weak relationships culminating in marriage. McGoldrick (2005) also suggests that living with one or multiple partners before marriage lessens the sense of marriage as a turning point in the life cycle.

## The Transition to Parenthood

The transition to parenthood comes with many of the same changes couples experience when adjusting to marriage (Sillars & Wilmot, 1989). The couples' initial emotional high begins to settle as the realities of marriage and, eventually, parenting become real. In addition, the introduction of a child makes the family a permanent system (McGoldrick & Carter, 2003). That is, even if the marriage relationship ends, both individuals remain parents to their children. This provides a different but important perspective on the nature of marriage as a long-term relationship. Rather than making a verbal commitment at a wedding ceremony, the act of having a child (through birth or adoption) symbolically demonstrates a desire and willingness to stay in the relationship for the long run, even if the relationship consists simply of greeting one's ex-spouse when transferring children from one home to the other.

The transition to parenthood begins with the wife's pregnancy (Huston & Holmes, 2004). Pre-birth couples, who have been putting their primary energy into careers and becoming financially stable, may now refocus on their relationship as they plan and ready their home and relational system for the new child. This includes renegotiating the balance between individuality and mutuality, as well as managing emotions, expectations, the sexual relationship, and preparation details for the baby (C. P. Cowan & Cowan, 1992). This time may also include shared activities such as buying materials for the baby, planning the baby's room, choosing names, and attending birth classes (Huston & Holmes, 2004). What is clear is that a "secure and satisfying" couple relationship is critical to making this adjustment (Feeney, Hohaus, Noller, & Alexander, 2001, p. 87).

The transition to parenthood, post-birth, increases the risk for distress and dysfunction for married couples (C. P. Cowan & Cowan, 1995). This transition requires the renegotiation of roles and responsibilities and is affected by physical and emotional stress, shifts in couples' roles and expectations regarding intimacy or social time with one another, decision making regarding issues such as childcare, management of extended family relationships, the learning associated with childcare, and the new emotional bond that grows between the child and parents (Huston & Holmes, 2004; McGoldrick, 2003; Stamp, 1994). Failure to negotiate these changes satisfactorily can result in lower levels of satisfaction. For example, fathers who have children soon after the wedding experience greater loss in relational satisfaction than those who wait, presumably because they have had less time to negotiate and stabilize the changing roles and responsibilities of the marriage relationship (Doss et al., 2009). Similarly, couples who have unplanned pregnancies may struggle in their relationship post-birth, especially if the pregnancy is unwanted (C. P.

Cowan & Cowan, 1992). Interestingly, Doss et al. (2009) found that couples with high levels of relationship functioning experience the greatest relationship deterioration (e.g., satisfaction and maternal dedication) following the birth of a child. The researchers speculate that couples who experience high levels of romance may have the hardest time adjusting to parenthood. Likewise, Lawrence, Nylen, and Cobb (2007) found that husbands and wives with high prenatal expectations experienced greater declines in marital satisfaction post-birth; although it should be noted that a significant number of couples reported their expectations met or exceeded.

Elements of the birth context itself can affect the couples' relationship. For example, age of the parents plays a factor. When the wife is under 24 years of age, first-birth couples experience greater decline in marital satisfaction than do their cohorts who wait longer (Helms-Erikson, 2001). Likewise, those who become fathers later tend to be more active and feel more positively about parenting, possibly due to reduced role demands outside the family system (Cooney, Pedersen, Indelicato, & Palkovitz, 1993). Gender is another birth context element. Male births are associated with higher marital satisfaction and lower rates of divorce (Raley & Bianchi, 2006), whereas female children are associated with larger decreases in mother's satisfaction and larger increases in father's reports of problem intensity (Doss et al., 2009). Doss et al. (2009) surmise that this effect is due to fathers' lower involvement with female children. Income is a third context element that affects the marriage relationship. In the Doss et al. study, fathers' satisfaction was also tied to individual income level, such that lower income dads exhibited lowered relationship functioning after birth.

Apparently, premarital relational experience also influences the transition to parenthood. According to Doss et al. (2009), several types of enduring vulnerabilities (C. P. Cowan & Cowan, 1995) are associated with relationship deterioration after birth. For mothers, a history of parental conflict and divorce is related to greater deterioration of relationship satisfaction after birth. Other research has also shown family of origin relationship functioning to affect current relationship functioning for the female partner

(D'Onofrio et al., 2007; Story, Karney, Lawrence, & Bradbury, 2004). Additionally, Doss et al. (2009) found that both mothers and fathers who had cohabited before marriage had more difficulty after birth than individuals who had not cohabited. This is consistent with a variety of research that demonstrates that married couples who cohabit before marriage engage in more negative interactions and physical violence, fewer positive interactions, higher rates of wife infidelity, and lower marital quality (Rhoades, Stanley, & Markman, 2006).

### Communication Changes for New Parents
It is clear that the transition to parenthood results in changes in communication between the partners (C. P. Cowan & Cowan, 1992). At the most fundamental level, communication may decrease, resulting in lowered marital satisfaction as couples struggle to balance career, household duties, and childcare (P. A. Cowan & Cowan, 1988; Stamp & Banski, 1992). In terms of marital functioning, poor communication and conflict during pregnancy predict further decline in marital functioning after birth (Doss et al., 2009). Doss et al. (2009) also found that, after birth, mothers tended to experience larger sudden increases in poor conflict management and problem intensity than fathers. In contrast, fathers experienced more consistent decline in relationship confidence and problem intensity in the years following birth. Consistent with other research (Belsky & Hsieh, 1998; Belsky & Rovine, 1990), however, it should be noted that certain individuals reported increases in relationship functioning.

The transition to parenthood is also typified by an increased focus on instrumental functions and a decrease in emotional expression, as reflected by a decrease in affection and frequency of joint leisure activities (Belsky, Spanier, & Rovine, 1983). Miller, Yorgason, Sandberg, and White (2003) found husbands married three to ten years (typically the beginning of the childbearing years; and as compared to those married fewer than three and more than ten years) more likely to report leisure activity and emotional intimacy as a problem area. These changes in time demands and responsibilities force the new parents to make relationship adjustments. It also appears that these trends persist as parents continue to have children (Belsky et al., 1983). That is, first-time parents engage in more leisure activities, view their relationship as more romantic than partnership-based, and have more marital interaction (especially regarding the new baby) than do parents with multiple children.

### Renegotiation of Autonomy and Interdependence

The introduction of a child into the couples' relational system also creates the need for renegotiation of autonomy (individuality) and interdependence (mutuality) in their relationship (C. P. Cowan & Cowan, 1992). Stamp and Banski (1992), in interviews with couples pre- and post-birth, found *constrained autonomy* – "the overwhelming feeling that one's sense of independence is severely compromised by factors outside one's control" (pp. 285–286) – to be often mentioned regarding parents' postpartum experience. Married partners perceive their autonomy to be compromised due to time pressures, restructuring of activities, anticipation of baby's needs, loss of control, social comparison, and engaging in difficult tasks. Interestingly enough, pre-birth couples described activity coordination as a significant challenge because of the need to constrain one's personal choices. After birth, couples still described activity coordination as a significant challenge; however, the reason it was considered significant shifted from constraining one's own personal choices to responding to increased couple interdependence and changes in responsibilities. Importantly, Stamp and Banski point out that it is virtually impossible for the couple to have accurate expectations as to how caring for a baby will impact their individual and couple autonomy. In addition, they note that postpartum changes and stress may cause some individuals to remember higher levels of pre-birth autonomy than they actually had. Of course, all of these factors contribute to making the transition to parenthood challenging at best.

Stamp and Banski (1992) identify three ways in which the tension between autonomy and interdependence is mediated. The first is excessive constraint on autonomy. This typically occurs when one spouse considers the other to be engaged in excessive activity or limited concessions regarding childcare. Second is voluntary restraint of autonomy. Here, one spouse voluntarily limits a particular activity in order to accommodate the spouse or child. For example, upon coming home from work a spouse may wait until both spouse and child have gone to bed before training for an upcoming 10k run. Third, negotiation of autonomy represents direct talk about the issue at hand.

C. P. Cowan and Cowan (1992) identify three qualities of couples who successfully manage the tension between individuality and mutuality. First, both partners feel secure in themselves as individuals (firm sense of self-identity). Second, spouses are able to tolerate the ambiguity that comes with trying to understand one's partner. Individuals are willing to defend their views, but do not feel the need to change their partner's view. Third, they don't avoid conflict but have a process for decision making, and they avoid staying stuck on issues.

An interesting twist on the management of individuality and mutuality issues is the tendency for couples to bring their children into their own private struggles (C. P. Cowan & Cowan, 1992). This triangulation of the conflict may occur as couples fail to distinguish between their own individual needs and what they think the child needs. Additionally, couples may fight over their children as a means of avoiding their own issues. Triangulation may also occur when couples become so enmeshed in their children's lives that they neglect issues in their own relationship.

### Changing Roles

The move to parenthood results in the execution of new roles and the renegotiation of existing roles (Stamp, 1994). This process affects marital satisfaction for the new parents (C. P. Cowan et al., 1985), such that some parents struggle with the transition while others find that the positive experience of being a new mother or father offsets the difficulties (Huston & Holmes, 2004).

According to Huston and Holmes (2004), renegotiation of relationship roles is precipitated by a substantial increase in family-related activities/chores following the birth of the child, on average from 5.8 to 36.2 per day. Wives increase household tasks from 3.9 to 5.3 per day, with the addition of 22.7 childcare tasks. Husbands increase from 1.9 to 2.4 per day, with an additional 5.9 childcare tasks.

These changes contribute to a traditionalization of gender roles for the couple (Feeney et al., 2001; McGoldrick & Carter, 2003; Sillars & Wilmot, 1989). In addition, biological considerations affect role shifts. For example, women are the ones who carry the developing child and the bulk of the responsibility for feeding, especially if the choice has been made to breast feed (C. P. Cowan et al., 1985). Often wives take on the responsibility for household tasks because they are home more after the birth of the child. Silberstein (1992) found maternity leave to be a significant turning point for dual career couples, especially as wives considered whether to take extended time off from outside work to become full-time mothers. In Huston and Holmes' (2004) sample, women were more likely than men to diminish their outside work involvement post-birth, and increase their household work; husbands saw their role as lightening the wife's childcare burden – playing with the child, setting rules, handling misbehaviors, picking up after the child, and getting up with the child at night. C. P. Cowan et al. (1985) also suggest that many couples take on traditional gender roles when they experience role confusion associated with the birth of the first child because they turn to their parents as models. Other researchers have suggested that wives may become "gatekeepers" in such a way that they limit their husbands' ability to develop childcare skills (Allen & Hawkins, 1999; Huston & Holmes, 2004). And, as we have seen, father–child involvement is related to marital quality (Doss et al., 2009). Whatever the reason for the traditionalization of roles, satisfaction with the process rests largely on what the partners believe constitutes appropriate marital roles (Huston & Holmes, 2004).

In spite of the tendency to adopt more traditional roles, McGoldrick and Carter (2003) suggest that couples can learn to balance gender roles: for example, fathers who lack experience with young children can learn these skills, and mothers can be encouraged to let fathers make mistakes. Interestingly, Grote, Naylor, and Clark (2002), in a longitudinal study of new parents, found that women perceive a lopsided household and childcare workload as fair when they enjoy performing family work. When viewed as competent by both themselves and their wives, husbands perceived greater fairness and increased how much housework and childcare they performed. Moreover, wives are more likely to adapt to their husbands' childcare preferences because of love for their husbands and a desire to create a harmonious family climate, and also when both partners see the wife as more skilled in early childcare (Huston & Holmes, 2004).

## Dual-Earner Couples with Children

Special role challenges present themselves for dual-earner couples with young children. At the center of these challenges is determining the nature of surrogate childcare. Couples in Silberstein's (1992) sample struggled in determining the amount and type of childcare. Women expressed concern that they would be "replaced" by the surrogate childcare providers, and frustration when they could not be there for their children in specific times of need. Perhaps these issues explain why most childcare decisions are left up to the mother (Huston & Holmes, 2004). Huston and Holmes (2004) found total work burden rarely balanced for dual-career couples; in addition to working outside the home, wives took on a larger burden of household responsibilities and childcare. However, many wives are resistant to handing over responsibility to their husbands or afraid that pushing them to increase participation may result in their husbands' increased dissatisfaction. Often, to manage the increased workload that accompanies the first child, dual-earner couples choose efficiency over companionship. That is, one parent (often the mother) spends more time managing the child while accomplishing other tasks, instead of both parents spending time together with the child (Huston & Holmes, 2004).

## Couples with Adolescents

Although stress is not necessarily the primary feature of families with adolescents, it is often a significant characteristic. Couples with adolescent children must renegotiate family boundaries in order to adapt to children's independence and grandparents' frailties (Carter & McGoldrick, 2005). As discussed previously, some research has revealed lower marital satisfaction during this stage of the life cycle (S. A. Anderson et al., 1983; Belsky et al., 1985; Glenn, 1990; McGoldrick & Carter, 2003). Presumably the increase in parent–youth conflict exacerbates differences between the parents, thus increasing couple conflict (Roloff & Miller, 2006). In my own research with long-term married couples (Waldron & Kelley, 2008), parenting differences were some of the most frequently reported sources of conflict. In addition, emotional and psychological distance that can develop between partners when children are young later may become evident with the additional stress of parent–adolescent conflict.

Couples with adolescents are often managing multiple sources of stress. Many middle-aged adults are feeling the pressure to provide emotional, physical, and financial support to their aging parents as well as to their adolescent children (Fingerman et al., 2004). Marital communication may revolve around "Mom and Dad's" change in health or limited, fixed finances. In addition, the reality of the couples' own retirement, career changes, or additional civic involvements may dominate conversations.

## Couples without Children in the Home

Another major transition that influences couples' communication is the transition from having children in the household to "launching" these children. Carter and McGoldrick (2005) suggest that couples at this stage of life must renegotiate the marital system, develop adult relationships with their children who are no longer living at home, potentially form relationships with children's in-laws and grandchildren, and possibly deal with disability or death of parents. Eventually, the couple must deal with the transition to retirement, realignment of social support systems, and their own physiological decline (Carter & McGoldrick, 2005; Dickson, Christian, & Remmo, 2004; Fingerman et al., 2004).

## Communication at Midlife: Launching Children and Centerstage Couples

Fingerman et al. (2004) note that midlife is a time of relative emotional stability and well-being. They suggest that during the transition to a child-free household, couples may find themselves embroiled in complex discussion regarding three developmental issues. First, midlife partners become more aware of their relationships with others, and their responsibilities to those relationships. This likely affects the execution of immediate and extended family roles. Second, often midlife, couples discuss perceived changes in self-identity. Third, partners become aware 'of time – time remaining in their lives, connection with the past, and possible discontinuities into the future (Blacker, 2005). This reorientation to time may generate significant discussions regarding doing something "significant" with the rest of one's life, or may be a call for forgiveness of past events (Waldron & Kelley, 2009).

Vince Waldron and I (2009) have labeled couples transitioning to a life without children at home "centerstage couples" (see Box 5.2). The term *centerstage* indicates the period of time that is in the center of a, hopefully, long life and relationship. Centerstage is also a metaphor indicating a period wherein couples have fewer responsibilities competing with their relationship for the "spotlight." This spotlight can result in reinvigorated investment in a healthy relationship or can reveal negative issues now that children cease to be a distraction. Either way, the couple have to deal with the realities of their relationship. This may mean making relationship choices, but also may include grieving the loss of children at home and the joint mission of parenting. Couple dialogue may center on choices regarding their couple identity and issues related to increased opportunity for joint activities, increased mobility (e.g., "Should we sell the house?"), increasing demands at work, possible career shifts or further education, support of launched children, and illness or disability of one of the partners or one of the partners' parents.

The multifaceted issues confronting centerstage couples, including multiple exits and entries of family members (McGoldrick

## Box 5.2: Concept Check: Centerstage Couples

Waldron and I (2009) identified midlife couples as experiencing *centerstage* marriage. Centerstage as a time dimension focuses on relationship tasks that occur in the middle of a long-term relationship. Centerstage as metaphor calls attention to the renewed focus on the marriage. Whereas, children, careers, and finances may have competed for each marriage partner's attention for the first half of the marriage, this centerstage may afford renewed attention on the couples' own relationship. We (Waldron & Kelley, 2009) suggest that certain couples, as they transition into centerstage marriage, will need help in overcoming inadequate relationship maintenance practices, rigid communication patterns, deficits in communication skills, and the physiological effects of aging. In addition, time to think about relational patterns of the past may precipitate a need for forgiveness and emotional healing. As they look to the future, the centerstage couple may feel the need for meaningful, joint activities as they rebuild a sense of intimacy and companionship.

Special issues confront centerstage couples as children depart from the house. Married partners may struggle with a loss of identity, relational boredom, the "too quiet" house, social isolation, uncertainty and fear, and unrealistic post-parenting expectations. In addition, couples may need to deal with job loss or a partner returning to school or beginning a new career, managing boundaries with adult children and aging parents, relocation, illness, or caregiving.

Clearly there are myriad issues that may arise during this phase of life. Waldron and I suggest seven communication-related strategies to help manage potential problems and keep one's relationship *centerstage*: renew the relationship commitment, prioritize the relationship, negotiate changing expectations, find a common voice, maintain external support, sustain intimacy, and develop the habit of dialogue.

& Carter, 2003), contribute to the development of complex role identities. For example, as children exit the family system, the married couple must maintain appropriate controlling and dominant behaviors as their children transition to adulthood, while at the same time they must demonstrate appropriate submission and respect to their own parents (Fingerman et al., 2004). Fingerman et al. (2004) argue that the complexity of these role relationships is demonstrated by the fact that middle-aged adults tend to be both more positive and negative about their parents and children than are younger and older adults.

Another example of the complex roles couples must negotiate occurs when launched children move back home. These "boomerang" children can create significant difficulties for the marriage relationship as well as the parent–child relationship. Parent–child relationships tend to stay connected (White & Edwards, 1990) and may actually improve (Troll, 1994) after the child leaves the home. However, the independence and autonomy the child gains while on her own may lead to conflict when she chooses to move back home. In addition, the causes of the child's return home may add stress to the marriage relationship. For example, boomerang children may return home for financial reasons, childcare or pregnancy, recovery from divorce, or for physical and emotional support (Waldron & Kelley, 2009). The presenting situation may result in significant discussion and conflict for the married couple. For example, differences of opinion regarding letting the child move home or helping him financially may be difficult for a couple who are in the middle of renegotiating their own relationship.

Other shifts for centerstage couples are role changes regarding the coordination of kinship communication and parental care (Blacker, 2005). For example, parental illness may result in an increase in sibling communication and coordination of caretaking activity. This may lead to married partner conversation regarding emotional and financial investment in the extended family.

Communication for couples who are successfully navigating the transition to centerstage may be rather nuanced and efficient. Managing the various roles required at this stage of life often leads to the development of productive communication skills.

In addition, psychological development by this age may result in communication styles that are able to take into account others' perspectives and appropriately manage emotions (Fingerman et al., 2004). Of course, individuals' idiosyncratic psychological development and unique relational history can lead to exceptions to these trends, yet centerstage couples have the potential to be very happy and successful in their relationships. Blacker (2005) suggests that the removal of stress, simplification of household routines, and development of positive relationship skills during childraising lead to a boost in marital happiness as children leave the home. In addition, fewer financial demands may diminish stress and difficult decision making for the couple (McGoldrick & Carter, 2003). Couples at centerstage may also emphasize friendship, companionship, equality, tolerance, and shared interests in their relationship (Blacker, 2005).

## Couples in Later Life

Understanding older adults as family or marriage communicators is no simple task. Certain research has conceptualized the life of the older adult as in decline (Walsh, 2005), characterized by relationship loss through illness, death, relocation, or a deterioration in social skills (Pecchioni et al., 2005). Older adults who experience these declines and losses may struggle as they resist change, find it difficult to establish new relationships, and experience isolation or depression (Dickson et al., 2004; McGoldrick & Carter, 2003). However, many positive changes occur with maturity (Walsh, 2005). For instance, some older adults may actually prefer smaller, more intense support networks (Carstensen, 1992), placing more emphasis on the family and the marriage relationship. In fact, familiarity with one's partner may lead to an increase in interpersonal communication skills within the marriage, and more reliance on one's spouse in the face of physiological barriers to effective communication (e.g., loss of hearing; Hansson & Carpenter, 1994). Marital satisfaction may increase as the couple have more resources, more time for shared pursuits, and deepened intimacy from a long history together (Walsh, 2005).

Later-life couples face unique challenges, as do couples at every stage of the life cycle, but many experience the rich rewards of numerous years together. When asked about the benefits of long-term marriage, one wife from my research echoed the feelings expressed by many couples: "This is the payoff" (Waldron & Kelley, 2008). Waldron and I often heard from our long-term, happily married couples that marriage after retirement has many benefits: companionship, working together with someone who knows you well, living with someone you trust, support during illness, having a partner when dealing with issues regarding adult children, and perspective. As one couple told us regarding perspective, "The things we fought about early in our marriage just don't seem that important any longer."

In spite of these many potential benefits, older-adult couples do have significant challenges at this stage of the relationship which they must negotiate together. They must maintain their relationship in the face of physiological decline (e.g., illness or disability and family caregiving); explore new familial (e.g., grandparenting) and social (e.g., changes associated with retirement) roles which may influence how they function as a couple; support a more central role in the family system for the middle generation; and deal with the loss of friends, family members, and possibly one's spouse (Carter & McGoldrick, 2005; Walsh, 2005). Couples may also experience sexual challenges due to illness or physiological changes; however, it appears that older-adult couples find ways to adapt to sexual barriers and still find sex as an important component that communicates commitment, trust, love, and selflessness in the relationship (Hinchliff & Gott, 2004).

Dickson et al. (2004) summarize the previous discussion as they present seven challenges (based on Arp & Arp, 1996) with which couples in later life are typically confronted. First, older-adult couples must negotiate their relationship after one member retires. Dickson et al. suggest that levels of satisfaction and conflict are dependent on the couple's ability to negotiate post-retirement issues. Second, later-life couples must shift from a child-focused relationship to one that is partner-focused. While this process may begin with children exiting the home, it is often retirement that facilitates a more complete shift from a child-focused to partner-focused relationship. Third, the shift to a partner focus in the relationship may create the need to deal with past relationship disappointments. Interestingly, this may be a prime time to manage past relationship hurts and disappointments as certain research has demonstrated that couples express less negativity in their later years (Carstensen, Gottman, & Levenson, 1995; Dickson et al., 2001). Fourth, couples must integrate health-related issues into their roles and marital relationship. For example, numerous studies have demonstrated health issues to have a negative impact on marital satisfaction (Booth & Johnson, 1994; Levenson et al., 1993). Fifth, older-adult couples may have difficulty rekindling romance and maintaining a pleasurable sexual relationship. Poor health and an unsuccessful shift of focus from children to partner may lead to difficulties for couples regarding romance and sex. Sixth, later-life couples must adjust the roles they play in the family system. For example, they may now play an advisory role to middle-aged children. Finally, older-adult couples must adapt to later life stresses, such as terminal illness.

## Couples without Children

Often forgotten when considering how married relationships change over time are couples who never had children. Couples may be childless by choice, inability to conceive, or through loss of a child pre- or post-birth. Couples who are child*less* by choice may suffer the stigma of being "only a couple" as others assume the couple are childless because of infertility or miscarriage (McGoldrick & Walsh, 2005). On the other hand, couples who experience infertility often incur high levels of stress as they struggle with the inability to conceive (Berliner, Jacob, & Schwartzberg, 2005; Carter, 2005). The couple may experience this disappointment with grief, mourning, and depression. This unexpected crisis in a couple's life requires joint emotional support between partners (as well as extended family and friends) and the ability to reformulate a life plan. Thus, couples need to work through their grief and begin to consider alternatives to having biological children.

Over time, nonparent couples tend to experience similar amounts of relationship decline to parent couples (Clements & Markman, 1996; Huston & Holmes, 2004). However, some research points to parent couples experiencing less joint activity (Kurdek, 1993), while other research suggests that couples still spend time together, it is just that the type of time together changes (e.g., less leisure activity; Feeney et al., 2001). Doss et al. (2009) discovered that couples who transition to parenthood and those who do not demonstrate similar amounts of change in relationship functioning over an eight-year period. However, parents experience sudden change that stabilizes over time, while nonparents experience more gradual change over time and demonstrate less change in negativity, conflict, and problem intensity.

The communication of childless couples is also likely affected in terms of topic. Of course, most noticeable is the relative absence of child-related talk. While childless young couples may engage in child-related talk as it pertains to pregnancy or fertility (C. P. Cowan & Cowan, 1992), talk related to the coordination and management of children in the household is mostly missing. Childless couple conversations differ from those of their parent peers in that they do not have to concern themselves with issues such as boomerang children, giving financial help to adult children, and potential grandchildren. While absence of these topics from their couple talk may reduce stress for the couple, it may also stimulate additional emotionally laden conversation. For example, older childless couples may find it challenging to discuss issues of inheritance and how to secure social support as they age.

Couples without children may also experience differences in how they process problems in their marriage. C. P. Cowan and Cowan (1995) report that in a six-year follow-up study only 20% of couples who had become parents divorced, whereas childless couples experienced a 50% divorce rate over the same period of time. The stabilizing effect of children on marriage may be due to constraints on communication within the household, a married-for-life mindset, or expectations to "stay together for the good of the child" that may be held by the couple themselves or the couple's social network. Absence of this stabilizing effect of children may allow certain "freedoms" in the way in which childless couples resolve relational difficulties.

## Blended Families and Couple Communication across the Life Cycle

Blended families, commonly referred to as stepfamilies (e.g., stepmother, stepfather, stepchildren), have become a familiar and common family structure. About half of all marriages in the U.S. are remarriages of some type (M. Coleman, Fine, Ganong, Downs, & Pauk, 2001). Pertinent to a focus on marital communication, McGoldrick and Carter (2005) refer to blended families as *remarried families* to emphasize that it is the marital relationship that forms the basis of this complex family system. Cissna, Cox, and Bochner (1990) also emphasize the marriage relationship as essential in making a successful transition from single-parent family to blended family. They note that blended families must struggle with a difficult dialectic between the chosen marriage relationship and the not-so-chosen family relationship. In order to manage this dialectic successfully it is necessary to establish the solidarity of the marriage in the mind of the children and use that solidarity to create a sense of authority for the stepparent with the stepchildren.

Specific challenges for remarried couples include bringing emotional baggage from one's family of origin, from one's first marriage, and from the process of ending the first marriage (e.g., separation, divorce or death, and the single period between marriages), and managing the ambiguity involved in creating new roles in the new couple system (McGoldrick & Carter, 2005). At the same time, couples may feel they have matured and learned from their first marriage. As such, they may come into the new marriage feeling better equipped and with high hopes. However, high second marriage divorce rates would suggest that simply learning new relationship lessons is not sufficient to override habitual relationship patterns. Mindlessness and high levels of arousal (see Chapters 1 and 4) may serve to throw the couple into negative spirals of behavior unless the partners work intentionally to change past patterns.

Remarried couples with children face numerous challenges as they seek to develop their relationship. These challenges include: no "honeymoon" period without children; the fact that parent–child bonds predate marriage bonds; possible revisioning of gender and parental roles; and management of relationships with stepchildren's biological parents (McGoldrick & Carter, 2005). Often newly remarried couples have short courtships and, as such, are highly motivated to communicate and continue to learn about one another (M. Coleman et al., 2004). Sometimes, however, partners are not as motivated to communicate with their new stepchildren, creating additional stress for the newly forged marriage union. In addition, relationship difficulties (e.g., conflict or termination) with ex-spouses, children, parents, and grandparents may be a source of conflict for the remarried couple (McGoldrick & Carter, 2005). Loyalty issues between parents and children and boundary negotiation within the new family system may create considerable challenges (Afifi, 2003; Petronio & Caughlin, 2006). Clinicians suggest that forging a particularly strong parental unit (e.g., adult couple) is important in stabilizing the new family system (Cissna et al., 1990; M. Coleman et al., 2004; Visher & Visher, 1998). Interestingly, M. Coleman et al. (2004) suggest that older stepfamilies (those whose children are grown or nearly grown at the start of the family) may be more couple-focused, presumably without the distraction of children to manage during the family transition.

Research focusing on stepfamily transitions provides another lens into the remarried couple's experience. Papernow (1993) offers a seven-stage model describing blended family development over time. Although this model is not focused solely on the remarried couple, the various stages provide a perspective on the kinds of issues they must deal with. The first stages manage the realignment of unrealistic expectations. The middle stages focus on conflict and negotiation of a foundation for the new, blended family system. In the last stages, the family creates positive bonds and identity as a healthy family unit. Clearly this process places demands on the newly joined couple to facilitate how the family adapts to these major life transitions.

Taking a different approach, Baxter, Braithwaite, and Nicholson

(1999) identified turning points in stepfamily experience all of which could typically affect couples' communication (e.g., coordinating and problem solving, celebrating, or dealing with conflict). Family members most frequently described blended family turning points in terms of changes in household configuration, conflict, holidays/special events, quality time, and family crisis. In addition, turning points such as reconciliation/problem solving, prosocial action (e.g., gift giving), and unmet expectations/disappointment likely place a demand on couples' communication as they attempt to manage this challenging family transition.

Similarly, Braithwaite, Olson, Golish, Soukup, and Turman (2001) determined that boundary management, solidarity, and adaptation were essential issues that had to be negotiated in "becoming a family" (p. 221). For example, families who developed a sense of closeness typically were patient, expected or accepted change, and realized that the transition would take time. Each of these issues requires the remarried couple to discuss and negotiate their own perspectives and coordinate with one another as they communicate their perspective to the children. Likewise, couples can model and encourage flexibility, open communication, and constructive conflict management to help the newly constructed family system weather coming challenges.

The development of rituals is a specific means for successfully managing the transition into the new blended family. Braithwaite, Baxter, and Harper (1998) found that blended families use rituals to manage the ongoing tension between "old family" and "new family." Rituals that productively manage this tension have elements that value the old while embracing the new. Once again, primary responsibility for the development of useful rituals typically falls to the adult couple, which may lead to stress, conflict, or creative problem solving.

## Adoptive Couples

Adoptive families are a type of blended family; however, couples planning to adopt have special issues to consider. For example, most couples considering adoption will have discussions focusing on the differences between having biological or adopted children. Also, couples will necessarily discuss how to manage external and internal boundaries (Galvin, 2006). For example, boundary practices such as labeling ("This is my adopted son." vs. "This is my son."), explaining ("We adopted you, because Mommy and I wanted you very much."), and naming ("You can call me Mom.") will likely precipitate important discussions for the married couple.

If the reason for adoption involves physiological limits on the part of the partners, couples will necessarily discuss these problems as they move toward the decision to adopt. This type of discussion is essential (Myers & Wark, 1996) as research has shown that couples who choose in-vitro fertilization (IVF) may experience depression and anxiety after unsuccessful attempts at IVF (Schmidt, 2006) and often experience infertility in terms of crisis and mourning (Shapiro, 1982). On the other hand, certain research suggests that infertility may actually strengthen the marital relationship for some couples (Schmidt, Holstein, Christensen, & Boivin, 2005). For example, increased communication about the infertility and use of active-confronting coping (e.g., letting feelings out, asking for others' advice) are associated with high marital benefit (Schmidt, Holstein, et al., 2005; Schmidt, Tjørnhøj-Thomsen, Boivin, & Nyboe Andersen, 2005).

## Final Thoughts

Couples, and the families they are a part of, encounter multiple stressors throughout the family life cycle. Particularly challenging are transitions to marriage, parenthood, childless homes, and eventually later adulthood and retirement. Couple and family systems that are able to successfully negotiate these transitions have been characterized as resilient (Luthar, Cicchetti, & Becker, 2000; Waldron & Kelley, 2009). Resilience is "the ability to withstand and rebound from disruptive life challenges" (Walsh, 2003, p. 399). The resilience framework provides a useful summary of how couples can adapt communicatively to developmental challenges (Walsh, 2003). Waldron and I (2009), in our recommendations for centerstage couples, suggest that the resilience characteristics of optimism and flexibility are key to managing change. Optimism may be communicated through maintenance behaviors such as assurances, compliments, and positive assessments that breed hope; whereas flexibility is a hallmark of healthy couples who avoid rigid, negative patterns of communication, such as attack–attack, or demand–withdraw. Walsh (2003) identifies communication as one of three key components of family resilience. Specifically, she identifies clarity, open emotional expression, and collaborative problem solving as central communication processes. Clarity involves using clear consistent words and actions. Open expression includes mutual empathy, taking responsibility for one's feelings, and pleasurable communication, such as humor. Collaborative problem solving is based on creative brainstorming, conflict resolution, development of shared goals, and acting proactively.

Remarkably, many couples and families manage expected and unexpected crises with great resilience. However, some who suffer trauma may find themselves trapped by anger and blame (Goman & Kelley, 2010; Walsh, 2003). It is this topic of destructive marital patterns and forgiveness for which I have reserved the final chapter.

**Basic Principles: Couple Communication across the Life Cycle**

1 Marriage relationships change across the life cycle.
2 Life cycle and developmental transition create unique communication challenges for couples as they move from security and balance, to uncertainty and change, and eventually return to security and balance.
3 Rituals help to maintain security and balance during times of transition.
4 Typically salient life cycle transitions for couples include: marriage, parenthood, children leaving the home, and retirement.
5 Successful transition management involves setting and recalibrating expectations, pre-transition quality of the relationship, and the couple's ability to adapt individually and relationally to changing circumstances (e.g., having an infant in the home).
6 Positive communication (e.g., the ability to renegotiate roles and engage in constructive conflict) is essential to individual partner and relationship adaptation.
7 For dual-earner families, determining the nature of surrogate childcare is central; and wives continue to take on a larger share of home-related tasks.
8 Parents of adolescents are needed for emotional, physical, and financial support by their children as well as their aging parents.
9 Centerstage and older/retired couples typically must renegotiate their relationship from parent-focused to partner-focused, as well as manage changing social/family networks and manage health-related issues.
10 Remarried couples (blended families) must manage the past (e.g., ending of the first marriage) as well as the future (e.g., uncertain blending of the two families).
11 Mindless patterns from the previous marriage, and existing relationship with one's own children, complicate the ability to create a successful blended family system.
12 Remarried couples' communication focuses on issues related to creating and maintaining the new family identity, including the creation of family rituals.
13 Resiliency (e.g., optimism and flexibility) enables couples to successfully manage life cycle transitions. Resilient communication is clear, emotionally expressive, and collaborative regarding problem solving.

**Questions You Should Ask**
*(as a Researcher or as a Relational Partner)*

1 How do relational partners respond to uncertainty during transition?

2  What types of rituals help partners manage relational transition?
3  How do partners set realistic expectations for predictable transitions (e.g. marriage, birth of a child)?
4  How do couples manage perceived unmet expectations regarding relational transitions?
5  How do couples learn positive communication skills to help prepare for and manage relationship change? (For example, the ability to renegotiate aspects of the relationship and manage conflict constructively.)
6  How do mindless communication patterns from previous relationships affect relationship transitions?
7  What are the communication hallmarks of resilient couples? For example, how does a couple's communication reflect the following: optimism, flexibility, clarity, open emotional expression, and collaborative problem solving?

# 6

## Destructive and Restorative Marital Processes

*Kathy had been suspicious for some time. And, yet, she was stunned when Rob said, yes, he had been involved in an affair with his administrative assistant. All Kathy could say through her tears was, "How could you?" Rob told her he would move out by morning. Even the way he left that night – books deposited by her bedside on how to deal with a spouse's affair – betrayed the power imbalance of their marriage. The following months were characterized by emotional hardship, personal growth, and, surprising them both, healing through forgiveness. They laugh now as they tell the story of Rob accompanying Kathy to dance lessons. Rob watched as Kathy moved across the floor seemingly unencumbered, confident, attractive. When we interviewed them, they had been happily living together again for over 20 years.*

Rob's affair almost destroyed the relationship he and Kathy had built over 28 years. Their marriage had experienced its ups and downs but, overall, seemed somewhat stable – until Rob had the brief affair. When Kathy discovered his infidelity, Rob said he would move out. He did, but not before paper-clipping sections in several books on *handling your spouse's affair* for Kathy to read. During the time Rob was out of the house, Kathy made the decision to restore her own sense of well-being. Years of unequal partnering and parenting had left her confused, frustrated, and broken. Over time, she began to heal and develop her sense of self. She began dancing with friends, taking college classes, and, eventually, reconnecting with Rob. Rob was regretting the affair and was finding the new, stronger Kathy very attractive. However, this time, as they rebuilt their relationship, Kathy was a much more equal partner.

Rob and Kathy were confronted with a choice: allow destructive forces to weaken and possibly destroy their marriage, or work to stabilize the relationship and possibly restore high levels of intimacy. They chose to stop the destructive forces that had been developing in their relationship – the unbalanced sense of power, the extramarital relationship, and poor communication patterns that were contributing to a low sense of intimacy and emotional connection. They chose to restore individual well-being, the relationship, and the moral order of the relationship.

In this chapter I explore some of the major destructive forces that affect marriage relationships. I begin by looking at the nature of relational hurt and transgression. Then, I examine patterns of abuse and relational betrayal. Because these "dark" relational forces often destroy relationships and individuals' sense of self, I shift focus for the second half of the chapter to communication processes that are able to restore. After an overview of relational repair strategies, I examine forgiveness, in particular. I do not assume that forgiveness demands reconciliation or that every relationship that encounters destructive forces should move toward reconciliation. However, I focus on forgiveness in this chapter because it can serve as a means of restoring personal well-being, the damaged relationship, and a sense of morality in the relationship (D. L. Kelley, in press).

## Destructive Processes

Early communication scholars generally approached communication as a positive component of relationships (Duck, 1994). And, yet, various researchers have begun to examine communication as a phenomenon that may be used to tear down and destroy as well as build up and enhance (Cupach & Sptizberg, 1994; Spitzberg & Cupach, 1998, 2007). Much of what is considered "dark" communication is considered so because of perceived damage to self and relationship (Vangelisti, Young, Carpenter-Thuene, & Alexander, 2005). As such, I use the concepts of relationship-based hurt and transgression to frame our discussion of destructive processes.

## Relationship Hurt

Hurtful messages can be understood as communication that results in emotional injury (Vangelisti, 2007; Vangelisti, Young, Carpenter-Thuene, & Alexander, 2005). Leary and Leder (2009) suggest that hurt occurs as a result of relational devaluation (e.g., rejection). From this perspective, hurtful messages are a function of the relational meanings in messages (see discussion in Chapter 4). As Sillars et al. (2000) suggest, couples make distinctions between the literal substance of messages and their relational implications. Burgoon and Hale (1984) conceptualize relational messages as individuals' perceptions, within a specific relationship context, of themselves, their partner, and the relationship itself. Therefore, hurt may include threats to one's personal identity, reassessment of one's partner, and violations of relationship norms. Vangelisti's (1994, 2001) emphasis on vulnerability and violation of relational rules reflects this same focus on relational communication. Feeney (2005, 2009) adds additional insight into the process, proposing that hurt in couple relationships is due to transgressions (Vangelisti, 2001) or devaluation (Leary, 2001) that results in a sense of "personal injury." Perceived personal injury results from events in which one's sense of being lovable or one's partner being available and trustworthy is lowered.

Viewing hurt as the result of interpersonal events, Vangelisti (1994) proposed the following as types of hurtful message speech acts: accusation, evaluation, directive, advise, express desire, inform, question, threat, joke, and lie. More specific to marriage relationships, Feeney (2004; see Box 6.1) adapted work by Leary, Springer, Negel, Ansell, and Evans (1998) and examined hurtful events specifically related to romantic couples. Her analyses produced five categories of hurtful events: active disassociation, passive disassociation, criticism, infidelity, and deception. Her data revealed infidelity as the most serious of hurtful events and

## Box 6.1: Theory Checkpoint: Attachment Theory and Hurtful Events in Couple Relationships

Feeney (2005, 2009) proposes that hurtful events in the lives of couples be understood in light of attachment theory. Building on work that focuses on relationship transgression (Vangelisti, 2001) and monitoring one's relational standing (Leary, 2001), Feeney (2009) understands the effects of hurtful events in light of individuals' "mental models of attachment" (p. 316).

Attachment theorists (e.g., Ainsworth et al., 1978; Bowlby, 1982; Trees, 2006; see Chapter 3) posit that, based on personal relational experience, individuals develop working mental models of attachment. These models begin taking shape during infancy, and are based upon one's experience with a primary caregiver. From these models emerge perceptions and expectations of one's loveworthiness and one's partner's availability, responsiveness, and trustworthiness (Feeney, 2005). In particular, the attachment perspective emphasizes individuals' need for "felt security" and the resultant intense emotion when attachment models are threatened (Feeney, 2009).

Critical for Feeney (2005, 2009) is the notion that threat to positive mental attachment models, due to relationship transgressions, elicits feelings of *personal injury*. In essence, personal injury triggers self- and partner-reassessment and orients the victim to potential relational meanings of behaviors. For example, relationship anxiety is associated with victim distress, self-blame, and a sense of being unlovable (Feeney, 2004; 2009). In addition, the partner is viewed as unavailable and no longer trustworthy. Feeney's research has demonstrated five categories of hurtful events: active disassociation (e.g. relationship termination, denial of feelings), passive disassociation (being ignored or excluded from plans/conversations), criticism (negative verbal comments regarding personal characteristics), infidelity (extrarelationship sexual activity), and deception (misleading acts).

associated with greater feelings of hurt and powerlessness, in addition to other negative relationship effects. Interestingly, in spite of differences in relational hurt, all five event types were associated with similar levels of negative affect.

Vangelisti and Crumley (1998) demonstrated that communication surrounding hurtful events more strongly affects romantic relationships than family and non-family relationships. Yet, these findings may be balanced with the fact that intimate relationships have been found to be less affected by single hurtful actions (Vangelisti, 1994). Vangelisti (1994) discovered that hurtful messages in more intimate relationships were less harmful to the relationship, perhaps because intimate partners attribute less damaging meaning to a single event or events involving their partners, or because intimate partners have idiosyncratic means of managing their hurt. It seems that intensity of hurt feelings may primarily be a function of the ability of the recipient (the hurt partner) to respond, the intentionality associated with the hurtful event, and the degree to which the recipient expects to be hurt by his or her partner (Vangelisti, 2007).

It is important to recognize that hurtful episodes, and their accompanying responses, are complex events. That is, hurtful episodes are often combinations of specific actions (Vangelisti & Gerstenberger, 2004). For example, infidelity and deception typically occur together. This creates complex emotional responses characterized as emotional blends (Vangelisti, 2009; Vangelisti & Young, 2000). As such, a victimized partner may feel a mixture of anger, sadness, hurt, and even compassion for an offending partner.

Interestingly, hurt is not all bad. In a recent review, Vangelisti (2009) concludes that hurt in any given interaction may serve three functions: it may be informative, persuasive, and supportive. Hurt may be *informative* as it serves as a relational indicator. Relational hurt often instigates evaluation of the relationship and one's partner. Hurt may also be *persuasive*. Hurtful messages may directly (e.g., accusations and criticism) or indirectly (e.g., information that threatens the relationship, "I'm confused about how I feel about us.") influence the relational partners.

Hurtful messages that function to *support* one's partner are well-intended messages that are delivered in a hurtful manner or carry information that is hurtful. For example, messages that signal disappointment may be intended to motivate the other toward positive behavior.

## Relationship Transgressions

Interruptions of typical behavior or violations of expected behavior often result in increased negatively labeled arousal (e.g., anger or hurt; Vangelisti, 1994, 2001). This effect is particularly poignant for marriage relationships because the long-term nature of the relationship is certainly associated with development of behavioral patterns, relational expectations, and implicit and explicit rules.

Metts and Cupach (2007) identify transgressions as involving rule violations (see Box 6.2) and hurtful events, noting that infidelity is often cited as a "prototype" of transgression behavior. Metts (1994) argues that, while multiple types of events can act as stressors and create uncertainty in the relationship, transgressions are violations of "relationally relevant rules" (p. 218). This is an important distinction as later I argue that transgressions have a moral component to them (e.g., "It was wrong to violate our relationship agreement."). Metts (1994) posits that couples maintain regulative rules that coordinate relationship behaviors, and constitutive rules that are essential to ascertaining the meaning of certain relationship activities or characteristics. For example, couples may regulate interactions with rules for conflict (regulative) and may demonstrate love and commitment through monogamy (constitutive). Similarly, Rusbult, Hannon, Stocker, and Finkel (2005) identify transgressions as incidents that harm the victim and are perceived by the victim (and possibly the perpetrator) as a knowing departure from relationship-governing norms. Norms are identified as courses of action, implicitly or explicitly agreed upon, that determine mandated or forbidden behavior under certain circumstances.

## Box 6.2: Interdependence Theory: Transgression and Reconciliation as Rule Violation and Restoration

Interdependence Theory is a social exchange approach to viewing relationships that makes predictions about relationship satisfaction, dependence, and stability based on relational outcomes, comparison levels (CL), and comparison levels of alternatives (CLalt) (Dainton & Zelley, 2006; Thibaut & Kelley, 1959). Outcome is derived by perception of rewards minus costs (Rewards − Costs = Outcome), whereas CL represents the rewards and costs one expects from a specific relationship, and CLalt is one's assessment of the current relationship compared to alternatives.

According to Rusbult et al. (2005), Interdependence Theory frames a relational transgression as "an incident in which a perpetrator is perceived (by the victim and perhaps by the perpetrator as well) to have knowingly departed from the norms that govern their relationship, thereby harming the victim" (p. 186). Metts and Cupach (2007) concur, identifying rule violations as the most inclusive understanding of relational transgressions. Further, Metts (1994) conceptualizes transgressions as relationship disruptions characterized by salience, focus, and consequence. Salience refers to transgressions recognized by participants. Focus references particular standards of behavior ("How could you do X?"). Consequence implies a response (explanation, apology, remediation) that neutralizes negative emotion generated by the transgression.

Rule (norm) violation has been linked to relationship termination and interpersonal forgiveness (D. L. Kelley & Waldron, 2006; Metts, 1994). Baxter (1986) found that romantic couples ended relationships due to rule violations regarding such things as autonomy, supportiveness, and loyalty. For those maintaining their relationships after relationship transgression, my early forgiveness study found that forgiveness episodes often led to the restoration of relational

167

rules or generation of new rules (D. L. Kelley, 1998). Some individuals used conditional forgiveness ("I will forgive you if ...") as a means of establishing relational boundaries (rules).

Transgressions manifest themselves in a variety of ways. Metts (1994) highlights six categories of transgression. *Sexual infidelity* represents sexual involvement outside the primary relationship. *Privacy/secrets* represents a misuse of information. *Commitments* is characterized by making a commitment or promise and subsequently not fulfilling what was promised. *Privileging the primary relationship* includes acts that fail to acknowledge the primacy of the relationship, such as putting other persons or events ahead of the relationship/partner. *Interaction management* involves abusive behavior and destructive conflict strategies. *Appropriate emotions* is violation of expectations for reciprocation and acceptance of love and affection.

Waldron and I (2008) distinguish between traumatic events and transgressions. The source for traumatic events is typically outside the relationship. Thus, the relationship between the offender and offended is somewhat indirect. For example, a job layoff may create economic stress wherein the layed-off partner is blamed for not accepting a job transfer earlier in the year. In contrast, transgressions are defined as deliberate acts that harm one's partner. Examples of transgressions were evident during analysis of long-term married couple data: verbal aggression, expressions of anger, public embarrassments, betrayal, unilateral decision making, infidelity and substance abuse (Harvey, 2004; Waldron & Kelley, 2008). These types can be understood in terms of three basic themes: threats to identity, violations of the "relationship covenant" (Hargrave, 1994), and acts of injustice/unfairness (Hargrave & Sells, 1997).

The third theme, injustice, highlights the fact that couple transgressions may often be conceptualized as moral violations (D. L. Kelley, in press; Waldron & Kelley, 2008). When individuals perceive behavior as "wrong" or "bad," they perceive an offending act as a moral transgression. This may create special challenges for partners who are no longer dealing with behavior that is simply irritating or inefficient. Moral transgressions may create the necessity for partners to renegotiate moral standards, establish guidelines for relational justice (e.g., relational equity), and ensure safety and certainty for partners to continue the relationship.

Up to this juncture I have focused on destructive relational processes as they create hurt for one or both partners and violate one's sense of identity, morality, or the relationship covenant. In this light I now turn to two specific communication-focused transgression types: abusive/controlling behavior and infidelity as betrayal. I focus on abusive behavior because power and control are ubiquitous concepts in the interpersonal relationship literature (Burgoon & Hale, 1984) and, generally, married partners have rules regarding aggression in their relationship (Metts, 1994). I focus on infidelity as betrayal, because the strong emotional responses make it one of the most difficult issues for marriage partners to confront (Feeney, 2009).

### Abusive/Controlling Behavior

Most marriages have rules related to non-aggression; though what constitutes a transgression, or "sufficiently untoward" behavior, is largely determined by the offending partner (Metts, 1994). This subjective nature of abuse has made it difficult for researchers to agree on terminology. For example, Marshall (1994) argues that the negative connotation of the term *abuse* may result in underreporting relationship violence. On the other hand, Spitzberg (2009) states that certain researchers prefer the term *abuse* because it implies violence or aggression that occurs over time. Related to this, distinctions between *aggression* and *violence* are not always clear. According to Marshall (1994), *aggression* includes the intent or perceived intent to harm, while the term *violence* avoids many of the meanings (e.g., intent, victimization) associated with aggression. However, Spitzberg (2009) defines violence as behavior that is intended to physically harm another person, although he recognizes gray areas, such as self-protection or parental discipline, that are often not labeled as violence.

For our purposes here, I focus on research that examines

behavior typically occurring over a period of time and intended to hurt one's partner. However, it is important to recognize that while intent is an important criterion (e.g., perception of intent to harm has been related to increased violence in relationships; Betancourt & Blair, 1992), it is difficult to assess in actual relationships. Spitzberg (2009) identifies four ways in which intent is problematic conceptually: it is not observable, it can be denied by perceived aggressors, assessment of intent may lead to further violence, and behavior without proximal effects to hurt may have distal effects. Also, the fact that intent implies that there is an aggressor and a victim in the interaction (Marshall, 1994) may complicate attempts to engage constructive conflict.

Three additional conceptual frameworks help frame our discussion. First, couple aggression can be conceptualized as either patriarchal terrorism or common couple violence (Johnson, 1995, 2004). The patriarchal terrorism perspective derives from feminist research focusing on battered women and emphasizes systematic male violence by focusing on family structure and psychological gender. Research in this area has identified the following power and control tactics: coercion and threats, intimidation, emotional abuse, isolation, minimizing, denying, blaming, and use of children, male privilege, and economics to gain control (Johnson, 2004; Pence & Paymer, 1993). In contrast, the common couple violence perspective largely arose from the study of family conflict and emphasizes violence that can more readily be characterized as husbands and wives who have occasional outbursts.

Second, aggressive/violent acts may be understood as communication tools used to achieve instrumental and expressive goals (K. L. Anderson, Umberson, & Elliott, 2004; Marshall, 1994; Spitzberg, 2009). In this context, instrumental aggression is used to achieve a goal or task (e.g., to gain compliance from one's partner). Expressive aggression is associated with the conveyance of strong emotion (e.g., anger or rage). Of course, violent acts may be both expressive and instrumental.

Third, communicative aggression in intimate relationships has been conceptualized as tantamount to psychological abuse (Spitzberg, 2009). Dailey, Lee, and Spitzberg (2007) define psychological abuse as "any recurring set of messages that function to impair a person's enduring preferred self-image" (p. 303). Critical to this definition is the emphasis on time. That is, psychologically abusive messages are recurring and affect one's desired sense of self *over time*.

**Arousal** The three conceptual frameworks just reviewed emphasize that aggressive behavior may be abusive when used instrumentally to gain power (e.g., patriarchal), or result from intermittent outbursts of strong emotion. Regarding the latter condition, heightened arousal accompanying expressive aggression may facilitate the intent to do harm to a partner. In short, high arousal and negative affect, when coupled with aggressive impulses and aggression-related thoughts, may lead to cycles of increasing arousal and cognitively complex processes (e.g., attributions of cause/blame) that increase the likelihood of an aggressive response (Marshall, 1994).

Research has demonstrated that verbal aggression is often a precursor to physical aggression (Sabourin, 1991, 1995). Feldman and Ridley (2000) propose four reasons for this effect. First, couples tend to "lock in" to negative reciprocal communication patterns (e.g., cross-complaining). Second, conflict escalates through the issue level, personality level, and relational level. Third, retaliation becomes more likely in order to save face or prevent future hurt. And, fourth, high arousal levels in one partner become mirrored in the other. As discussed previously (see Chapter 4), high arousal level impairs the complex cognitive processing needed for constructive conflict.

It is important to note that aggression is not simply the result of runaway conflict episodes. Marshall (1994) suggests that high arousal triggers of this cycle need not be directly related to the relationship. That is, highly arousing events unrelated to the aggressor's partner may still trigger violent episodes. In addition, Marshall also reports anecdotal evidence that suggests battered women are sometimes hit without warning, not due to escalating conflict. In fact, a problem associated with use of the term *violence* is its association with high intensity and severity, when actually most forceful acts in close relationships occur at relatively low to moderate levels of intensity and severity (Marshall, 1994).

Work by Gottman (Gottman, Jacobson, Rushe, & Shortt, 1995; Jacobson, Gottman, & Shortt, 1995) has described two types of batterers based on heart rate. Type I batterers (cobras) reduce heart rate over the course of marital interaction, while Type II (pit bulls) increase heart rates. Type I batterers typically have a family history of violence, have been engaged in substance abuse, and extend their violent tendencies to a variety of relationships (e.g., with friends or coworkers). They are more severely violent in their marriages. Type II batterers are more likely to be motivated by dependency and emotional insecurity, and are less severely violent in their interactions with their wives. Their pattern of violence results from emotional reactions that spiral out of control.

*Communication-related variables*  In interviews in which couples talked about a "typical day," Sabourin and Stamp (1995) identified seven communication-based differences that differentiated couples with abusive histories from nonabusive couples: vague vs. precise language, opposition vs. collaboration, relational vs. content talk, despair vs. optimism, interfering vs. facilitating interdependence, complaints vs. compliments, and ineffective vs. effective change. In essence, couples with abusive histories had communication interactions characterized by lack of detail, opposition and argumentation regarding daily activities (e.g., cooking), the inability to describe daily tasks without digressing to criticizing, expression of anger and frustration, misunderstanding, negative reciprocity, enmeshment, chronic complaining, and self-focus and ambiguity regarding handling problems or change in the relationship.

As suggested by Sabourin and Stamp's (1995) work, couple violence has been related to a lack of problem-solving skills (K. L. Anderson et al., 2004; Feldman & Ridley, 2000). Problem-solving skills provide relational partners with response choices that include cooperative options as well as help to moderate arousal levels. In addition, research on couples who experience abuse shows spouses to be less argumentative (constructive defense of one's position), more verbally aggressive, more likely to recipro-

172

cate aggression, and to experience stronger, longer lasting feelings of anger, frustration, and contempt (K. L. Anderson et al., 2004; Feldman & Ridley, 2000). Feldman and Ridley's (2000) work with couples who experience male domestic violence toward female partners found a number of distinguishing communication and outcome variables. Compared to nonviolent relationships, those experiencing male domestic violence demonstrated more male and female unilateral aggression, mutual verbal aggression, male demand/female withdraw, and less constructive (relative to destructive) communication and mutual problem solving, as well as poorer problem resolution and more emotional distance after problem arguments and discussions.

*Relational variables* Christopher and Lloyd (2000) identify a number of relational variables associated with violent couples. First, violent couples exhibit marital skill deficits. As discussed earlier, they have difficulty problem solving. This may be due, in part, to couples' inability to extract themselves from patterns of competitive symmetry (one-up statements followed by one-up statements) (Sabourin, 1995). Constructive interaction may also be inhibited by males' use of fewer positive communication elements such as sympathy and support. Attribution of hostile intent regarding their wives' actions may also contribute to males' skill deficit. In addition, research indicates that violent husbands use more negativity, including attacking strategies such as blaming, interrupting, invalidating, and threat (Christopher & Lloyd, 2000; Murphy & O'Farrell, 1997). Christopher and Lloyd (2000) suggest that skill deficits may be most pronounced when partners feel threat, such as perceived public embarrassment, character threats, or rejection.

Second, Christopher and Lloyd (2000) suggest violent couples describe their daily interactions and conflict differently than nonviolent couples. In particular, violent couples' daily conflict is highly ritualized and reactive, violent husbands see themselves as giving more than they receive, and distressed-violent couples report their daily interactions as volatile and enmeshed (Christopher & Lloyd, 2000; Lloyd, 1996). As discussed previously, Sabourin and Stamp

(1995) found abusive couples' daily interactions to be character-ized by complaints, ineffective change, opposition, despair, and vague language that focused on relational topics to such an extent that it interfered with effective problem solving and the develop-ment of a healthy sense of interdependence.

Third, according to Christopher and Lloyd (2000), violent-distressed couples struggle for relational control. This may include patterns of competitive symmetry characterized by domi-neering statements (Sabourin, 1995), husbands asserting their rights (Rogers, Castleton, & Lloyd, 1996), and husband and wife demand–withdraw patterns (Babcock, Waltz, Jacobson, & Gottman, 1993; Feldman & Ridley, 2000). Specific to demand–withdraw patterns, it should be noted that the literature is complex. It seems that while withdrawal is more often the strategy of the dominant partner (K. L. Anderson et al., 2004), for violent couples who are distressed (e.g., Holtzworth-Munroe, Smutzler, & Stuart, 1998) or include Type I batterers (Berns, Jacobson, & Gottman, 1999), the dominant partner may take the demand role.

Finally, Christopher and Lloyd (2000) argue that there is a strong relationship between marital distress and husband vio-lence. Yet, they recognize that the distress–violence relationship is not clear. For example, K. L. Anderson et al. (2004) indicate that communication interaction may both facilitate couple violence and become victim to it. Likewise, while psychological abuse is typically associated with lower marital satisfaction (Dailey et al., 2007), it should be noted that violence also occurs in relationships with high marital satisfaction, and that distress may primarily be a factor when coupled with other variables (e.g., husband's alcohol-ism; Christopher & Lloyd, 2000).

*Effects of intimate violence*    As mentioned previously, communica-tion interaction may both facilitate couple violence and be affected by it (K. L. Anderson et al., 2004). For example, while skills deficit perspectives posit the inability to problem solve productively as a contributing factor leading to violence, Feldman and Ridley (2000) also present poor problem solving as a result of male vio-lence. Additionally, in their study, partners in violent relationships also experienced more emotional distance after an argument or conflict discussion: that is, one or both partners felt distant, withdrawn, discouraged, or hopeless.

Spitzberg (2009) presents 10 effect clusters, originally identified by Cupach and Spitzberg (2004), that he believes encompass all forms of intimate violence. *General trauma* includes effects on life satisfaction and quality of life. General trauma may manifest such effects as posttraumatic stress syndrome. *Affective* health is characterized by elements such as hurt, sadness, and depression; and *cognitive* health represents changes in one's cognitive/rational quality of life, such as distrust, suspicion, and lack of concentration. *Physical/physiological, behavioral,* and *social* health effects may include sleep disorders and appetite disturbance, disruption of typical behavioral routines, and changes in the quality of one's relational life: for instance, experiencing loneliness. *Resource* health recognizes changes in tangible resources, such as change or loss of home or finances. *Spiritual* and *societal* health identifies changes in one's belief systems, such as faith in God and faith in people (e.g., fear of crime or stereotyping). *Resilience* effects refers to enhanced experience of any of the previous categories with an emphasis on the inability to recover from change as one might typically. Importantly, Spitzberg notes that most hurt is likely to reside within multiple categories.

At one level, the preceding information on aggression, violence, and abuse may seem overwhelming. And, yet, after reviewing the literature, Spitzberg (2009) concludes that while some relational violence may be deeply traumatizing, especially if accompanied by communicative aggression (psychological abuse), other violence is short term and has minimal to moderate negative relational effects. These conclusions set the stage for the second half of this chapter wherein I deal with relationship restoration and, specifically, forgiveness. Before examining relationship restoration, I turn to one other potentially destructive relationship event – betrayal.

### Infidelity as Betrayal

Most marriages have rules related to monogamy and deception (Metts, 1994). Yet, researchers have noted the predominance of marital infidelity throughout Western societies, most often among men (Buunk & Dijkstra, 2004; Wiederman, 1997). Presently, the state of infidelity is somewhat complex. Allan and Harrison (2009) note that the terms *extradyadic relationship* and *extradyadic sex* have entered more common usage because they are freer of value-based meaning, as compared to terms such as *adultery* and *infidelity*, which may seem "old-fashioned or overly moralistic" (p. 192). *Having an affair* or, even, *being unfaithful* may be seen as less morally rigid than infidelity (Allan & Harrison, 2002). At the same time, research collected from public archives in Britain indicates that a vast majority of individuals see affairs as inappropriate (Allan & Harrison, 2002), and Tafoya and Spitzberg (2007) conclude that most infidelity definitions converge on the idea that there is a violation of "expectations and standards of relationship exclusivity" (p. 202). Later in this chapter I argue that forgiveness is a particularly relevant response to infidelity because of partners' perceptions that a moral covenant has been broken (Hargrave, 1994), and I have labeled the current section of this chapter *infidelity as betrayal* because I focus the discussion on couples who experience infidelity as betrayal of the relationship agreement.

Allan and Harrison (2009) state that, commonly, individuals experience infidelity as betrayal. Violation of explicit and implicit rules in the relationship, particularly for relationship exclusivity (Tafoya & Spitzberg, 2007), may lead a partner to feel "cheated," and undercut the perception of "coupleness" or a sense that the relationship is "special" (Allan & Harrison, 2009, p. 199). As such, partners may experience a betrayal of the relationship contract and betrayal of emotional vulnerability. Most significant is the loss of trust that often accompanies the experience of betrayal. Most infidelity involves deceit, whether passive (e.g., simply not telling one's partner of the extradyadic relationship) or active (e.g., direct lying about why one is late coming home from work), which undermines openness and vulnerability in the relationship. In addition, some infidelity may be communication-based. That is, infidelity may serve a relational or communicative function, such as revenge or attention getting (Tafoya & Sptizberg, 2007).

Infidelity as betrayal presumes negative relational and personal effects. Because living as a couple remains a "cherished ideal," it is likely that secret affairs will be viewed and experienced negatively (Jamieson, 2004). Feeney (2004, 2009) points out that since sexual involvement and exclusivity are typically characteristic of marriage relationships and used as indicators of partners' love for one another, sexual infidelity may be more hurtful than other types of relational transgressions. Additionally, the deception that typically accompanies affairs (Jamieson, 2004; Vangelisti & Gerstenberger, 2004) and guilt associated with potential harm to one's children (Allan & Harrison, 2002) may create added relational pain. This thinking is consistent with the suggestion that couples who are involved in infidelity experience emotional responses akin to the experience of general trauma, thus making infidelity one of the most difficult issues with which to deal by couples and their therapists (Gordon, Baucom, & Snyder, 2005).

Responses to infidelity may vary according to culture, the gender of the transgressor, whether the transgression is a one-time encounter or an enduring event, and whether the infidelity has been terminated (Allan & Harrison, 2009). However, according to Gordon et al. (2005), central responses to the discovery of infidelity parallel those related to the experience of trauma. Partners' experience vacillates between outwardly directed emotion, such as rage toward the participating partner, to inwardly directed emotion, such as feelings of shame, depression, powerlessness, victimization, and abandonment. Cognitive responses often include rumination about the event (often to the extent that it affects daily functioning), change of beliefs about the offending partner, and loss of trust. Behavioral effects may include avoidance, hypervigilance, obsessive questioning, and negative, punitive exchanges.

Allan and Harrison (2009) also recognize shame, worthlessness, and rejection as responses to infidelity. However, they focus on jealousy, betrayal, and loss of identity as common responses to discovering a partner's indiscretion. Here I discuss jealousy and identity (see previous discussion of betrayal). Jealousy can be cognitive (e.g., mental suspicion and rumination), behavioral (e.g., questioning about previous relationships), and emotional (e.g., upset feelings when contemplating possible jealous scenarios)

(Tafoya & Spitzberg, 2007). Jealousy has been linked to such personality variables as low self-esteem, high neuroticism, and insecure attachment style, possibly because such individuals feel dependent on their partners (Buunk & Dijkstra, 2000). Gender differences have also been identified regarding jealousy, such that women are perceived as more prone to jealousy. Allan and Harrison (2009) suggest this gender difference may result from a double standard that gives men more freedom to stray from their relationship commitments or men's and women's differing views of sexual and emotional unfaithfulness. It is argued that a partner's extradyadic sexual involvement is most upsetting for men, whereas women are more affected by their partner's emotional involvement with another person (Buss, Larsen, Westen, & Semmelroth, 1992; Tafoya & Spitzberg, 2007). Evolutionary psychologists propose this effect is due to males' desire for paternity and females' desire to secure resources (e.g., economic stability when pregnant or caring for young children). Consistent with this thinking, Allan (2004) found women's reasons for having an affair typically embedded in dissatisfaction with their marriage, whereas men's reasons tended to be independent of their current relationship. Others have blurred the focus on gender and, instead, suggest that those who see emotional and sexual intimacy as closely tied also experience a broader or deeper sense of betrayal as a result of infidelity (Allan & Harrison, 2009; DeSteno, Bartlett, Salovey, & Braverman, 2002; DeSteno & Salovey, 1996). This perspective is consistent with our earlier discussion of intimacy (see Chapter 3) in which greater access (e.g., physical and psychological/emotional) is associated with greater intimacy.

Infidelity is also associated with identity struggles for the victimized partner (Allan & Harrison, 2009; M. M. Olson, Russell, Higgins-Kessler, & Miller, 2002). During this difficult time, individuals often experience a sense of loss of relationship and identity (Allan & Harrison, 2009). Because couple relationships are central to maintaining personal identity (Jamieson, 2004), the sense of betrayal that accompanies the discovery of an affair often is interpreted as personal rejection. And, as presented previously, rejection, or relational devaluation, is clearly associated with relational hurt (Leary & Leder, 2009).

Waldron and I (2008) suggest that individuals who experience transgressions go through a period of sense making, wherein they seek to assess the meaning of what has happened. Gordon and Baucom (1998) note that during this time, uncertainty limits the injured party's ability to make predictions about the future, which heightens a sense of confusion and lack of control. For instance, an individual may wonder, "If my partner is willing to break one rule, will he/she be willing to break another? Is there no longer a moral anchor in our marriage?" (VanderVoort & Duck, 2004). The substantial emotional pain, sense of rejection, and need to make sense of the situation may lead to questions of intent or motive (e.g., "Why would you do this to me?"), relational assessment ("What was wrong with *us*?"), self-blame ("What did I do wrong?"), personal shame ("What is wrong with me?"), or other shame ("What is wrong with you?"). Likewise, individuals who suspect their partner of an affair may experience an *interrogative dilemma* (Vangelisti & Gerstenberger, 2004). That is, the jealousy and increased uncertainty experienced by the suspecting partner may generate the desire to question (interrogate) the spouse about perceived changes in behavior; however, the suspecting partner will likely also experience fear that, if mistaken, he or she will damage the relationship by exhibiting lack of trust.

## Restorative Processes

Having focused on infidelity (perceived as relational betrayal) and abusive behavior within the broader context of interpersonal hurt and relationship transgression, I now transition to restorative processes. I begin with a review of research focusing on relational repair, then argue that because certain relationship transgressions are perceived as moralistic in nature (e.g., abuse and infidelity), forgiveness is a reasonable response if one seeks to restore the relationship. The chapter finishes with a discussion of how couples reconcile, particularly after one partner has had an affair.

The nature of intimate relationships is vulnerability with one's partner and inevitable hurt over time. As such, I begin this section with a brief overview of research on relational repair. I focus here only on a few studies that are not specifically conflict-oriented (Chapter 4 provides an extensive review of the conflict literature). The bulk of the following section centers on forgiveness as it creates space for relationship transformation and interpersonal reconciliation.

## Relational Repair

Married partners typically take corrective action when they perceive their relationship to have diminished in quality (Thompson-Hayes & Webb, 2008). Specifically, relationship responses when "something has gone awry" have been conceptualized as repair (Dindia & Baxter, 1987). Early work by Dindia and Baxter (1987) sought empirically to determine behaviors associated with relational repair and to distinguish these behaviors, if possible, from relational maintenance strategies. They asked couples to list things they had done when: (1) they felt their relationship was good and wanted to keep it from deteriorating (maintenance); and (2) they felt like the relationship was not as good as it once was and wanted to bring it back to its previous state (repair). Although 12 categories of maintenance/repair strategies were identified, the authors concluded that married partners primarily use a narrow band of strategies that focus on communication or activity (e.g., togetherness activities). Communication strategies included prosocial "warmness," metacommunication (e.g., communication about the problem), and expressions of affection. Few differences were found between repair and maintenance strategies, although metacommunication was used more, and anti-ritualizing (e.g., spontaneity) less, as repair strategies. It seems that repair, versus maintenance, encourages the use of direct talk about the problem and a focus on keeping things predictable (less spontaneous). The relatively few differences discovered between repair and maintenance strategies may be in part because repair was not conceptualized as response to a damaging event or transgression.

Thompson-Hayes and Webb (2008) found similar results to Dindia and Baxter (1987), noting that talking about the problem was the repair strategy most frequently used by couples. Couples also used two somewhat opposite strategies, apologizing and avoiding. Apologizing admits a wrong done, while avoiding "hopes that things will smooth over" (Thompson-Hayes & Webb, 2008, p. 154). Interestingly, Thompson-Hayes and Webb (2008) report two wives in their sample who said they either never thought about, or their relationships never needed, repair. I have found similar individuals in my studies with married couples. For example, one husband reported that he never had to forgive his wife because she had never done anything to intentionally hurt him (Waldron & Kelley, 2008).

J. M. Lewis (1998) suggests that relational repair is an alternative to relational conflict. He proposes the following elements as essential to facilitating effective repair and avoiding destructive conflict. To begin, partners should be encouraged to share feelings about the experience in question or about one's self, before discussing feelings about one's partner. In essence, sharing feelings about one another is an advanced skill, only to be used once the event and one's self can reasonably be discussed. Skills such as active listening can help this process. Couples must also learn to have "repair" discussions at appropriate times and places. In addition, Lewis believes that repair is facilitated by couple vulnerability. For partners to feel safe being vulnerable, it is likely that negative communication patterns will have to change and be closely monitored by the couple.

This short review has focused on processes and strategies intended to restore relationships to previous levels of functioning. However, the presented studies have focused on variables other than hurt and moral disruption within the relationship. As such, I now turn our attention to forgiveness because of its ability to respond to moral and emotional disturbance as a means of achieving restoration.

## Forgiveness

Forgiveness has been conceptualized as a means of facilitating relational repair or reconciliation (Gordon & Baucom, 2003; Rusbult et al., 2005; Waldron & Kelley, 2008). For example, in a recent review of emerging trends in marriage research, Fincham, Stanley, and Beach (2007) identify forgiveness as a transformative process in marriage. Metts and Cupach (2007), as well, emphasize forgiveness as including the enactment of relationship-constructive behaviors.

Recently I have argued that forgiveness is a form of positive communication designed to restore (D. L. Kelley, in press). Specifically, people seek or grant forgiveness in order to restore self or other well-being, the relationship, and a sense of moral order. Various researchers have found that forgiveness can play an important role in the restoration of marital relationships (e.g., Fincham, Hall, & Beach, 2005). Because my goal in this section is somewhat narrow – to focus on aspects of forgiveness that set the stage for personal and relational restoration – I offer the following definition of forgiveness, as developed by Vince Waldron and myself (2008):

> *Forgiveness is a relational process whereby harmful conduct is acknowledged by one or both partners; the harmed partner extends undeserved mercy to the perceived transgressor; one or both partners experience a transformation from negative to positive psychological states; and the meaning of the relationship is renegotiated, with the possibility of reconciliation.* (p. 19)

This definition highlights six issues that are essential to consider regarding restoration: relational context, recognition of harmful conduct, undeserved mercy, perceived transgressor, transformation from negative to positive, and renegotiated meaning. First, the definition locates forgiveness within a *relational context*. This is not to presume forgiveness is not appropriate in other contexts (e.g., self-forgiveness); however, forgiveness certainly has a significant role to play in what happens between people. Rusbult et al. (2005) suggest that in ongoing relationships, the forgiveness process is "inherently interpersonal – it is a process to which both victim *and* perpetrator contribute" (p. 185). Second, the definition emphasizes the recognition of *harmful conduct*. This essential element separates forgiveness from many related, but non-forgiveness concepts. For example, excuse is typically identified as a non-forgiveness concept because excuses imply the nullification of any "wrong" action (Enright & Fitzgibbons, 2000; Waldron & Kelley, 2008). That is, although certain hurtful actions may have occurred, if there is an excuse for one's behavior, there is no longer responsibility or blame for the harmful conduct. Similarly, while it is important to accept one's partner for who he or she is, acceptance is not forgiveness (Waldron & Kelley, 2008).

Third, the definition also calls for *undeserved mercy* for a perceived transgressor. Underserved mercy highlights the gift nature of forgiveness from victim to perpetrator (Worthington, 1998, 2001). Forgiveness is not offered because someone deserves it or has earned it. Forgiveness is undeserved. Undeserved mercy also calls attention to relationship morality and justice. That is, while mercy may bypass immediate justice, it can set the stage for the creation of relational justice over time. For example, Canary and Stafford's (1992) emphasis on equity as a guiding process that affects relational outcomes (see Chapter 2) reflects this concern for a relational justice. In essence, relational justice may be conceptualized as balance or equity (Exline, Worthington, Hill, & McCullough, 2003).

*Perceived transgressor* recognizes that relational rule breaking is based on perception (Metts, 1994). As such, partners may disagree as to whether a transgression has taken place. Yet, forgiveness is offered because one partner perceives harm and moral violation (Rusbult et al., 2005).

The final two components of the definition are focused on potential forgiveness outcomes. First, there is a *transformation from negative to positive*. Both forgivers and offenders may experience a move from negative to positive behavior and/or psychological or emotional states. Forgiveness research has indicated that when married partners forgive, they experience a reduction in negative motivational states (e.g., desire to seek revenge) and an increase in positive motivational states (e.g., willingness to engage in conciliatory behavior; Fincham et al., 2005). The second forgiveness outcome is *renegotiated meaning*. The renegotiation may or may not be verbal, may lead to the establishment of new rules or a new relationship definition (e.g., change from married to ex-spouses coordinating their children's lives), and may result in returning to normal, weakening, strengthening, or even terminating the relationship (D. L. Kelley, 1998). In addition, because transgressions are often conceived as having a moral component to them ("What you did to me was wrong."; Allan & Harrison, 2002; Rusbult et al., 2005), renegotiation involves the reestablishment of the relationship moral order (Enright & Fitzgibbons, 2000), leading to possible reconciliation.

### Forgiveness within the Marriage Context

Forgiveness is particularly salient in marriage relationships because "those we love are paradoxically the ones we are most likely to hurt" (Fincham et al., 2005, p. 207). The high level of interdependence and emotional connection between partners results in the frequent need for forgiveness for many couples. My research (Waldron & Kelley, 2008) with long-term married couples revealed that while some couples report little need for forgiveness, others report "forgiveness is every day." Significantly, forgiveness may be conceptualized as a "self-repair" process that has the potential to positively alter couple exchanges (Fincham et al., 2007, p. 279).

Harvey (2004) identified various traumatic relational experiences reported by long-term couples in their relationship histories (e.g., money, parenting, substance dependence, verbal aggression, infidelity, deception, public embarrassment). In a review of Harvey's work, Waldron and I (2008) identified three types of transgressions that seem particularly related to forgiveness and, I suggest, have particular relevance for married couples. The first is transgressions that attack one's personal identity. This transgression category includes showing disrespect, public embarrassment, and communication that devalues one's partner. Second is violation of the "relationship covenant" (see Hargrave, 2004). This includes behaviors that violate implicit or explicit relational rules (e.g., extradyadic sexual relationships, trust, loyalty, collaborative decision making). The third category of transgression includes acts of injustice or unfairness. Abuse of power, inequity, or favoritism fit here. In married relationships this category may be represented by inequities related to household chores, childcare, or outside work. Note that perception of injustice places a transgression within a moral context (Freedman, Enright, & Knutson, 2005) and that these three categories are not mutually exclusive. For instance, in the case of infidelity, the victim of the transgression may perceive the act as unfair, a violation of the relationship covenant, and damaging to his or her personal identity.

Waldron and I (2008) argue that transgressions that "require" forgiveness are often perceived as moral in nature. We assume that relationships are values-based entities and, as such, that individuals are constantly negotiating (implicitly or explicitly) moral guidelines unique to their specific relationships. As couples develop a sense of "right" or "wrong" in their relationship, they develop a moral code (Freedman et al., 2005). For example, when couples say vows as a part of their wedding ceremony, they are explicitly developing part of their moral code – "in sickness and in health" signifies that it would be "wrong" for one partner to leave another over issues of illness. Similarly, research by Allan and Harrison (2002) reflects the idea that many couples view extramarital affairs as violations of a moral code, religious or otherwise, that is the "bedrock of stable and ordered family life" (p. 53). This code of exclusivity may be implicit and, yet, guide partner behavior and expectations.

Research has demonstrated the ability of forgiveness to aid in the management of everyday hurts and major transgressions, and found that couples perceive forgiveness as important to marital longevity and satisfaction (Fenell, 1993; Fincham et al., 2005; Waldron & Kelley, 2008). Regarding satisfaction, Kachadourian, Fincham, and Davila (2005) found that forgiveness was positively associated with marital satisfaction, and negatively associated with rumination and ambivalence. My work with Vince Waldron (2005) revealed that marital satisfaction drops after a relational transgression and then increases significantly (although not always to pre-transgression levels) after forgiveness. In particular, we also found communication-granting behaviors to be associated with relational outcomes. For example, explicit (e.g., saying "I forgive you.") and nonverbal strategies were associated with relationship strengthening, whereas conditional strategies were associated with relationship deterioration. Our work has also demonstrated forgiveness-seeking behaviors (e.g., explicit acknowledgement, nonverbal assurance, and compensation) associated with relationship recovery.

Consistent with these findings, Karremans, Van Lange, Ouwerkerk, and Kluwer (2003) discovered that partner-specific forgiveness is positively related to life satisfaction, even more than general attitudes regarding forgiveness. Likewise, Allemand, Amberg, Zimprich, and Fincham (2007) found trait forgiveness positively related to relationship satisfaction. However, they also discovered that relationship satisfaction moderated the relationship between trait forgiveness and episodic forgiveness, such that couples with high satisfaction levels exhibited a positive relationship between trait and episodic forgiveness, and those with low satisfaction exhibited a negative relationship between trait and episodic forgiveness. Similarly, Guerrero and Bachman (2010) found positive pre-transgression relationship evaluations (relationship quality, high investment, low-quality alternatives) to be associated with conciliatory response patterns when offenses were perceived as mild, and associated with conditional response patterns when offenses were perceived as severe. Negative pre-transgression relationship evaluations were associated with minimizing when offenses were perceived as mild, and with retaliation when offenses were perceived as severe.

Waldron and I (2008) suggest seven communication tasks essential to the forgiveness process for couples. While not exclusive to marriage, these tasks were developed from our research based primarily on married couples. We have labeled each of the following elements as *tasks* in an effort to avoid thinking about each as a stage in the forgiveness process. Instead, tasks may be worked on concurrently or repeatedly throughout the forgiveness process (see Box 6.3).

---

## Box 6.3: The Overlapping Nature of the Seven Communication Tasks of Forgiveness

It is common for the seven tasks of forgiveness to overlap and be repeated throughout the forgiveness process (Waldron & Kelley, 2008). The following example demonstrates how the seven forgiveness tasks interplay with one another.

Stan and Tracey had been married for 20 years when Stan made a significant financial investment without telling Tracey. When the economy slowed, they needed to draw against their savings to meet their mortgage needs. Unfortunately, the slowed economy also affected Stan's investment and Tracey found out that much of their savings had been depleted. Tracey discovered the transgression while examining bank statements (which she rarely did) and found records to indicate that much of their savings had been reinvested in what were now fairly worthless stocks. When she asked Stan about the reallocation of funds, he became defensive, but admitted that he had done it on the advice of a friend. When she asked him why he didn't tell her about the move, he replied that they normally don't talk about their finances, especially money that is in savings or allocated for retirement. Tracey felt angry that Stan had not told her about the transfer of funds and confusion about their financial situation. Stan felt angry and defensive when Tracey approached him, but after they discussed the issue he apologized for not telling her what he had done; he had been nervous to tell her because he knew she did not like the friend from whom he had taken advice. Tracey apologized for "coming on too strong" when she first approached him. They hugged. Eventually they talked about the financial decisions in which to include Tracey and reemphasized the moral value of their relationship, "that they should never keep secrets from one another" (except positive secrets like birthday parties), and Tracey stated her desire to talk further about Stan's friend.

In this event, the nature of the transgression was discovered

---

over time, first when Tracey was looking at bank statements, then in her initial discussion with Stan, then again later when Stan admitted that he did not tell her about the transfer because he knew she did not like his friend. During each of these times, Tracey's emotions changed. She was angry and confused at first. When she realized Stan's secrecy was because of his perception of her possible reaction, she was disappointed that he did not trust her. During this time she was trying to make sense of what had happened: If he keeps a secret about this, what other secrets do I not know about? Can I still trust him? Have I given him too much control with our finances? Note that many of these questions drive the final tasks of renegotiation and transition: setting new financial guidelines, reemphasizing the moral value of honesty, and setting up a time to talk more about Stan's friend. Additionally, emotional responses and sense making were affected when Stan apologized, prompting an apology from Tracey as well.

The first task, *confront the transgression*, involves acknowledging the transgression and determining an initial response. At least one partner recognizes that a transgression (e.g., relational hurt, rule violation, violation of the relationship's moral code) has taken place. Communication behaviors may include questioning perceived unethical behavior or perceived insincerity, truth telling, confession, requests for information, and description of the offense from either partner's perspective. During this task individuals are trying to assess personal hurt, what relational rules or mores were actually violated, and the magnitude of the violation.

*Manage emotion* is a second task of the forgiveness process. As we discussed previously in the chapter, response to a perceived transgression may precipitate hurt and anger, or even fear and shock. During this emotion-focused task, spouses will likely engage a number of the following elements in response to their, or their partner's, felt emotions: express, label, acknowledge, legitimize, accept, or deintensify. Specific communication behaviors that characterize this task include verbal and nonverbal expression of the emotion, listening and observing to discern emotional responses, affirming the right to have an emotional response, reciprocating emotional states, or engaging in a "cooling off" period.

Task three, *engage in sense making*, focuses on the need to reduce uncertainty and reestablish meaning in the relationship, or one's life, after experiencing the transgression. The task may involve questioning, information sharing, and explanation. When partners discuss what has happened, they jointly negotiate the meaning of the event in light of the past, possible future, and current state of the relationship. Specific communication behaviors may include seeking or offering various accounts (e.g., excuses, justifications, apologies), sharing of motive for the offense, a consideration of responsibility, perspective taking, assessment of personal and relational harm, and determination if the event is reflective of a larger pattern in the relationship (e.g., whether this is a repeat offense). Eventual components of this task are determining if the offense is forgivable, understanding the partner's perspective, and assessing the current and future implications of the offense for each partner and for the relationship itself.

*Seeking forgiveness* is a fourth task that, when done sincerely, may have a great impact on relationship reconstruction, but does not always occur as part of the forgiveness process. In my early work I determined that people sought forgiveness primarily for self or other well-being, or to restore the relationship (D. L. Kelley, 1998). These motives are pursued through explicit acknowledgement (e.g., apology, remorse), explanation (e.g., discussing reasons and circumstances), nonverbal assurance (e.g., hugs, crying), compensation (e.g., gifts), and humor (e.g., joking). Use of explicit acknowledgement, nonverbal assurance, and compensation are most strongly related with relationship recovery (D. L. Kelley & Waldron, 2005).

A fifth task is *forgiveness granting*. Forgiveness granting is driven by a variety of motives. The wounded party may be motivated to forgive to restore well-being (self or other) or the relationship, because of the offender's response after the transgression (e.g., apology), out of love for the partner, or as a response to reframing (e.g., from "You don't care about me." to "You have a different means of showing love."). It is important to emphasize that reframing is closely related to empathy, which has been demonstrated to have a strong relationship to willingness to forgive (McCullough, Worthington, & Rachal, 1997; Paleari, Regalia, & Fincham, 2005). For example, individuals often reframe an event ("He was just trying to help me when he said that."), resulting in empathy ("So I know he felt badly when he found out he had hurt my feelings."). Consonant with this perspective, Paleari et al. (2005) found rumination and empathy to predict concurrent unforgiveness and benevolence, respectively. Empathy, conceptualized as perspective taking, has also been shown to mediate the relationship between emotion management and forgiveness (Hodgson & Wertheim, 2007).

Our research has revealed five main strategies couples use to grant forgiveness (Waldron & Kelley, 2008). First, the *explicit statement* is typically represented by the phrase "I forgive you." Second, *discussion* is partners' talk about the offense. Often they come away feeling like forgiveness has taken place although "forgive" was never stated directly. Third, *nonverbal displays* may be used with other strategies to demonstrate sincerity. Specific nonverbal behaviors can be used alone (e.g., giving a hug to let someone know they are forgiven), but are also used to indicate a "return to normal." Fourth, *minimization* grants forgiveness by deflecting the significance of the transgression (e.g., "Forget it, it was no big deal."). Fifth, the *conditional approach* puts limits on one's willingness to give forgiveness ("I told him I'd forgive him if he stayed off the booze."). Our research has demonstrated that the conditional strategy is used more often with severe transgressions, and minimization with less severe transgressions (Waldron & Kelley, 2005). Explicit and nonverbal strategies were most often associated with relationship strengthening, whereas conditional forgiveness was most often associated with relationship deterioration.

A significant choice to make during forgiveness granting is whether to express forgiveness verbally. This can be a difficult decision with significant relationship risks. For example, one's partner may feel offended because the forgiven partner may perceive the forgiveness granting as a "one-up" strategy. As such, the following may be used as guidelines when determining whether to include one's partner in the forgiveness process. First, determine if both partners will be safe, physically and psychologically, if contact is initiated to offer forgiveness. Second, determine if it is appropriate to offer forgiveness to the offending party. For example, in certain cultures offering forgiveness from wife to husband may be not be sanctioned. Third, assess whether healing can occur without some sort of verbal, nonverbal, or mediated contact between partners.

The sixth forgiveness task, *renegotiating relationship values and rules*, involves the decision whether to continue and renegotiate the relationship "covenant" (Hargrave, 1994). Partners examine the moral structure of the relationship and create new, or reinvest in previous, moral values that ensure relational justice, psychological safety, and restored levels (or mutually determined new levels) of trust and intimacy. Communication during this time includes metacommunication about existing communication rules, negotiation of new rules, planning, and creating a vision for the future. This task may also include asking hard, hypothetical questions (e.g., "How are you going to stop?" "What if I fail?").

*Transition* is the seventh task. Here partners must monitor, maintain, and renegotiate the agreement that has been, or is being, forged between the two partners. Married couples in our interviews shared reconstructed joint relationship narratives that included their negotiated understanding of the transgression. Couple narratives demonstrated two central components of the task of transition: rebuilding trust and maintaining hope in the relationship. During this time, communication focuses on noting successes and "lessons learned" from the process, and continual adjustment of the new relationship agreement. Typical during transition is editing relational talk to deemphasize blame and negative affect, and focus on positive future goals.

A final look at forgiveness comes from the work of Gordon and Baucom (1999; 2003; Gordon, Baucom, & Snyder, 2000, 2005). Their extensive experience with couples wherein at least one partner has experienced an affair provides insight into the communication tasks of forgiveness (Waldron & Kelley, 2008). Gordon and colleagues propose a forgiveness model that consists of three stages that parallel those that individuals may face when experiencing general trauma. The first stage, *impact*, is characterized by individuals trying to comprehend the transgression and is accompanied by a wide array of emotions such as fear, hurt, and anger. These strong emotions may alternate with a sense of numbness or disbelief. The victim may, uncharacteristically, lash out at the offending partner in punitive, vindictive words and actions. Stage two, *meaning*, is analogous to *sense making*, discussed previously (Waldron & Kelley, 2008). The goal of this stage is to minimize uncertainty and restore control. As such, it may be characterized by questioning ("Why did this happen to me?" "Did I do something wrong?"), and explanations and accounts, assurances and promises from the offender. The final stage, *recovery or moving on*, represents restoration of personal well-being and, possibly, the relationship.

## Reconciling Couples

The definition of forgiveness offered in this chapter includes the suggestion that forgiveness creates the "possibility of reconciliation" (Waldron & Kelley, 2008). In addition, certain forgiveness models, focused on relationship restoration, conflate the process of forgiveness and reconciliation. For instance, Hargrave (1994) discusses the forgiveness process as including exoneration (insight and understanding) and forgiveness (opportunity for compensation and overt act of forgiveness). The Latin root of *conciliate* means "to bring together or unite." Therefore, re-conciliation occurs any time partners are brought together following relational distancing.

Interpersonal reconciliation has been primarily conceptualized as restoring trust (Worthington, 2001). Worthington and Drinkard (2000) define reconciliation as "the restoration of trust in an interpersonal relationship through mutual trustworthy behavior" (p. 93). Importantly, they emphasize that reconciliation does not imply that all differences or discord have been eliminated, or that conflict has ceased. For example, research by Keeley (2007) found reconciliation to be a function of final conversations between dying family members and survivors. In this context, reconciliation represents peace and healing for previously unresolved relationship issues.

Rusbult et al. (2005) conceptualize reconciliation as centering on the restoration of trust and commitment. They define trust as "the strength of each partner's conviction that the other can be counted on to behave in a benevolent manner," and commitment as "the extent to which each partner intends to persist in the relationship, feels psychologically attached to it, and exhibits long-term orientation toward it" (p. 187). These two concepts are integrally related. Because trust is focused on the perception that one's partner will act prosocially toward one's self, it is also related to perception of one's partner's commitment.

Although Rusbult et al. (2005) define reconciliation as the "resumption of pretransgression relationship status," reconciliation may take various forms. My own research demonstrates that post-forgiveness relationships are characteristically typified by change (D. L. Kelley, 1998; D. L. Kelley & Waldron, 2005; Waldron & Kelley, 2005). They may be strengthened, weakened, or may continue with renegotiated rules or relationship definitions.

B. Patterson and O'Hair (1992) take a narrower approach to reconciliation, viewing it as a response to the actualization or threat of relationship termination. In this light, they argue that while reconciliation strategies may share commonalities with relational repair strategies, they are a unique strategic approach. The reconciliation approach described by Rusbult et al. (2005) suggests that overcoming significant transgressions entails mutual investment and coordinated effort by each relational partner, characterized by prosocial action, energy, and motivation over time. For the victim, this involves setting aside blame and the desire for retaliation, and instead showing good will and a willingness to start with a "clean slate." Perpetrators have to suppress the tendency to justify actions, and move toward responsibility and restitution, when appropriate. Together the partners must renegotiate the rules and norms of the relationship, including the couples' moral code (D. L. Kelley, in press).

Worthington and Drinkard (2000) identify the enactment of reconciliation as implicit or explicit. Implicit strategies include giving up aggressive responses and working toward peace, showing affection, resuming communication, or engaging in a joint pleasing activity or task together. The latter response is similar to my finding that individuals often try to "return to normal" to forgive and reconcile. Explicit reconciliation involves choosing to move on in the relationship ("bury the hatchet") or to reconcile because it is the "right" thing to do.

Worthington and Drinkard (2000) suggest six specific steps, or planks (imagine a bridge with six planks), to facilitate explicit reconciliation. First, *decide whether to reconcile*. Considerations here parallel the previous discussion regarding the decision to include one's partner in the forgiveness process: is it safe and appropriate for both parties? Second, partners must *"soften"* toward one another. This may involve openness to changing the perception of the transgression or the perception of one's partner, and rethinking one's perspective on relational justice. The sense-making and empathy components of the forgiveness process can aid with this step.

*Forgiveness* is the third plank. While a certain level of reconciliation may occur without forgiveness, restoration of personal well-being and of the relationship are unlikely without the emotion-healing properties of forgiveness (D. L. Kelley, in press; Worthington, Lerner, & Sharp, 2005). The fourth step, *reverse the negative cascade*, involves reestablishing the emotional connection with one's partner. This is followed by step five, *deal with failures in trustworthiness*. The final step, *actively build love*, is acting in ways that are perceived as loving by one's partner. For instance, it has been suggested that "love languages" may be thought of as speaking words of affirmation, spending quality time, affectionate touch, acts of service, and gifts (Chapman, 1995; Worthington & Drinkard, 2000).

Worthington and Drinkard's final three steps parallel two of Waldron's and my (2008) communicative tasks of forgiveness:

negotiating values and rules and monitoring the transition. These crucial steps of the forgiveness process also serve as important components of reconciling the relationship. Discussion is had and plans are made to lessen negative (or distant) emotions and, simultaneously, begin building toward the future with benevolent, relationship-benefiting actions (also see work by Fincham & Beach, 2002; Fincham, Beach, & Davila, 2004; Fincham et al., 2005). In addition, I should highlight that our research has found conditional forgiveness (giving forgiveness with conditions or boundaries – "You are forgiven if . . .") to be associated with weakening the relationship (Waldron & Kelley, 2005). It may be that conditional forgiveness often falls short because it fails to separate the forgiveness and reconciliation processes, is unilateral (one party sets the conditions), and signals an unwillingness to trust one's partner.

## Final Thoughts

This chapter explores topics often considered the "dark side" of interpersonal communication. Relational hurt creates a foundation from which to examine events, such as abuse and infidelity, that typically generate a great deal of relational pain. And, yet, there are responses to these negative life events that could be described as the "light" side of interpersonal communication. Forgiveness offers hope for the restoration of personal and other well-being, one's relational moral code, and, when appropriate, the relationship. Relationship restoration, in particular, requires a return to conciliatory communication. Worthington and Drinkard (2000) suggest that this re-conciliation "is more than simply getting past a bad period in a relationship" (p. 100). They propose the development of reconciliation as a character virtue that permeates one's relational world. Such a proposal suggests that relational partners cultivate a reconciliation worldview that influences how partners approach relationships when "bad" things happen, but also provides guidelines for rebuilding relationships with healthy personal boundaries and shared moral codes.

**Basic Principles: Destructive and Restorative Marital Processes**

1 Relational hurt occurs from emotional injury within a relational context.
2 Relational hurt in couple relationships is due to transgressions or devaluation that results in a sense of personal injury.
3 Intensity of hurt feelings may primarily be a function of the ability of the recipient (the hurt partner) to respond, the intentionality associated with the hurtful event, and the degree to which the recipient expects to be hurt by his or her partner.
4 Emotional responses to transgressions are at times emotional blends (e.g., a mixture of anger, sadness, hurt, or even compassion for an offending partner).
5 Relationship transgressions are violations of relationally relevant rules or norms.
6 Transgressions can be conceptualized as threats to identity, violations of the "relationship covenant," and acts of injustice/unfairness.
7 Transgressions are often viewed within a moral framework (e.g., behavior as right or wrong).
8 Transgressions (e.g., abuse and infidelity) may be traumatizing to individuals.
9 Transgressions often initiate a process of sense making and communication focused on discovering meaning (e.g., questioning, interrogating).
10 Abuse is typically considered violent behavior that is intentional and occurs over time.
11 Communicative aggression is tantamount to psychological abuse (e.g., affects one's sense of self over time).
12 Couple violence is associated with a lack of social skills – in particular, problem-solving skills – and is related to power and control.
13 Infidelity is often viewed by relational partners as betrayal.
14 Responses to discovered infidelity may include jealousy, betrayal, loss of identity, shame, worthlessness, and rejection.
15 Infidelity may be conceptualized as sexual and/or emotional.
16 Couples use prosocial communication (e.g., warmth and affection), metacommunicaiton, and activity to repair relationships.
17 Interpersonal forgiveness is a transformative process, focused on limitation of negative responses and development of benevolent responses.
18 Forgiveness may restore individual well-being, the relationship (e.g., satisfaction), and the relationship moral order.
19 There are seven communicative forgiveness tasks that focus on the transgression, emotion, sense making, requesting and granting forgiveness, and renegotiating and monitoring the relationship.

20  Reconciliation focuses on reestablishing trust and commitment.
21  Reconciliation takes various forms, including relationship strengthening and weakening, and a change in relationship rules or type.

### Questions You Should Ask
*(as a Researcher or as a Relational Partner)*

1   How does relationship hurt function in marital relationships?
2   How do relationship characteristics (e.g., relationship quality) affect partners' responses to hurtful events?
3   How do marital partners explicitly or implicitly negotiate relationship rules and norms?
4   Are partners able to predict their own (or partner's) response to hurtful events?
5   How do couples negotiate what is considered *abusive* behavior in their relationship?
6   What obstacle prevents relational partners from identifying behavior as "abusive"?
7   How do partners express the perception of infidelity as betrayal?
8   Do couples talk about the distinction between sexual and emotional betrayal?
9   What factors influence couples' willingness to reconcile after infidelity?
10  How do couples repair their relationships after severe relationship transgressions?
11  What are the most predominant obstacles to forgiveness in marriage relationships?
12  Which of the seven communicative forgiveness tasks present the most challenges for couples to implement?
13  What is the process for trust restoration in marriage relationships?

# References

Adams, J. S. (1965). Inequity in social change. *Advances in Experimental Social Psychology, 2,* 267–299.

Adelmann, P. K., Chadwick, K., & Baerger, D. R. (1996). Marital quality of black and white adults over the life course. *Journal of Social and Personal Relationships, 13,* 361–384.

Afifi, T. D. (2003). "Feeling caught" in stepfamilies: Managing boundary turbulence through appropriate communication privacy rules. *Journal of Social and Personal Relationships, 20,* 729–755.

Ainsworth, M. D. S., Blehar, M. C., Waters, E., & Wall, S. (1978). *Patterns of attachment: A psychological study of the strange situation.* Hillsdale, NJ: Erlbaum.

Alberts, J. K. (1988). An analysis of couples' conversational complaints. *Communication Monographs, 55,* 184–197.

Allan, G. (2004). Being unfaithful: His and her affairs. In J. Duncombe, K. Harrison, G. Allan, & D. Marsden (Eds.), *The state of affairs: Explorations in infidelity and commitment* (pp. 121–140). Mahwah, NJ: Erlbaum.

Allan, G., & Harrison, K. (2002). Affairs. In R. Goodwin & D. Cramer (Eds.), *Inappropriate relationships: The unconventional, the disapproved, and the forbidden* (pp. 45–64). Mahwah, NJ: Erlbaum.

Allan, G., & Harrison, K. (2009). Affairs and infidelity. In A. Vangelisti (Ed.), *Feeling hurt in close relationships* (pp. 191–208). New York: Cambridge University Press.

Allemand, M., Amberg, I., Zimprich, D., & Fincham, F. D. (2007). The role of trait forgiveness and relationship satisfaction in episodic forgiveness. *Journal of Social and Clinical Psychology, 26,* 199–217.

Allen, S. M., & Hawkins, A. J. (1999). Maternal gatekeeping: Mothers' beliefs and behaviors that inhibit greater father involvement in family work. *Journal of Marriage and Family, 61,* 199–212.

Allred, K. G. (2000). Anger and retaliation in conflict: The role of attribution.

# References

In M. Deutsch & P. T. Coleman (Eds.), *The handbook of conflict resolution: Theory and practice* (pp. 236–255). San Francisco, CA: Jossey-Bass.

Altman, I., & Taylor, D. A. (1973). *Social penetration: The development of interpersonal relationships.* New York: Holt, Rinehart and Winston.

Altman, I., Vinsel, A., & Brown, B. B. (1981). Dialectic conceptions in social psychology: An application to social penetration and privacy regulation. *Advances in Experimental Social Psychology, 14,* 107–160.

Andersen, P. A. (1985). Nonverbal immediacy in interpersonal communication. In A. W. Siegman & S. Feldstein (Eds.), *Multichannel integrations of nonverbal behavior* (pp. 1–36). Hillsdale, NJ: Erlbaum.

Anderson, K. L., Umberson, D., & Elliot, S. (2004). Violence and abuse in families. In A. L. Vangelisti (Ed.), *Handbook of family communication* (pp. 629–646). Mahwah, NJ: Erlbaum.

Anderson, S. A., Russell, C. S., & Schumm, W. R. (1983). Perceived marital quality and family life-cycle categories: A further analysis. *Journal of Marriage and Family, 45,* 127–139.

Anderson, T. B., & McCulloch, B. J. (1993). Conjugal support: Factor structure for older husbands and wives. *Journals of Gerontology, 48,* S133–S142.

Antonucci, T. C., & Akiyama, H. (1987a). An examination of sex differences in social support among older men and women. *Sex Roles, 17,* 737–749.

Arp, D., & Arp, C. (1996). *The second half of marriage.* New York: Zondervan.

Aune, K. S., Buller, D. B., & Aune, R. K. (1996). Display rule development in romantic relationships: Emotion management and perceived appropriateness of emotions across relationship stages. *Human Communication Research, 23,* 115–145.

Avis, J. M. (1986). "Working together": An enrichment program for dual-career couples. *Journal of Psychotherapy & the Family, 2,* 29–45.

Babcock, J. C., Waltz, J., Jacobson, N. S., & Gottman, J. M. (1993). Power and violence: The relation between communication patterns, power discrepancies, and domestic violence. *Journal of Consulting and Clinical Psychology, 61,* 40–50.

Bailey, T. C., & Snyder, C. R. (2007). Satisfaction with life and hope: A look at age and marital status. *The Psychological Record, 57,* 233–240.

Bakhtin, M. M. (1981). *The dialogic imagination: Four essays by M. M. Bakhtin* (M. Holquist, Ed.; C. Emerson & M. Holquist, Trans.). Austin: University of Texas Press.

Bakhtin, M. M. (1984). *Problems of Dostoevsky's poetics* (C. Emerson, Ed. and Trans.). Minneapolis: University of Minnesota Press.

Bakhtin, M. M. (1986). *Speech genres and other late essays* (C. Emerson & M. Holquist, Eds.; V. McGee, Trans.). Austin: University of Texas Press.

Barnett, L. R., & Nietzel, M. T. (1979). Relationship of instrumental and affectional behaviors and self-esteem to marital satisfaction in distressed and

# References

nondistressed couples. *Journal of Consulting and Clinical Psychology, 47,* 946–957.

Bavelas, J. B., & Coates, L. (1992). How do we account for the mindfulness of face-to-face dialogue? *Communication Monographs, 59,* 301–305.

Baxter, L. A. (1985). Accomplishing relationship disengagement. In L. A. Baxter (Ed.), *Understanding personal relationships: An interdisciplinary approach* (pp. 243–265). London: Sage.

Baxter, L. A. (1986). Gender differences in the heterosexual relationship rules embedded in break-up accounts. *Journal of Social and Personal Relationships, 3,* 289–306.

Baxter, L. A. (1987). Symbols of relationship identities in relationship cultures. *Journal of Social and Personal Relationships, 4,* 261–280.

Baxter, L. A. (2004). Relationships as dialogues. *Personal Relationships, 11,* 1-22.

Baxter, L. A. (2006). Relational Dialectics Theory: Multivocal dialogues of family communication. In D. O. Braithwaite & L. A. Baxter (Eds.), *Engaging theories in family communication: Multiple perspectives* (pp. 130–145). Thousand Oaks, CA: Sage.

Baxter, L. A., & Braithwaite, D. O. (2002). Performing marriage: The marriage renewal ritual as cultural performance. *Southern Communication Journal, 67,* 94–109.

Baxter, L. A., & Braithwaite, D. O. (2006). Family rituals. In L. H. Turner & R. West (Eds.), *The family communication sourcebook* (pp. 259–280). Thousand Oaks, CA: Sage.

Baxter, L. A., Braithwaite, D. O., & Nicholson, J. H. (1999). Turning points in the development of blended families. *Journal of Social and Personal Relationships, 16,* 291–313.

Baxter, L. A., & Dindia, K. (1990). Marital partners' perceptions of marital maintenance strategies. *Journal of Social and Personal Relationships, 7,* 187–208.

Baxter, L. A., & Erbert, L. A. (1999). Perceptions of dialectical contradictions in turning points of development in heterosexual romantic relationships. *Journal of Social and Personal Relationships, 16,* 547–569.

Baxter, L. A., & Montgomery, B. M. (1996). *Relating: Dialogues and dialectics.* New York: Guilford Press.

Belsky, J., & Hsieh, K. (1998). Patterns of marital change during the early childhood years: Parent personality, coparenting, and division-of-labor correlates. *Journal of Family Psychology, 12,* 511–528.

Belsky, J., Lang, M. E., & Rovine, M. (1985). Stability and change in marriage across the transition to parenthood: A second study. *Journal of Marriage and Family, 47,* 855–865.

Belsky, J., & Rovine, M. (1990). Patterns of marital change across the transition to parenthood: Pregnancy to three years postpartum. *Journal of Marriage and Family, 52,* 5–19.

# References

Belsky, J., Spanier, G. B., & Rovine, M. (1983). Stability and change in marriage across the transition to parenthood. *Journal of Marriage and Family, 45,* 567–577.

Berg-Cross, L., Daniels, C., & Carr, P. (1992). Marital rituals among divorced and married couples. *Journal of Divorce & Remarriage, 18,* 1–30.

Berliner, K., Jacob, D., & Schwartzberg, N. (2005). The single adult and the family life cycle. In B. Carter & M. McGoldrick (Eds.), *The expanded family life cycle: Individual, family, and social perspectives* (3rd ed., pp. 362–372). Boston: Allyn and Bacon.

Berns, S. B., Jacobson, N. S. & Gottman, J. M. (1999). Demand–withdraw interactions in couples with a violent husband. *Journal of Consulting and Clinical Psychology, 67,* 666–674.

Berscheid, E. (1983). Emotion. In H. H. Kelley, E. Berscheid, A. Christensen, J. H. Harvey, T. L. Huston, G. Levinger, E. McClintock, L. A. Peplau, & D. R. Peterson (Eds.), *Close relationships* (pp. 110–168). New York: Freeman.

Berscheid, E., & Walster, E. (1978). *Interpersonal attraction* (2nd ed.). Reading, MA: Addison-Wesley.

Betancourt, H., & Blair, I. (1992). A cognition (attribution)-emotion model of violence in conflict situations. *Personality and Social Psychology Bulletin, 18,* 343–350.

Birchler, G. R., Weiss, R. L., & Vincent, J. P. (1975). Multimethod analysis of social reinforcement exchange between maritally distressed and nondistressed spouse and stranger dyads. *Journal of Personality and Social Psychology, 31,* 349–360.

Blacker, L. (2005). The launching phase of the life cycle. In B. Carter & M. McGoldrick (Eds.), *The expanded family life cycle: Individual, family, and social perspectives* (3rd ed., pp. 287–306). Boston: Allyn and Bacon.

Blanck, R., & Blanck, G. (1968). *Marriage and personal development.* New York: Columbia University Press.

Bochner, A. P., Krueger, D. L., & Chmielewski, T. L. (1982). Interpersonal perceptions and marital adjustment. *Journal of Communication, 32,* 135–147.

Booth, A., & Johnson, D. R. (1994). Declining health and marital quality. *Journal of Marriage and Family, 56,* 218–223.

Bowlby, J. (1982). Attachment and loss: Retrospect and prospect. *American Journal of Orthopsychiatry, 52,* 664–678.

Bowlby, J. (1988). *A secure base.* London: Routledge.

Bowling, T. K., Hill, C. M., & Jencius, M. (2005). An overview of marriage enrichment. *The Family Journal, 13,* 87–94.

Braithwaite, D. O., & Baxter, L. A. (1995). "I do" again: The relational dialectics of renewing marriage vows. *Journal of Social and Personal Relationships, 12,* 177–198.

Braithwaite, D. O., Baxter, L. A., & Harper, A. M. (1998). The role of rituals

# References

in the management of the dialectical tension of "old" and "new" in blended families. *Communication Studies, 49*, 101–120.

Braithwaite, D. O., McBride, M. C., & Schrodt, P. (2003). "Parent teams" and the everyday interactions of co-parenting in stepfamilies. *Communication Reports, 16*, 93–111.

Braithwaite, D. O., Olson, L. N., Golish, T. D., Soukup, C., & Turman, P. (2001). "Becoming a family": Developmental processes represented in blended family discourse. *Journal of Applied Communication Research, 29*, 221–247.

Bruess, C. J. S., & Pearson, J. C. (1997). Interpersonal rituals in marriage and adult friendship. *Communication Monographs, 64*, 25–46.

Buck, R. (1989). Emotional communication in personal relationships: A developmental-interactionist view. In C. Hendrick (Ed.), *Close relationships* (pp. 144–163). Newbury Park, CA: Sage.

Buck, R. (1999). The biological affects: A typology. *Psychological Review, 106*, 301–336.

Buehlman, K. T., Gottman, J. M., & Katz, L. F. (1992). How a couple views their past predicts their future: Predicting divorce from an oral history interview. *Journal of Family Psychology, 5*, 295–318.

Burgoon, J. K. (1982). Privacy and communication. In M. Burgoon (Ed.), *Communication Yearbook, 6*, 206-249. Beverly Hills, CA: Sage.

Burgoon, J. K. (1983). Nonverbal violations of expectations. In J. M. Wiemann & R. P. Harrison (Eds.), *Nonverbal interaction* (pp. 77–111). Beverly Hills, CA: Sage.

Burgoon, J. K. (1993). Interpersonal expectations, expectancy violations, and emotional communication. *Journal of Language and Social Psychology. Special Issue: Emotional Communication, Culture, and Power, 12*, 30–48.

Burgoon, J. K., Berger, C. R., & Waldron, V. R. (2000). Mindfulness and interpersonal communication. *Journal of Social Issues, 56*, 105–127.

Burgoon, J. K., Buller, D. B., & Woodall, W. G. (1989). *Nonverbal communication: The unspoken dialogue*. New York: Harper & Row.

Burgoon, J. K., & Hale, J. L. (1984). The fundamental topoi of relational communication. *Communication Monographs, 51*, 193–214.

Burgoon, J. K., & Hale, J. L. (1987). Validation and measurement of the fundamental themes of relational communication. *Communication Monographs, 54*, 19–41.

Burgoon, J. K., Kelley, D. L., Newton, D. A., & Keeley-Dyreson, M. P. (1989). The nature of arousal and nonverbal indices. *Human Communication Research, 16*, 217–255.

Burgoon, J. K., & Langer, E. J. (1995). Language, fallacies, and mindlessness-mindfulness. *Communication Yearbook, 18*, 105–132.

Burgoon, J. K., Parrott, R., LePoire, B. A., Kelley, D. L., Walther, J. B., & Perry, D. (1989). Maintaining and restoring privacy through communication in

# References

different types of relationships. *Journal of Social and Personal Relationships,* *6, 131–158.*

Burke, P. J., & Stets, J. E. (1999). Trust and commitment through self-verification. *Social Psychology Quarterly, 62,* 347–366.

Burleson, B. R., & Denton, W. H. (1997). The relationship between communication skill and marital satisfaction: Some moderating effects. *Journal of Marriage and Family, 59,* 884–902.

Burpee, L. C., & Langer, E. J. (2005). Mindfulness and marital satisfaction. *Journal of Adult Development, 12,* 43–51.

Buss, D. M. (1988). The evolution of human intrasexual competition: Tactics of mate attraction. *Journal of Personality and Social Psychology, 54,* 616–628.

Buss, D. M. (2006). Strategies of human mating. *Psychological Topics, 15,* 239–260.

Buss, D. M., Larsen, R. J., Westen, D., & Semmelroth, J. (1992). Sex differences in jealousy: Evolution, physiology, and psychology. *Psychological Science, 3,* 251–255.

Butler, M. H., Stout, J. A., & Gardner, B. C. (2002). Prayer as a conflict resolution ritual: Clinical implications of religious couples' report of relationship softening, healing perspective, and change responsibility. *The American Journal of Family Therapy, 30,* 19–37.

Buunk, B. P., & Dijkstra, P. (2000). Extradyadic relationships and jealousy. In C. Hendrick & S. Hendrick (Eds.), *Close relationships: A sourcebook* (pp. 317–329). Thousand Oaks, CA: Sage.

Buunk, B. P., & Dijkstra, P. (2004). Men, women, and infidelity: Sex differences in extradyadic sex and jealousy. In J. Duncombe, K. Harrison, G. Allan, & D. Marsden (Eds.), *The state of affairs: Explorations in infidelity and commitment* (pp. 103–120). Mahwah, NJ: Erlbaum.

Cahn, D. D. (1992). *Conflict in intimate relationships.* New York: Guilford Press.

Call, V. R. A., & Heaton, T. B. (1997). Religious influence on marital stability. *Journal for the Scientific Study of Religion, 36,* 382–392.

Canary, D. J., Cupach, W. R., & Serpe, R. T. (2001). A competence-based approach to examining interpersonal conflict: Test of a longitudinal model. *Communication Research, 28,* 79–104.

Canary, D. J., & Lakey, S. G. (2006). Managing conflict in a competent manner. In J. G. Oetzel & S. Ting-Toomey (Eds.), *The Sage handbook of conflict communication: Integrating theory, research, and practice* (pp. 185–210). Thousand Oaks, CA: Sage.

Canary, D. J., & Spitzberg, B. H. (1989). A model of the perceived competence of conflict strategies. *Human Communication Research, 15,* 630–649.

Canary, D. J., & Stafford, L. (1992). Relational maintenance strategies and equity in marriage. *Communication Monographs, 59,* 243–267.

Canary, D. J., & Stafford, L. (1993). Preservation of relational characteristics:

# References

Maintenance strategies, equity, and locus of control. In P. J. Kalbfleisch (Ed.), *Interpersonal communication: Evolving interpersonal relationships* (pp. 237–259). Hillsdale, NJ: Erlbaum.

Canary, D. J., & Stafford, L. (2001). Equity in the preservation of personal relationships. In J. H. Harvey & A. Wenzel (Eds.), *Close romantic relationships: Maintenance and enhancement* (pp. 133–151). Mahwah, NJ: Erlbaum.

Cappella, J. N., & Greene, J. O. (1982). A discrepancy–arousal explanation of mutual influence in expressive behavior for adult and infant–adult interaction. *Communication Monographs, 49,* 89–114.

Carrère, S., Buehlman, K. T., Gottman, J. M., Coan, J. A., & Ruckstuhl, L. (2000). Predicting marital stability and divorce in newlywed couples. *Journal of Family Psychology, 14,* 42–58.

Carstensen, L. L. (1992). Social and emotional patterns in adulthood: Support for socioemotional selectivity theory. *Psychology and Aging, 7,* 331–338.

Carstensen, L. L., Gottman, J. M., & Levenson, R. W. (1995). Emotional behavior in long-term marriage. *Psychology and Aging, 10,* 140–149.

Carter, B. (2005). Becoming parents: The family with young children. In B. Carter & M. McGoldrick (Eds.), *The expanded family life cycle: Individual, family, and social perspectives* (3rd ed., pp. 249–273). Boston: Allyn and Bacon.

Carter, B., & McGoldrick, M. (2005). Overview: The expanded family life cycle: Individual, family, and social perspectives. In B. Carter & M. McGoldrick (Eds.), *The expanded family life cycle: Individual, family, and social perspectives* (3rd ed., pp. 1–26). Boston: Allyn and Bacon.

Caughlin, J. P. (2002). The demand/withdraw pattern of communication as a predictor of marital satisfaction over time. *Human Communication Research, 28,* 49–85.

Caughlin, J. P., & Huston, T. L. (2002). A contextual analysis of the association between demand/withdraw and marital satisfaction. *Personal Relationships, 9,* 95–119.

Caughlin, J. P., & Petronio, S. (2004). Privacy in families. In A. L. Vangelisti (Ed.), *Handbook of family communication* (pp. 379–412). Mahwah, NJ: Erlbaum.

Caughlin, J. P., & Vangelisti, A. L. (1999). Desire for change in one's partner as a predictor of the demand/withdraw pattern of marital communication. *Communication Monographs, 66,* 66–89.

Caughlin, J. P., & Vangelisti, A. L. (2000). An individual difference explanation of why married couples engage in the demand/withdraw pattern of conflict. *Journal of Social and Personal Relationships. Special Issue: Relationship Conflict, 17,* 523–551.

Caughlin, J. P., & Vangelisti, A. L. (2006). Conflict in dating and marital relationships. In J. G. Oetzel & S. Ting-Toomey (Eds.), *Sage handbook of conflict communication: Integrating theory, research, and practice* (pp. 129–157). Thousand Oaks, CA: Sage.

# References

Chapman, G. D. (1995). *The five love languages: How to express heartfelt commitment to your mate.* Chicago: Northfield.

Chesser, B. J. (1980). Analysis of wedding rituals: An attempt to make weddings more meaningful. *Family Relations, 29,* 204–209.

Christensen, A. (1988). Dysfunctional interaction patterns in couples. In P. Noller & M. A. Fitzpatrick (Eds.), *Perspectives on marital interaction* (pp. 31–52). Philadelphia, PA: Multilingual Matters.

Christensen, A., & Heavey, C. L. (1990). Gender and social structure in the demand/withdraw pattern of marital conflict. *Journal of Personality and Social Psychology, 59,* 73–81.

Christensen, A., & Shenk, J. L. (1991). Communication, conflict, and psychological distance in nondistressed, clinic, and divorcing couples. *Journal of Consulting and Clinical Psychology, 59,* 458–463.

Christopher, F. S., & Kisler, T. S. (2004). Exploring marital sexuality: Peeking inside the bedroom and discovering what we don't know – but should! In J. H. Harvey, A. Wenzel, & S. Sprecher (Eds.), *The handbook of sexuality in close relationships* (pp. 371–384). Mahwah, NJ: Erlbaum.

Christopher, F. S., & Lloyd, S. A. (2000). Physical and sexual aggression in relationships. In C. Hendrick & S. S. Hendrick (Eds.), *Close relationships: A sourcebook* (pp. 331–343). Thousand Oaks, CA: Sage.

Cissna, K. N., Cox, D. E., & Bochner, A. P. (1990). The dialectic of marital and parental relationships within the stepfamily. *Communication Monographs, 57,* 44–61.

Clements, M. L., Cordova, A. D., Markman, H. J., & Laurenceau, J.-P. (1997). The erosion of marital satisfaction over time and how to prevent it. In R. J. Sternberg & M. Hojiat (Eds.), *Satisfaction in close relationships* (pp. 335–355). New York: Guilford Press.

Clements, M., & Markman, H. J. (1996). The transition to parenthood: Is having children hazardous to marriage? In M. Clements & H. J. Markman (Eds.), *A lifetime of relationships* (pp. 290–310). Belmont, CA: Thomson Brooks/ Cole.

Cohan, C. L., & Bradbury, T. N. (1997). Negative life events, marital interaction, and the longitudinal course of newlywed marriage. *Journal of Personality and Social Psychology, 73,* 114–128.

Coleman, M., Fine, M., Ganong, L., Downs, K. M., & Pauk, N. (2001). When you're not the Brady Bunch: Identifying perceived conflicts and resolution strategies in stepfamilies. *Personal Relationships, 8,* 55–73.

Coleman, M., Ganong, L., & Fine, M. (2004). Communication in stepfamilies. In A. Vangelisti (Ed.), *Handbook of family communication* (pp. 215–232). Mahwah, NJ: Erlbaum.

Coleman, P. T. (2000). Power and conflict. In M. Deutsch & P. T. Coleman (Eds.), *The handbook of conflict resolution: Theory and practice* (pp. 108–28). San Francisco, CA: Jossey-Bass.

# References

Conville, R. L. (1991). *Relational transitions: The evolution of personal relation-ships.* New York: Praeger.

Cooney, T. M., Pedersen, F. A., Indelicato, S., & Palkovitz, R. (1993). Timing of fatherhood: Is "on-time" good? *Journal of Marriage and Family, 55,* 205–215.

Cornelius, T. L., Alessi, G., & Shorey, R. C. (2007). The effectiveness of commu-nication skills training with married couples: Does the issue discussed matter? *The Family Journal, 15,* 124–132.

Cowan, C. P., & Cowan, P. A. (1992). *When partners become parents: The big life change for couples.* New York: Basic Books.

Cowan, C. P., & Cowan, P. A. (1995). Interventions to ease the transition to parenthood: Why they are needed and what they can do. *Family Relations, 44,* 412–423.

Cowan, C. P., Cowan, P. A., Heming, G., Garrett, E., Coysh, W. S., Curtis-Boles, H., & Boles, A. J., III. (1985). Transitions to parenthood: His, hers and theirs. *Journal of Family Issues, 6,* 451–481.

Cowan, P. A., & Cowan, C. P. (1988). Changes in marriage during the transi-tion to parenthood: Must we blame the baby? In G. Michaels & W. Goldberg (Eds.), *The transition to parenthood: Current theory and research* (pp. 114–154). Cambridge: Cambridge University Press.

Cramer, D. (1998). *Close relationships: The study of love and friendship.* London: Hodder Arnold.

Cupach, W. R., & Comstock, J. (1990). Satisfaction with sexual communication in marriage: Links to sexual satisfaction and dyadic adjustment. *Journal of Social and Personal Relationships, 7,* 179–186.

Cupach, W. R., & Metts, S. (1991). Sexuality and communication in close relationships. In K. McKinney, & S. Sprecher (Eds.), *Sexuality in close rela-tionships* (pp. 93–110). Hillsdale, NJ: Erlbaum.

Cupach, W. R., & Spitzberg, B. H. (Eds.) (1994). *The dark side of interpersonal communication.* Hillsdale, NJ: Erlbaum.

Cupach, W. R., & Spitzberg, B. H. (2004). *The dark side of relationship pursuit: From attraction to obsession to stalking.* Mahwah, NJ: Erlbaum.

Curtis, K. T., & Ellison, C. G. (2002). Religious heterogamy and marital conflict. *Journal of Family Issues, 23,* 551–576.

Dailey, R. M., Lee, C. M., & Spitzberg, B. H. (2007). Communicative aggression: Toward a more interactional view of psychological abuse. In B. H. Spitzberg & W. R. Cupach (Eds.), *The dark side of interpersonal communication* (2nd ed., pp. 297–326). Mahwah, NJ: Erlbaum.

Dainton, M., & Stafford, L. (1993). Routine maintenance behaviors: A com-parison of relationship type, partner similarity and sex differences. *Journal of Social and Personal Relationships, 10,* 255–272.

Dainton, M., & Zelley, E. D. (2006). Social exchange theories: Interdependence and equity. In D. O. Braithwaite & L. A. Baxter (Eds.), *Engaging theories in*

# References

*family communication: Multiple perspectives* (pp. 243–259). Thousand Oaks, CA: Sage.

Davis, M. S. (1973). *Intimate relations*. New York: Free Press.

Derlega, V., Metts, S., Petronio, S., & Margulis, S. (1993). *Self disclosure*. Newbury Park, CA: Sage.

DeSteno, D. A., Bartlett, M. Y., Salovey, P., & Braverman, J. (2002). Sex differences in jealousy: Evolutionary mechanism or artifact of measurement? *Journal of Personality and Social Psychology, 83,* 1103–1116.

DeSteno, D. A., & Salovey, P. (1996). Evolutionary origins of sex differences in jealousy? Questioning the "fitness" of the model. *Psychological Science, 7,* 367–372.

Dickson, F. C., Christian, A., & Remmo, C. J. (2004). An exploration of the marital and family issues of the later-life adult. In A. Vangelisti (Ed.), *Handbook of family communication* (pp. 153–174). Mahwah, NJ: Erlbaum

Dickson, F. C., Hughes, P. C., Manning, L. D., Walker, K. L., Bollis-Pecci, T., & Gratson, S. D. (2001). An analysis of conflict in long-term, later-life, married couples. *Southern Communication Journal, 67,* 110–121.

Dimidjian, S., Martell, C. R., & Christensen, A. (2002). Integrative behavioral couple therapy. In N. S. Jacobson & A. S. Gurman (Eds.), *Clinical handbook of couple therapy* (pp. 251–277). New York: Guilford Press.

Dindia, K. (2003). Definitions and perspectives on relational maintenance communication. In D. J. Canary & M. Dainton (Eds.), *Maintaining relationships through communication: Relational, contextual, and cultural variations* (pp. 1–28). Mahwah, NJ: Erlbaum.

Dindia, K. (2006). The effects of sex of subject and sex of partner on interruptions. *Human Communication Research, 13,* 345–371.

Dindia, K., & Baxter, L. A. (1987). Strategies for maintaining and repairing marital relationships. *Journal of Social and Personal Relationships, 4,* 143–158.

Dindia, K., & Canary, D. J. (1993). Definitions and theoretical perspectives on maintaining relationships. *Journal of Social and Personal Relationships, 10,* 163–173.

Dinkmeyer, D., & Carlson, J. (1984). *Time for a better marriage*. Circle Pines, Minnesota: American Guidance Service.

Dinkmeyer, D., & Carlson, J. (2003). *Training in marriage enrichment*. Bowling Green, KY: CMTI Press.

D'Onofrio, B. M., Turkheimer, E., Emery, R. E., Harden, K. P., Slutske, W. S., Heath, A. C., Madden, P. A. F., & Martin, N. G. (2007). A genetically informed study of the intergenerational transmission of marital instability. *Journal of Marriage and Family, 69,* 793–809.

Doss, B. D., Rhoades, G. K., Stanley, S. M., & Markman, H. J. (2009). The effect of the transition to parenthood on relationship quality: An 8-year prospective study. *Journal of Personality and Social Psychology, 96,* 601–619.

# References

Driver, J. L., & Gottman, J. M. (2004). Daily marital interactions and positive affect during marital conflict among newlywed couples. *Family Process, 43,* 301–314.

Driver, J., Tabares, A., Shapiro, A., Nahm, E. Y., & Gottman, J. M. (2003). In F. Walsh (Ed.), *Normal family processes: Growing diversity and complexity* (3rd ed., pp. 493–513). New York: Guilford Press.

Ducharme, F. (1994). Conjugal support, coping behaviors, and psychological well-being of the elderly spouse: An empirical model. *Research on Aging, 16,* 167–190.

Duck, S. (1982). A topography of relationship disengagement and dissolution. *Personal Relationships: Dissolving Personal Relationships, 4,* 1–30.

Duck, S. (1988). *Relating to others.* Chicago: Dorsey Press.

Duck, S. (1994). Stratagems, spoils, and a serpent's tooth: On the delights and dilemmas of personal relationships. In W. R. Cupach & B. H. Spitzberg (Eds.), *The dark side of interpersonal communication* (pp. 3–24). Hillsdale, NJ: Erlbaum.

Dudley, M. G., & Kosinski, F. A., Jr. (1990). Religiosity and marital satisfaction: A research note. *Review of Religious Research, 32,* 78–86.

Ellison, C. G., Bartkowski, J. P., & Anderson, K. L. (1999). Are there religious variations in domestic violence? *Journal of Family Issues, 20,* 87–113.

Enright, R. D., & Fitzgibbons, R. P. (2000). *Helping clients forgive: An empirical guide for resolving anger and restoring hope.* Washington, DC: American Psychological Association.

Epstein, N., & Baucom, D. H. (2002). *Enhanced cognitive-behavioral therapy for couples: A contextual approach.* Washington, DC: American Psychological Association.

Exline, J. J., Worthington, E. L, Jr., Hill, P., & McCullough, M. E. (2003). Forgiveness and justice: A research agenda for social and personality psychology. *Personality and Social Psychology Review, 7,* 337–348.

Feeney, J. A. (2004). Hurt feelings in couple relationships: Towards integrative models of the negative effects of hurtful events. *Journal of Social and Personal Relationships, 21,* 487–508.

Feeney, J. A. (2005). Hurt feelings in couple relationships: Exploring the role of attachment and perceptions of personal injury. *Personal Relationships, 12,* 253–271.

Feeney, J. A. (2009). When love hurts: Understanding hurtful events in couple relationships. In A. Vangelisti (Ed.), *Feeling hurt in close relationships* (pp. 313–335). New York: Cambridge University Press.

Feeney, J. A., Hohaus, L., Noller, P., & Alexander, R. P. (2001). *Becoming parents.* Cambridge: Cambridge University Press.

Feeney, J. A., & Noller, P. (1990). Attachment style as a predictor of adult romantic relationships. *Journal of Personality and Social Psychology, 58,* 281–291.

# References

Feeney, J. A., Noller, P., & Roberts, N., (2000). Attachment in close relationships. In C. Hendrick & S. S. Hendrick (Eds.), *Close relationships: A sourcebook* (pp. 185–202). Thousand Oaks, CA: Sage.

Feeney, J., Peterson, C., & Noller, P. (1994). Equity and marital satisfaction over the family life cycle. *Personal Relationships, 1*, 83–99.

Fehr, B. (1988). Prototype analysis of the concepts of love and commitment. *Journal of Personality and Social Psychology, 55*, 557–579.

Fehr, B. (2006). A prototype approach to studying love. In R. J. Sternberg & K. Weis (Eds.), *The new psychology of love* (pp. 225–246). New Haven, CT: Yale University Press.

Feldman, C. M., & Ridley, C. A. (2000). The role of conflict-based communication responses and outcomes in male domestic violence toward female partners. *Journal of Social and Personal Relationships. Special Issue: Relationship Conflict, 17*, 552–573.

Fenell, D. (1993). Characteristics of long-term first marriages. *Journal of Mental Health Counseling, 15*, 446–460.

Fiese, B. H. (1992). Dimensions of family rituals across two generations: Relations to adolescent identity. *Family Process, 31*, 151–162.

Fiese, B. H. (1993). Family rituals in alcoholic and nonalcoholic households. *Family Relations, 42*, 187–192.

Fiese, B. H., Hooker, K. A., Kotary, L., & Schwagler, J. (1993). Family rituals in the early stages of parenthood. *Journal of Marriage and Family, 55*, 633–642.

Fincham, F. D. (2004). Communication in marriage. In A. L. Vangelisti (Ed.), *Handbook of family communication* (pp. 83–103). Mahwah, NJ: Erlbaum.

Fincham, F. D., & Beach, S. R. H. (1999). Conflict in marriage: Implications for working with couples. *Annual Review of Psychology, 50*, 47–77.

Fincham, F. D., & Beach, S. R. (2002). Forgiveness in marriage: Implications for psychological aggression and constructive communication. *Personal Relationships, 9*, 239–251.

Fincham, F. D., Beach, S. R. H., & Davila, J. (2004). Forgiveness and conflict resolution in marriage. *Journal of Family Psychology, 18*, 72–81.

Fincham, F. D., & Bradbury, T. N. (1987). The assessment of marital quality: A reevaluation. *Journal of Marriage and Family, 49*, 797–809.

Fincham, F. D., Bradbury, T. N., & Scott, C. K. (1990). *The psychology of marriage*. New York: Guilford Press.

Fincham, F. D., Hall, J. H., & Beach, S. R. H. (2005). "'Til lack of forgiveness doth us part": Forgiveness and marriage. In E. L. Worthington, Jr. (Ed.), *Handbook of forgiveness* (pp. 207–226). New York: Routledge.

Fincham, F. D., Harold, G. T., & Gano-Phillips, S. (2000). The longitudinal association between attributions and marital satisfaction: Direction of effects and role of efficacy expectations. *Journal of Family Psychology, 14*, 267–285.

Fincham, F. D., & Linfield, K. J. (1997). A new look at marital quality: Can

209

# References

spouses feel positive and negative about their marriage? *Journal of Family Psychology, 11*, 489–502.

Fincham, F. D., Stanley, S. M., & Beach, S. R. H. (2007). Transformative processes in marriage: An analysis of emerging trends. *Journal of Marriage and Family. Special Issue: A Minisymposium on Transformative Process in Marriage, 69*, 275–292.

Fingerman, K. L., Nussbaum, J., & Birditt, K. S. (2004). Keeping all five balls in the air: Juggling family communication at midlife. In A. Vangelisti (Ed.), *Handbook of family communication* (pp. 135–152). Mahwah, NJ: Erlbaum.

Fitzpatrick, M. A. (1984). A typological approach to marital interaction: Recent theory and research. *Advances in Experimental Social Psychology, 18*, 1–47.

Fitzpatrick, M. A. (1987). Marriage and verbal intimacy. In V. J. Derlega & J. H. Berg (Eds.), *Self-disclosure: Theory, research, and therapy* (pp. 131–154). New York: Plenum Press.

Fitzpatrick, M. A. (1988). *Between husbands and wives: Communication in marriage.* Beverly Hills, CA: Sage.

Fitzpatrick, M. A., Fey, J., Segrin, C., & Schiff, J. L. (1993). Internal working models of relationships and marital communication. *Journal of Language and Social Psychology, 12,* 103–131.

Floyd, K. (2006). *Communicating affection: Interpersonal behavior and social context.* Cambridge: Cambridge University Press.

Floyd, K., Boren, J. P., Hannawa, A. F., Hesse, C., McEwan, B., & Veksler, A. E. (2009). Kissing in marital and cohabiting relationships: Effects on blood lipids, stress, and relationship satisfaction. *Western Journal of Communication, 73,* 113–133.

Floyd, K., & Morman, M. T. (2002). Human affection exchange: III. Discriminative parental solicitude in men's affection with their biological and non-biological sons. *Communication Quarterly, 49,* 310–327.

Folkes, V. S. (1985). Mindlessness or mindfulness: A partial replication and extension of Langer, Blank and Chanowitz. *Journal of Personality and Social Psychology, 48,* 600–604.

Frankl, V. E. (1963). *Man's search for meaning.* New York: Pocket Books.

Freedman, S., Enright, R. D., & Knutson, J. (2005). A progress report on the process model of forgiveness. In E. L. Worthington, Jr. (Ed.), *Handbook of forgiveness* (pp. 393–406). New York: Routledge.

Gallo, L. C., Troxel, W. M., Matthews, K. A., & Kuller, L. H. (2003). Marital status and quality in middle-aged women: Associations with levels and trajectories of cardiovascular risk factors. *Health Psychology, 22,* 453–463.

Galvin, K. M. (2006). Diversity's impact on defining the family: Discourse-dependence and identity. In L. H. Turner & R. West (Eds.), *The family communication sourcebook* (pp. 3–20). Thousand Oaks, CA: Sage.

Gilbert, L. A. (1985). *Men in dual-career families: Current realities and future prospects.* Hillsdale, NJ: Erlbaum.

# References

Givertz, M., Segrin, C., & Hanzal, A. (2009). The association between satisfaction and commitment differs across marital couple types. *Communication Research, 36*, 561–584.

Glenn, N. D. (1990). Quantitative research on marital quality in the 1980s: A critical review. *Journal of Marriage and Family, 52*, 818–831.

Glenn, N. D. (1998). The course of marital success and failure in five American 10-year marriage cohorts. *Journal of Marriage and Family, 60*, 569–576.

Goman, C., & Kelley, D. L. (2010, October). Conceptualizing forgiveness in the face of historical trauma. Presentation at New Approaches to Trauma: Bridging Theory and Practice conference. Tempe, AZ.

Gordon, K. C., & Baucom, D. H. (1998). Understanding betrayals in marriage: A synthesized model of forgiveness. *Family Process, 37*, 425–449.

Gordon, K. C., & Baucom, D. H. (1999). A multitheoretical intervention for promoting recovery from extramarital affairs. *Clinical Psychology: Science and Practice, 6*, 382–399.

Gordon, K. C., & Baucom, D. H. (2003). Forgiveness and marriage: Preliminary support for a measure based on a model of recovery from a marital betrayal. *American Journal of Family Therapy, 31*, 179–199.

Gordon, K. C., Baucom, D. H., & Snyder, D. K. (2000). The use of forgiveness in marital therapy. In M. E. McCullough, K. I. Pargament, & C. E. Thoreson (Eds.), *Forgiveness: Theory, research, and practice* (pp. 203–227). New York: Guilford Press.

Gordon, K. C., Baucom, D. H., & Snyder, D. K. (2005). Treating couples recovering from infidelity: An integrative approach. *Journal of Clinical Psychology, 61*, 1393–1405.

Gottman, J. M. (1982). Temporal form: Toward a new language for describing relationships. *Journal of Marriage and Family, 44*, 943–962.

Gottman, J. M. (1993). A theory of marital dissolution and stability. *Journal of Family Psychology, 7*, 57–75.

Gottman, J. M. (1994). *What predicts divorce? The relationship between marital processes and marital outcomes.* Hillsdale, NJ: Erlbaum.

Gottman, J. M. (1998). Psychology and the study of marital processes. *Annual Review of Psychology, 49*, 169–197.

Gottman, J. M. (1999). *The marriage clinic: A scientifically based marital therapy.* New York: Norton.

Gottman, J. M., Jacobson, N. S., Rushe, R. H., & Shortt, J. W. (1995). The relationship between heart rate reactivity, emotionally aggressive behavior, and general violence in batterers. *Journal of Family Psychology, 9*, 227–248.

Gottman, J. M., & Krokoff, L. J. (1989). Marital interaction and satisfaction: A longitudinal view. *Journal of Consulting and Clinical Psychology, 57*, 47–52.

Gottman, J. M., & Levenson, R. W. (1992). Marital processes predictive of later dissolution: Behavior, physiology, and health. *Journal of Personality and Social Psychology, 63*, 221–233.

# References

Gottman, J. M., & Notarius, C. I. (2002). Marital research in the 20th century and a research agenda for the 21st century. *Family Process, 41*, 159–197.

Gottman, J. M., Notarius, C., Gonso, J., & Markman, H. (1976). *A couple's guide to communication.* Champaign, IL: Research Press.

Gottman, J. M., Notarius, C., Markman, H., Bank, S., Yoppi, B., & Rubin, M. E. (1976). Behavior exchange theory and marital decision making. *Journal of Personality and Social Psychology, 34*, 14–23.

Gray-Little, B., Baucom, D. H., & Hamby, S. L. (1996). Marital power, marital adjustment, and therapy outcome. *Journal of Family Psychology, 10*, 292–303.

Greeff, A. P., & Malherbe, H. L. (2001). Intimacy and marital satisfaction in spouses. *Journal of Sex & Marital Therapy, 27*, 247–257.

Greenberg, L. S., & Johnson, S. M. (1988). *Emotionally focused therapy for couples.* New York: Guilford Press.

Gross, J. J., & Levenson, R. W. (1997). Hiding feelings: The acute effects of inhibiting negative and positive emotion. *Journal of Abnormal Psychology, 106*, 95–103.

Grote, N. K., & Frieze, I. H. (1994). The measurement of friendship-based love in intimate relationships. *Personal Relationships, 1*, 275–300.

Grote, N. K., Naylor, K. E., & Clark, M. S. (2002). Perceiving the division of family work to be unfair: Do social comparisons, enjoyment, and competence matter? *Journal of Family Psychology, 16*, 510–522.

Guerrero, L. K., & Andersen, P. A. (2000). Emotions in close relationships. In C. Hendrick & S. S. Hendrick (Eds.), *Close relationships: A sourcebook* (pp. 171–184). Thousand Oaks, CA: Sage.

Guerrero, L. K., and Bachman, G. F. (2010). Forgiveness and forgiving communication in dating relationships: An expectancy–investment explanation. *Journal of Social and Personal Relationships, 27*, 801–823.

Guerrero, L. K., & Floyd, K. (2006). *Nonverbal communication in close relationships.* Mahwah, NJ: Erlbaum.

Guerrero, L. K., & La Valley, A. G. (2006). Conflict, emotion, and communication. In J. G. Oetzel & S. Ting-Toomey (Eds.), *The Sage handbook of conflict communication: Integrating theory, research, and practice* (pp. 69–96). Thousand Oaks, CA: Sage.

Hansson, R. O., & Carpenter, B. N. (1994). *Relationships in old age.* New York: Guilford Press.

Hanzal, A., & Segrin, C. (2009). The role of conflict resolution styles in mediating the relationship between enduring vulnerabilities and marital quality. *Journal of Family Communication, 9*, 150–169.

Hargrave, T. D. (1994). *Families and forgiveness: Healing wounds in the intergenerational family.* New York: Brunner/Mazel.

Hargrave, T. D., & Sells, J. N. (1997). The development of a forgiveness scale. *Journal of Marital and Family Therapy, 23*, 41–62.

# References

Harvey, J. (2004). *Trauma and recovery strategies across the lifespan of long-term married couples*. Phoenix: Arizona State University Press.

Hatch, L. R., & Bulcroft, K. (2004). Does long-term marriage bring less frequent disagreements? Five explanatory frameworks. *Journal of Family Issues, 25,* 465–495.

Hatfield, E. (1988). Passionate and companionate love. In R. J. Sternberg & M. L. Barnes (Eds.), *The psychology of love* (pp. 191–217). New Haven, CT: Yale University Press.

Hatfield, E., Traupmann, J., Sprecher, S., Utne, M., & Hay, J. (1985). Equity and intimate relations: Recent research. In W. Ickes (Ed.), *Compatible and incompatible relationships* (pp. 91–117). New York: Springer-Verlag.

Hazan, C., & Shaver, P. (1987). Romantic love conceptualized as an attachment process. *Journal of Personality and Social Psychology, 52,* 511–524.

Heavey, C. L., Christensen, A., & Malamuth, N. M. (1995). The longitudinal impact of demand and withdrawal during marital conflict. *Journal of Consulting and Clinical Psychology, 63,* 797–801.

Heavey, C. L., Layne, C., & Christensen, A. (1993). Gender and conflict structure in marital interaction: A replication and extension. *Journal of Consulting and Clinical Psychology, 61,* 16–27.

Helms-Erikson, H. (2001). Marital quality ten years after the transition to parenthood: Implications of the timing of parenthood and the division of housework. *Journal of Marriage and Family, 63,* 1099–1110.

Hendrick, C., & Hendrick, S. S. (1983). *Liking, loving, and relating*. Monterey, CA: Brooks/Cole.

Hendrick, C., & Hendrick, S. S. (2006). Styles of romantic love. In R. J. Sternberg & K. Weis (Eds.), *The new psychology of love* (pp. 149–170). New Haven, CT: Yale University Press.

Hendrick, S. S., & Hendrick, C. (1992). *Romantic love*. Beverly Hills, CA: Sage.

Hinchliff, S., & Gott, M. (2004). Intimacy, commitment, and adaptation: Sexual relationships within long-term marriages. *Journal of Social & Personal Relationships, 21,* 595–609.

Hodgson, L. K., & Wertheim, E. H. (2007). Does good emotion management aid forgiving? Multiple dimensions of empathy, emotion management and forgiveness of self and others. *Journal of Social and Personal Relationships, 24,* 931-949.

Holmes, J. G., & Rempel, J. K. (1989). Trust in close relationships. In C. Hendrick (Ed.), *Close relationships* (pp. 187–220). Newbury Park, CA: Sage.

Holtzworth-Munroe, A., & Jacobson, N. S. (1985). Causal attributions of married couples: When do they search for causes? What do they conclude when they do? *Journal of Personality and Social Psychology, 48,* 1398–1412.

Holtzworth-Munroe, A., Smutzler, N. & Stuart, G. L. (1998). Demand and withdraw communication among couples experiencing husband violence. *Journal of Consulting and Clinical Psychology, 66,* 731–743.

# References

Honeycutt, J. M., Cantrill, J. G., Kelly, P., & Lambkin, D. (1998). How do I love thee? Let me consider my options: Cognition, verbal strategies, and the escalation of intimacy. *Human Communication Research*, 25, 39–63.

Honeycutt, J. M., & Wiemann, J. M. (1999). Analysis of functions of talk and reports of imagined interactions (IIs) during engagement and marriage. *Human Communication Research*, 25, 399–419.

Horwitz, A. V., White, H. R., & Howell-White, S. (1996). Becoming married and mental health: A longitudinal study of a cohort of young adults. *Journal of Marriage and Family*, 58, 895–907.

Huston, T. L., & Holmes, E. K. (2004). Becoming parents. In A. Vangelisti (Ed.), *Handbook of family communication* (pp. 105–133). Mahwah, NJ: Erlbaum.

Imber-Black, E. (2005). Creating meaningful rituals for new life cycle transitions. In B. Carter & M. McGoldrick (Eds.), *The expanded family life cycle: Individual, family, and social perspectives* (3rd ed., pp. 202–214). Boston: Allyn and Bacon.

Jacob, T., Kornblith, S., Anderson, C., & Hartz, M. (1978). Role expectation and role performance in distressed and normal couples. *Journal of Abnormal Psychology*, 87, 286–290.

Jacobson, N. S., Gottman, J. M., & Shortt, J. W. (1995). The distinction between Type 1 and Type 2 batterers – further considerations: Reply to Ornduff et al. (1995), Margolin et al. (1995), and Walker (1995). *Journal of Family Psychology*, 9, 272–279.

Jamieson, L. (2004). Intimacy, negotiated nonmonogamy, and the limits of the couple. In J. Duncombe, K. Harrison, G. Allan, & D. Marsden (Eds.), *The state of affairs: Explorations in infidelity and commitment* (pp. 35–58). Mahwah, NJ: Erlbaum.

Janicki, D. L., Kamarck, T. W., Shiffman, S., Sutton-Tyrrell, K., & Gwaltney, C. J. (2005). Frequency of spousal interaction and 3-year progression of carotid artery intima medial thickness: The Pittsburgh healthy heart project. *Psychosomatic Medicine*, 67, 889–896.

Johnson, M. P. (1995). Patriarchal terrorism and common couple violence: Two forms of violence against women. *Journal of Marriage and Family*, 57, 283–294.

Johnson, M. P. (2004). Patriarchal terrorism and common couple violence: Two forms of violence against women. In H. T. Reis & C. E. Rusbult (Eds.), *Close relationships: Key readings* (pp. 471–482). New York: Psychology Press.

Johnson, M. P. (2006). Violence and abuse in personal relationships: Conflict, terror, and resistance in intimate partnerships. In A. L. Vangelisti & D. Perlman (Eds.), *The Cambridge handbook of personal relationships* (pp. 557–576). Cambridge: Cambridge University Press.

Jordan, C., Cobb, N., & McCully, R. (1989). Clinical issues of the dual-career couple. *Social Work*, 34, 29–32.

Kachadourian, L. K., Fincham, F., & Davila, J. (2005). Attitudinal ambivalence,

# References

rumination, and forgiveness of partner transgressions in marriage. *Personality and Social Psychology Bulletin, 31,* 334–342.

Kantor, D., & Lehr, W. (1975). *Inside the family.* San Francisco, CA: Jossey-Bass.

Kaplan, R. E. (1975–1976). Maintaining interpersonal relationships. *Interpersonal Development, 6,* 106–119.

Karremans, J. C., Van Lange, P. A., Ouwerkerk, J. W., & Kluwer, E. S. (2003). When forgiving enhances psychological well-being: The role of interpersonal commitment. *Journal of Personality and Social Psychology, 84,* 1011–1026.

Keeley, M. P. (2007). "Turning toward death together": The functions of messages during final conversations in close relationships. *Journal of Personal and Social Relationships, 24,* 225–253.

Kellermann, K. (1992). Communication: Inherently strategic and primarily automatic. *Communication Monographs, 59,* 288–300.

Kelley, D. L. (1998). The communication of forgiveness. *Communication Studies, 49,* 255–271.

Kelley, D. L. (1999). Relational expectancy fulfillment as an explanatory variable for distinguishing couple types. *Human Communication Research, 25,* 420–442.

Kelley, D. L. (2008). Doing meaningful research: From *no duh* to *aha!* (A personal record). *Journal of Family Communication, 8,* 1–18.

Kelley, D. L. (in press). Forgiveness as restoration: The search for well-being, reconciliation, and relational justice. In T. Socha & M. Pitts (Eds.), *Positive interpersonal communication.* New York: Peter Lang.

Kelley, D. L., & Burgoon, J. K. (1991). Understanding marital satisfaction and couple type as functions of relational expectations. *Human Communication Research, 18,* 40–69.

Kelley, D. L., & Waldron, V. (2005). An investigation of forgiveness-seeking communication and relational outcomes. *Communication Quarterly, 53,* 339–358.

Kelley, D. L., & Waldron, V. R. (2006). Forgiveness: Communicative implications in social relationships. *Communication Yearbook, 30,* 303–341.

Kelley, H. H., Berscheid, E., Christensen, A., Harvey, J. H., Huston, T. L., Levinger, G., McClintock, E., Peplau, L. A., & Peterson, D. R. (1983). *Close relationships.* San Francisco, CA: Freeman.

Kenrick, D. T. (2006). A dynamical evolutionary view of love. In R. J. Sternberg & K. Weis (Eds.), *The new psychology of love* (pp. 15–34). New Haven, CT: Yale University Press.

Kerber, K. B. (1994). The marital balance of power and quid pro quo: An evolutionary perspective. *Ethology & Sociobiology. Special Issue: Mental Disorders in an Evolutionary Context, 15,* 283–297.

Kiecolt-Glaser, J. K., & Newton, T. L. (2001). Marriage and health: His and hers. *Psychological Bulletin, 127,* 472–503.

Klein, W., Izquierdo, C., & Bradbury, T. N. (2007). Working relationships:

# References

Communicative patterns and strategies among couples in everyday life. *Qualitative Research in Psychology*, 4, 29–47.

Klinetob, N. A., & Smith, D. A. (1996). Demand–withdraw communication in marital interaction: Tests of interspousal contingency and gender role hypotheses. *Journal of Marriage and Family*, 58, 945–957.

Knapp, M. (2006). Lying and deception in close relationships. In A. L. Vangelisti & D. Perlman (Eds.), *The Cambridge handbook of personal relationships* (pp. 517–532). Cambridge: Cambridge University Press.

Komter, A. (1989). Hidden power in marriage. *Gender and Society*, 3, 187–216.

Kurdek, L. A. (1993). Nature and prediction of changes in marital quality for first-time parent and nonparent husbands and wives. *Journal of Family Psychology*, 6, 255–265.

Lambert, N. M., & Dollahite, D. C. (2006). How religiosity helps couples prevent, resolve, and overcome marital conflict. *Family Relations*, 55, 439–449.

Langer, E. J. (1978). Rethinking the role of thought in social interaction. *New Directions in Attribution Research*, 2, 35–58.

Langer, E. J. (1989). *Mindfulness*. Reading, MA: Addison-Wesley.

Langer, E. J., Blank, A., & Chanowitz, B. (1978). The mindlessness of ostensibly thoughtful action: The role of "placebic" information in interpersonal interaction. *Journal of Personality and Social Psychology*, 36, 635–642.

Larson, J. H., & Holman, T. B. (1994). Premarital predictors of marital quality and stability. *Family Relations: An Interdisciplinary Journal of Applied Family Studies*, 43, 228–237.

Laurenceau, J., Barrett, L. F., & Rovine, M. J. (2005). The interpersonal process model of intimacy in marriage: A daily-diary and multilevel modeling approach. *Journal of Family Psychology*, 19, 314–323.

Lawrence, E., Nylen, K., & Cobb, R. J. (2007). Prenatal expectations and marital satisfaction over the transition to parenthood. *Journal of Family Psychology*, 21, 155–164.

Lazarus, R. S. (1991). *Emotion and adaptation*. New York: Oxford University Press.

Leary, M. R. (2001). Toward a conceptualization of interpersonal rejection. In M. R. Leary (Ed.), *Interpersonal rejection* (pp. 3–20). New York: Oxford University Press.

Leary, M. R., & Leder, S. (2009). The nature of hurt feelings: Emotional experience and cognitive appraisals. In A. Vangelisti (Ed.), *Feeling hurt in close relationships* (pp. 15–33). New York: Cambridge University Press.

Leary, M. R, Springer, C., Negel, L., Ansell, E., & Evans, K. (1998). The causes, phenomenology, and consequences of hurt feelings. *Journal of Personality and Social Psychology*, 74, 1225–1237.

Lee, J. A. (1973). *The colors of love: An exploration of the ways of loving*. Don Mills, Ontario: New Press.

216

# References

Lee, J. A. (1977). A typology of styles of loving. *Personality and Social Psychology Bulletin, 3,* 173–182.

Lee, J. A. (1988). Love-styles. In R. J. Sternberg & M. L. Barnes (Eds.), *The psychology of love* (pp. 38–67). New Haven, CT: Yale University Press.

Lee, Y. S. (2005). Measuring the gender gap in household labor: Accurately estimating wives' and husbands' contributions. In B. Schneider & L. J. Waite (Eds.), *Being together, working apart: Dual-career families and the work–life balance* (pp. 229–247). Cambridge: Cambridge University Press.

Leeds-Hurwitz, W. (2002). *Wedding as text: Communicating cultural identities through ritual.* Mahwah, NJ: Erlbaum.

Levenson, R. W., Carstensen, L. L., & Gottman, J. M. (1993). Long-term marriage: Age, gender, and satisfaction. *Psychology and Aging, 8,* 301–313.

Levenson, R. W., & Gottman, J. M. (1983). Marital interaction: Physiological linkage and affective exchange. *Journal of Personality and Social Psychology, 45,* 587–597.

Levenson, R. W., & Gottman, J. M. (1985). Physiological and affective predictors of change in relationship satisfaction. *Journal of Personality and Social Psychology, 49,* 85–94.

Levy, M. B., & Davis, K. E. (1988). Lovestyles and attachment styles compared: Their relations to each other and to various relationship characteristics. *Journal of Social and Personal Relationships, 5,* 439.

Lewis, J. M. (1998). For better or worse: Interpersonal relationships and individual outcome. *The American Journal of Psychiatry, 155,* 582–589.

Lewis, M. A., & Butterfield, R. M. (2007). Social control in marital relationships: Effect of one's partner on health behaviors. *Journal of Applied Social Psychology, 37,* 298–319.

Lewis, R. A. (1978). Emotional intimacy among men. *Journal of Social Issues, 34,* 108–121.

Lewis, S. A., Langan, C. J., & Hollander, E. P. (1972). Expectation of future interaction and the choice of less desirable alternatives in conformity. *Sociometry, 35,* 440–447.

Lloyd, S. A. (1996). Physical aggression and marital distress: The role of everyday marital interaction. In D. D. Cahn & S. A. Lloyd (Eds.), *Family violence from a communication perspective* (pp. 177–198). Thousand Oaks, CA: Sage.

Luthar, S. S., Cicchetti, D., & Becker, B. (2000). The construct of resilience: A critical evaluation and guidelines for future work. *Child Development, 71,* 543–562.

Mace, D. R., & Mace, V. C. (1975). Marriage enrichment – wave of the future? *Family Coordinator, 24,* 131–135.

Main, F. O. (1996). David Olson: On assessment and families. *The Family Journal, 4*(2), 174–179.

Marshall, L. L. (1994). Physical and psychological abuse. In W. R. Cupach &

# References

B. H. Spitzberg (Eds.), *The dark side of interpersonal communication* (pp. 281–311). Hillsdale, NJ: Erlbaum.

McAllister, F. M., Mansfield, P., & Dormor, D. J. (1991). Expectations and experiences of marriage today. *Journal of Social Work Practice, 5,* 181–191.

McCarthy, B. (2003). Marital sex as it ought to be. *Journal of Family Psychotherapy, 14*(2), 1–12.

McCullough, M. E., Worthington, E. L., Jr., & Rachal, K. C. (1997). Interpersonal forgiving in close relationships. *Journal of Personality and Social Psychology, 73,* 321–336.

McDonald, G. W. (1980). Family power: The assessment of a decade of theory and research, 1970–1979. *Journal of Marriage and Family, 42,* 841–854.

McGoldrick, M. (2005). Becoming a couple. In B. Carter & M. McGoldrick (Eds.), *The expanded family life cycle: Individual, family, and social perspectives* (3rd ed., pp. 231–248). Boston: Allyn and Bacon.

McGoldrick, M., & Carter, B. (2003). The family life cycle. In F. Walsh (Ed.), *Normal family processes: Growing diversity and complexity* (3rd ed., pp. 375–398). New York: Guilford Press.

McGoldrick, M., & Carter, B. (2005). Remarried families. In B. Carter & M. McGoldrick (Eds.), *The expanded family life cycle: Individual, family, and social perspectives* (3rd ed., pp. 417–435). Boston: Allyn and Bacon.

McGoldrick, M., Heiman, M., & Carter, B. (1993). The changing family life cycle: A perspective on normalcy. In F. Walsh (Ed.), *Normal family processes* (2nd ed., pp. 405–443). New York: Guilford Press.

McGoldrick, M. & Walsh, F. (2005). Death and the family life cycle. In B. Carter & M. McGoldrick (Eds.), *The expanded family life cycle: Individual, family, and social perspectives* (3rd ed., pp. 185–201). Boston: Allyn and Bacon.

McHale, J. P., Kavanaugh, K. C., & Berkman, J. M. (2003). Sensitivity to infants' cues: As much a mandate for researchers as parents. In A. C. Crouter & A. Booth (Eds.), *Children's influence on family dynamics: The neglected side of family relationships* (pp. 91–108). Mahwah, NJ: Erlbaum.

McIlvane, J. M., Ajrouch, K. J., & Antonucci, T. C. (2007). Generational structure and social resources in mid-life: Influences on health and well-being. *Journal of Social Issues, 63,* 759–773.

Mellen, S. L. W. (1981). *The evolution of love.* San Francisco, CA: W. H. Freeman.

Metts, S. (1994). Relational transgressions. In W. R. Cupach & B. H. Spitzberg (Eds.), *The dark side of interpersonal communication* (pp. 217–239). Hillsdale, NJ: Erlbaum.

Metts, S., & Cupach, W. R. (2007). Responses to relational transgressions: Hurt, anger, and sometimes forgiveness. In B. H. Spitzberg & W. R. Cupach (Eds.), *The dark side of interpersonal communication* (2nd ed., pp. 243–274). Mahwah, NJ: Erlbaum.

# References

Michaels, J. W., Edwards, J. N., & Acock, A. C. (1984). Satisfaction in intimate relationships as a function of inequality, inequity, and outcomes. *Social Psychology Quarterly, 47*, 347–357.

Miller, R. B., Yorgason, J. B., Sandberg, J. G., & White, M. B. (2003). Problems that couples bring to therapy: A view across the family life cycle. *American Journal of Family Therapy, 31*, 395–407.

Montgomery, B. M. (1981). The form and function of quality communication in marriage. *Family Relations, 30*, 21–30.

Montgomery, M. J., & Sorell, G. T. (1997). Differences in love and attitudes across family life stages. *Family Relations, 46*, 55–61.

Moss, B. F., & Schwebel, A. I. (1993). Defining intimacy in romantic relationships. *Family Relations: An Interdisciplinary Journal of Applied Family Studies, 42*, 31–37.

Motley, M. T. (1992). Mindfulness in solving communicators' dilemmas. *Communication Monographs, 59*, 306–314.

Murphy, C. M., & O'Farrell, T. J. (1997). Couple communication patterns of maritally aggressive and nonaggressive male alcoholics. *Journal of Studies on Alcohol, 58*, 83–90.

Myers, L. B., & Wark, L. (1996). Psychotherapy for infertility: A cognitive-behavioral approach for couples. *American Journal of Family Therapy, 24*, 9–20.

Navran, L. (1967). Communication and adjustment in marriage. *Family Process, 6*, 173–184.

Nicola, J. S., & Hawkes, G. R. (1986). Marital satisfaction of dual-career couples: Does sharing increase happiness? *Journal of Social Behavior & Personality, 1*, 47–60.

Nielsen, M. R. (2005). Couples making it happen: Marital satisfaction and what works for highly satisfied couples. In B. Schneider & L. J. Waite (Eds.), *Being together, working apart: Dual-career families and the work–life balance* (pp. 196–216). New York: Cambridge University Press.

Noller, P. (1980). Misunderstanding in marital communication: A study of couples' nonverbal communication. *Journal of Personality and Social Psychology, 39*, 1135–1148.

Noller, P. (1981). Gender and marital adjustment level differences in decoding messages from spouses and strangers. *Journal of Personality and Social Psychology, 41*, 272–278.

Noller, P. (1993). Gender and emotional communication in marriage: Different cultures or differential social power? *Journal of Language and Social Psychology. Special Issue: Emotional Communication, Culture, and Power, 12*, 132–152.

Noller, P. (1996). What is this thing called love? Defining the love that supports marriage and family. *Personal Relationships, 3*, 97–115.

Norton, R. (1983). Measuring marital quality: A critical look at the dependent variable. *Journal of Marriage and Family, 45*, 141–151.

# References

Notarius, C., & Markman, H. (1993). *We can work it out: Making sense of marital conflict.* New York: Putnam.

Olson, D. H., Fournier, D., & Druckman, J. (1986). *PREPARE/ENRICH Counselor Manual.* Minneapolis, MN: Life Innovations, Inc.

Olson, D. H., & Gorall, D. M. (2003). Circumplex model of marital and family systems. In F. Walsh (Ed.), *Normal family processes: Growing diversity and complexity* (3rd ed., pp. 514–548). New York: Guilford Press.

Olson, D. H., Russell, C. S., & Sprenkle, D. (1989). *Circumplex Model: Systemic assessment and treatment of families.* New York: Haworth Press.

Olson, M. M., Russell, C. S., Higgins-Kessler, M., & Miller, R. B. (2002). Emotional proceses following disclosure of an extramarital affair. *Journal of Marital and Family Therapy, 28,* 423–434.

Paleari, F. G., Regalia, C., & Fincham, F. (2005). Marital quality, forgiveness, empathy, and rumination: A longitudinal analysis. *Personality and Social Psychology Bulletin, 31,* 368–378.

Papernow, P. L. (1993). *Becoming a stepfamily: Patterns of development in remarried families.* San Francisco, CA: Jossey-Bass.

Papp, L. M., Cummings, E. M., & Goeke-Morey, M. C. (2009). For richer, for poorer: Money as a topic of marital conflict in the home. *Family Relations, 58,* 91–103.

Parkman, A. M. (2004). The importance of gifts in marriage. *Economic Inquiry, 42,* 482–495.

Pasupathi, M., Carstensen, L. L., Levenson, R. W., & Gottman, J. M. (1999). Responsive listening in long-married couples: A psycholinguistic perspective. *Journal of Nonverbal Behavior, 23,* 173–193.

Patrick, S., Sells, J. N., Giordano, F. G., & Tollerud, T. R. (2007). Intimacy, differentiation, and personality variables as predictors of marital satisfaction. *The Family Journal, 15,* 359–367.

Patterson, B., & O'Hair, D. (1992). Relational reconciliation: Toward a more comprehensive model of relational development. *Communication Research Reports, 9,* 119–129.

Patterson, M. L. (1976). An arousal model of interpersonal intimacy. *Psychological Review, 83,* 235–245.

Patterson, M. L. (1982). A sequential functional model of nonverbal exchange. *Psychological Review, 89,* 231–249.

Pecchioni, L. L., Wright, K. B., & Nussbaum, J. F. (2005). *Life-span communication.* Mahwah, NJ: Erlbaum.

Pence, E., & Paymer, M. (1993). *Education groups for men who batter: The Duluth Model.* New York: Springer-Verlag.

Perlman, D., & Fehr, B. (1987). The development of intimate relationships. In D. Perlman & S. Duck (Eds.), *Intimate relationships: Development, dynamics, and deterioration* (pp. 13–42). Newbury Park, CA: Sage.

Perry-Jenkins, M., & Crouter, A. C. (1990). Men's provider-role attitudes:

# References

Implications for household work and marital satisfaction. *Journal of Family Issues*, *11*, 136–156.

Perry-Jenkins, M., Pierce, C. P., & Goldberg, A. E. (2004). Discourses on diapers and dirty laundry: Family communication about childcare and housework. In A. L. Vangelisti (Ed.), *Handbook of family communication* (pp. 541–561). Mahwah, NJ: Erlbaum.

Petronio, S. (1991). Communication boundary management: A theoretical model of managing disclosure of private information between marital couples. *Communication Theory*, *1*, 311–335.

Petronio, S. (2002). *Boundaries of privacy: Dialectics of disclosure*. Albany, NY: State University of New York Press.

Petronio, S., & Caughlin, J. P. (2006). Communication privacy management theory: Understanding families. In D. O. Braithwaite & L. A. Baxter (Eds.), *Engaging theories in family communication: Multiple perspectives* (pp. 35–49). Thousand Oaks, CA: Sage.

Petronio, S., & Reierson, J. (2009). The privacy of confidentiality: Grasping the complexities through communication privacy management. In T. D. Afifi & W. A. Afifi (Eds.), *Uncertainty and information regulation in interpersonal contexts: Theories and applications* (pp. 365–383). New York: Routledge.

Pickering, J. (2008). *Being in love: Therapeutic pathways through psychological obstacles to love*. London: Routledge.

Pienta, A. M., Hayward, M. D., & Jenkins, K. R. (2000). Health consequences of marriage for the retirement years. *Journal of Family Issues*, *21*, 559–586.

Poole, M. S. & Billingsley, J. (1989). The structuring of dyadic decisions. In D. Brinberg & J. Jaccard (Eds.), *Dyadic decision-making* (pp. 216–248). New York: Springer-Verlag.

Prager, K. J. (1995). *The psychology of intimacy*. New York: Guilford Press.

Prager, K. J. (2000). Intimacy in personal relationships. In C. Hendrick & S. S. Hendrick (Eds.), *Close relationships: A sourcebook* (pp. 229–242). Thousand Oaks, CA: Sage.

Putnam, L. L. (2006). Definitions and approaches to conflict and communication. In J. G. Oetzel & S. Ting-Toomey (Eds.), *The Sage handbook of conflict communication: Integrating theory, research, and practice* (pp. 1–32). Thousand Oaks, CA: Sage.

Quick, E., & Jacob, T. (1973). Marital disturbance in relation to role theory and relationship theory. *Journal of Abnormal Psychology*, *82*, 309–316.

Ragsdale, J. D. (1996). Gender, satisfaction level, and the use of relational maintenance strategies in marriage. *Communication Monographs*, *63*, 354–369.

Raley, S., & Bianchi, S. (2006). Sons, daughters, and family processes: Does gender of children matter? *Annual Review of Sociology*, *32*, 401–421.

Reis, H. T., & Patrick, B. C. (1996). Attachment and intimacy: Component processes. In E. T. Higgins & A. W. Kruglanski (Eds.), *Social psychology: Handbook of basic principles* (pp. 523–563). New York: Guilford Press.

# References

Reis, H. T., & Rusbult, C. E. (2004). Relationship science: A casual and some-what selective review. In H. T. Reis & C. E. Rusbult (Eds.), *Close relationships* (pp. 1–20). New York: Psychology Press.

Reis, H. T., & Shaver, P. (1988). Intimacy as an interpersonal process. In S. Duck (Ed.), *Handbook of personal relationships: Theory, relationships, and interventions* (pp. 367–389). Chichester: Wiley.

Rhoades, G. K., Stanley, S. M., & Markman, H. J. (2006). Pre-engagement cohabitation and gender asymmetry in marital commitment. *Journal of Family Psychology, 20,* 553–560.

Rhoades, G. K., Stanley, S. M., & Markman, H. J. (2009). The pre-engagement cohabitation effect: A replication and extension of previous findings. *Journal of Family Psychology, 23,* 107–111.

Roberts, L. J., & Krokoff, L. J. (1990). A time-series analysis of withdrawal, hostility, and displeasure in satisfied and dissatisfied marriages. *Journal of Marriage and Family, 52,* 95–105.

Rogers, L. E., Castleton, A., & Lloyd, S. A. (1996). Relational control and physi-cal aggression in satisfying marital relationships. In D. D. Cahn & S. A. Lloyd (Eds.), *Family violence from a communication perspective* (pp. 218–239). Thousand Oaks, CA: Sage.

Roloff, M. E., & Miller, C. W. (2006). Mulling about family conflict and com-munication: What we know and what we need to know. In L. H. Turner & R. West (Eds.), *The family communication sourcebook* (pp. 143–164). Thousand Oaks, CA: Sage.

Rubin, Z. (1970). Measurement of romantic love. *Journal of Personality and Social Psychology, 16,* 265–273.

Rubin, Z. (1973). *Liking and loving: An invitation to social psychology.* New York: Holt, Rinehart and Winston.

Rusbult, C. E., Hannon, P. A., Stocker, S. L., & Finkel, E. J. (2005). Forgiveness and relational repair. In E. L. Worthington, Jr. (Ed.), *Handbook of forgiveness* (pp. 185–206). New York: Routledge.

Rusbult, C. E., Olsen, N., Davis, J. L., & Hannon, P. A. (2001). Commitment and relationship maintenance mechanisms. In J. H. Harvey & A. Wenzel (Eds.), *Close romantic relationships: Maintenance and enhancement* (pp. 87–113). Mahwah, NJ: Erlbaum.

Sabatelli, R. M. (1988). Measurement issues in marital research: A review and critique of contemporary survey instruments. *Journal of Marriage and Family, 50,* 891–915.

Sabourin, T. C. (1991). Perceptions of verbal aggression in interspousal violence. In D. Knudsen & J. L. Miller (Eds.), *Abused and battered: Social and legal responses to family violence* (pp. 135–142). New York: Aldine de Gruyter.

Sabourin, T. C. (1995). The role of negative reciprocity in spouse abuse: A rela-tional control analysis. *Journal of Applied Communication Research. Special Issue: Applied Communication Research in Families, 23,* 271–283.

# References

Sabourin, T. C., & Stamp, G. H. (1995). Communication and the experience of dialectical tensions in family life: An examination of abusive and nonabusive families. *Communication Monographs, 62*, 213–242.

Sanford, K. (2003). Expectancies and communication behavior in marriage: Distinguishing proximal-level effects from distal-level effects. *Journal of Social & Personal Relationships, 20*, 391–402.

Sanford, K. (2007). The couples emotion rating form: Psychometric properties and theoretical associations. *Psychological Assessment, 19*, 411–421.

Schaefer, M. T., & Olson, D. H. (1981). Assessing intimacy: The PAIR inventory. *Journal of Marital and Family Therapy, 7*, 47–60.

Schmeeckle, M., & Sprecher, S. (2004). Extended family and social networks. In A. Vangelisti (Ed.), *Handbook of family communication* (pp. 349–375). Hillsdale, NJ: Erlbaum.

Schmidt, L. (2006). Psychosocial burden of infertility and assisted reproduction. *The Lancet, 367*, 379-380.

Schmidt, L., Holstein, B., Christensen, U., & Boivin, J. (2005). Does infertility cause marital benefit? An epidemiological study of 2250 women and men in fertility treatment. *Patient Education and Counseling. Special Issue: Social and Cultural Factors in Fertility, 59*, 244–251.

Schmidt, L., Tjørnhøj-Thomsen, T., Boivin, J., & Nyboe Andersen, A. (2005). Evaluation of a communication and stress management training programme for infertile couples. *Patient Education and Counseling. Special Issue: Social and Cultural Factors in Fertility, 59*, 252–262.

Schudlich, D. R., Papp, L. M., & Cummings, M. E. (2004). Relations of husbands' and wives' dysphoria to marital conflict resolution strategies. *Journal of Family Psychology, 18*, 171–183.

Segrin, C., & Fitzpatrick, M. A. (1992). Depression and verbal aggressiveness in different marital couple types. *Communication Studies, 43*, 79–91.

Segrin, C., & Flora, J. (2005). *Family communication*. Mahwah, NJ: Erlbaum.

Segrin, C., Hanzal, A., & Domschke, T. J. (2009). Accuracy and bias in newlywed couples' perceptions of conflict styles and the association with marital satisfaction. *Communication Monographs, 76*, 207–233.

Segrin, C., & Nabi, R. L. (2002). Does television viewing cultivate unrealistic expectations about marriage? *Journal of Communication, 52*, 247–263.

Sexton, C. S., & Perlman, D. S. (1989). Couples' career orientation, gender role orientation, and perceived equity as determinants of marital power. *Journal of Marriage and Family, 51*, 933–941.

Sexton, H. (2005). Spending time at work and at home: What workers do, how they feel about it, and how these emotions affect family life. In B. Schneider & L. J. Waite (Eds.), *Being together, working apart: Dual-career families and the work–life balance* (pp. 47–71). Cambridge: Cambridge University Press.

Shapiro, C. H. (1982). The impact of infertility on the marital relationship. *Social Casework, 63*, 387–393.

# References

Shaver, P. R., & Hazan, C. (1988). A biased overview of the study of love. *Journal of Social and Personal Relationships, 5,* 473–501.

Sherbourne, C. D., & Hays, R. D. (1990). Marital status, social support, and health transitions in chronic disease patients. *Journal of Health and Social Behavior, 31,* 328–343.

Shipman, B., & Smart, C. (2007). "It's made a huge difference": Recognition, rights and the personal significance of civil partnership. *Sociological Research Online, 12*(1).

Silberstein, L. R. (1992). *Dual-career marriage: A system in transition.* Hillsdale, NJ: Erlbaum.

Sillars, A. L., Canary, D. J., & Tafoya, M. (2004). Communication, conflict, and the quality of family relationships. In A. L. Vangelisti (Ed.), *Handbook of family communication* (pp. 413–446). Mahwah, NJ: Erlbaum.

Sillars, A. L. & Kalbfleisch, P. (1989). Implicit and explicit decision making styles in couples. In D. Brinberg & J. Jaccard (Eds.), *Dyadic decision making* (pp. 179–215). New York: Springer-Verlag.

Sillars, A. L., Roberts, L. J., Leonard, K. E., & Dun, T. (2000). Cognition during marital conflict: The relationship of thought and talk. *Journal of Social and Personal Relationships. Special Issue: Relationship Conflict, 17,* 479–502.

Sillars, A. L., & Wilmot, W. W. (1989). Marital communication across the life-span. In J. F. Nussbaum (Ed.), *Life-span communication: Normative processes* (pp. 225–254). Hillsdale, NJ: Erlbaum.

Solomon, R. C. (1981). *Love: Emotion, myth and metaphor.* New York: Anchor.

Solomon, R. C. (2006). *About love: Reinventing romance for our times.* Indianapolis, IN: Hackett Publishing.

Spade, J. Z. (1994). Wives' and husbands' perceptions of why wives work. *Gender & Society, 8,* 170–188.

Spanier, G. B. (1976). Measuring dyadic adjustment: New scales for assessing the quality of marriage and similar dyads. *Journal of Marriage and Family, 38,* 15–28.

Spitzberg, B. H. (2009). Aggression, violence, and hurt in close relationships. In A. Vangelisti (Ed.), *Feeling hurt in close relationships* (pp. 209–232). New York: Cambridge University Press.

Spitzberg, B. H., Canary, D. J., & Cupach, W. R. (1994). A competence-based approach to the study of interpersonal conflict. In D. D. Cahn (Ed.), *Conflict in personal relationships* (pp. 183–202). Hillsdale, NJ: Erlbaum.

Spitzberg, B. H., & Cupach, W. R. (Eds.). (1998). *The dark side of close relationships.* Mahwah, NJ: Erlbaum.

Spitzberg, B. H., & Cupach, W. R. (2007). *The dark side of interpersonal communication* (2nd ed.). Mahwah, NJ: Erlbaum.

Sprecher, S. (1986). The relation between inequity and emotions in close relationships. *Social Psychology Quarterly, 49,* 309–321.

Sprecher, S., & Cate, R. M. (2004). Sexual satisfaction and sexual

# References

expression as predictors of relationship satisfaction and stability. In J. H. Harvey, A. Wenzel, & S. Sprech (Eds.), *Handbook of sexuality in close relationships* (pp. 235–256). Mahwah, NJ: Erlbaum.

Stafford, L. (2003). Maintaining romantic relationships: A summary and analysis of one research program. In D. J. Canary & M. Dainton (Eds.), *Maintaining relationships through communication: Relational, contextual, and cultural variations* (pp. 51–77). Mahwah, NJ: Erlbaum.

Stafford, L., & Canary, D. J. (1991). Maintenance strategies and romantic relationship type, gender and relational characteristics. *Journal of Social and Personal Relationships, 8,* 217–242.

Stafford, L., & Canary, D. J. (2006). Equity and interdependence as predictors of relational maintenance strategies. *Journal of Family Communication, 6,* 227–254.

Stafford, L., Dainton, M., & Haas, S. (2000). Measuring routine and strategic relational maintenance: Scale revision, sex versus gender roles, and the prediction of relational characteristics. *Communication Monographs, 67,* 306–323.

Stafford, L., Kline, S. L., & Rankin, C. T. (2004). Married individuals, cohabiters, and cohabiters who marry: A longitudinal study of relational and individual well-being. *Journal of Social and Personal Relationships, 21,* 231–248.

Staines, G. L., & Libby, P. L. (1986). Men and women in role relationships. *The Social Psychology of Female–Male Relations: A Critical Analysis of Central Concepts, 1,* 211–258.

Stamp, G. H. (1994). The appropriation of the parental role through communication during the transition to parenthood. *Communication Monographs, 61,* 89–112.

Stamp, G. H. (1999). A qualitatively constructed interpersonal communication model: A grounded theory analysis. *Human Communication Research, 25,* 531–547.

Stamp, G. H., & Banski, M. A. (1992). The communicative management of constrained autonomy during the transition to parenthood. *Western Journal of Communication, 56,* 281–300.

Stanley, S. M., Blumberg, S. L., & Markman, H. J. (1999). Helping couples fight for their marriages: The PREP approach. In R. Berger & M. T. Hannah (Eds.), *Preventive approaches in couples therapy* (pp. 279–303). Philadelphia, PA: Brunner/Mazel.

Stanley, S. M., Markman, H. J., & Blumberg, S. L. (1997). The speaker/listener technique. *The Family Journal: Counseling and Therapy for Couples and Families, 5,* 82–83.

Stanley, S. M., Markman, H. J., & Whitton, S. W. (2002). Communication, conflict and commitment: Insights on the foundations of relationship success from a national survey. *Family Process, 41,* 659–675.

Stanley, S. M., Whitton, S. W., Sadberry, S. L., Clements, M. L., & Markman,

# References

H. J. (2006). Sacrifice as a predictor of marital outcomes. *Family Process, 45,* 289–303.

Starrels, M. E., & Holm, K. E. (2000). Adolescents' plans for family formation: Is parental socialization important? *Journal of Marriage and Family, 62,* 416–429.

Steffy, B. D., & Ashbaugh, D. (1986). Dual-career planning, marital satisfaction and job stress among women in dual-career marriages. *Journal of Business and Psychology, 1,* 114–123.

Sternberg, R. J. (1986). A triangular theory of love. *Psychological Review, 93,* 119–135.

Sternberg, R. J. (1988). *The triarchic mind: A new theory of human intelligence.* New York: Viking Press.

Sternberg, R. J. (1997). Construct validation of a triangular love scale. *European Journal of Social Psychology, 27,* 313–335.

Sternberg, R. J. (1998). *Love is a story: A new theory of relationships.* New York: Oxford University Press.

Sternberg, R. J. (2006). A duplex theory of love. In R. J. Sternberg & K. Weis (Eds.), *The new psychology of love* (pp. 184–199). New Haven, CT: Yale University Press.

Storaasli, R. D., & Markman, H. J. (1990). Relationship problems in the early stages of marriage: A longitudinal investigation. *Journal of Family Psychology, 4,* 80–98.

Story, L. B., Karney, B. R., Lawrence, E., & Bradbury, T. N. (2004). Interpersonal mediators in the intergenerational transmission of marital dysfunction. *Journal of Family Psychology, 18,* 519–529.

Tafoya, M. A., & Spitzberg, B. H. (2007). The dark side of infidelity: Its nature, prevalence, and communication functions. In B. H. Spitzberg & W. R. Cupach (Eds.), *The dark side of interpersonal communication* (2nd ed., pp. 201–242). Mahwah, NJ: Erlbaum.

Thayer, S. (1986). Touch: Frontier of intimacy. *Journal of Nonverbal Behavior, 10,* 7–11.

Thibaut, J. W., & Kelley, H. H. (1959). *The social psychology of groups.* New York: Wiley.

Thompson-Hayes, M., & Webb, L. M. (2008). Documenting mutuality: Testing a dyadic and communicative model of marital commitment. *Southern Communication Journal, 73,* 143–159.

Tichenor, V. J. (1999). Status and income as gendered resources: The case of marital power. *Journal of Marriage and Family, 61,* 638–650.

Ting-Toomey, S. (1983). Coding conversation between intimates: A validation study of the intimate negotiation coding system (INCS). *Communication Quarterly, 31,* 68–77.

Tolstedt, B. E., & Stokes, J. P. (1983). Relation of verbal, affective, and physical intimacy to marital satisfaction. *Journal of Counseling Psychology, 30,* 573–580.

# References

Trees, A. R. (2006). Attachment theory: The reciprocal relationship between family communication and attachment patterns. In D. O. Braithwaite & L. A. Baxter (Eds.), *Engaging theories in family communication: Multiple perspectives* (pp. 165–180). Thousand Oaks, CA: Sage.

Troll, L. (1994). Family connectedness of old women: Attachments in later life. In B. F. Turner & L. E. Troll (Eds.), *Women growing older* (pp. 169–201). Thousand Oaks, CA: Sage.

Umberson, D., Williams, K., Powers, D. A., Liu, H., & Needham, B. (2006). You make me sick: Marital quality and health over the life course. *Journal of Health and Social Behavior, 47,* 1–16.

Van de Vliert, E., & Euwema, M. C. (1994). Agreeableness and activeness as components of conflict behaviors. *Journal of Personality and Social Psychology, 66,* 674–687.

VanderVoort, L. & Duck, S. (2004). Sex, Lies, and . . . transformation. In J. Duncombe, K. Harrison, G. Allan, & D. Marsden (Eds.), *The state of affairs: Explorations in infidelity and commitment* (pp. 1–13). Mahwah, NJ: Erlbaum.

Vanfossen, B. E. (1981). Sex differences in the mental health effects of spouse support and equity. *Journal of Health and Social Behavior, 22,* 130–143.

Vangelisti, A. L. (1994). Messages that hurt. In W. R. Cupach & B. H. Spitzberg (Eds.), *The dark side of interpersonal communication* (pp. 53–82). Hillsdale, NJ: Erlbaum.

Vangelisti, A. L. (2001). Making sense of hurtful interactions in close relationships: When hurt feelings create distance. In V. Manusov & J. H. Harvey (Eds.), *Attribution, communication behavior, and close relationships* (pp. 38–58). New York: Cambridge University Press.

Vangelisti , A. L. (2007). Communicating hurt. In B. H. Spitzberg & W. R. Cupach (Eds.), *The dark side of interpersonal communication* (2nd ed., pp. 121–142). Mahwah, NJ: Erlbaum.

Vangelisti, A. L. (2009). Hurt feelings: Distinguishing features, functions, and overview. In A. L. Vangelisti (Ed.), *Feeling hurt in close relationships* (pp. 3–11). New York: Cambridge University Press.

Vangelisti, A. L., & Banski, M. A. (1993). Couples' debriefing conversations: The impact of gender, occupation, and demographic characteristics. *Family Relations, 42,* 149–157.

Vangelisti, A. L., & Crumley, L. P. (1998). Reactions to messages that hurt: The influence of relational contexts. *Communication Monographs, 65,* 173–196.

Vangelisti, A. L. & Gerstenberger, M. (2004). Communication and marital infidelity. In J. Duncombe, K. Harrison, G. Allan, & D. Marsden (Eds.), *The state of affairs: Explorations in infidelity and commitment* (pp. 59–78). Mahwah, NJ: Erlbaum.

Vangelisti, A. L., & Young, S. L. (2000). When words hurt: The effects of perceived intentionality on interpersonal relationships. *Journal of Social and Personal Relationships, 17,* 393–424.

# References

Vangelisti, A. L., Young, S. L., Carpenter-Theune, K. E., & Alexander, A. L. (2005). Why does it hurt? The perceived causes of hurt feelings. *Communication Research, 32*, 443–477.

VanLaningham, J., Johnson, D. R., & Amato, P. (2001). Marital happiness, marital duration, and the U-shaped curve: Evidence from a five-wave panel study. *Social Forces, 79*, 1313–1341.

Veroff, J., Douvan, E., Orbuch, T. L., & Acitelli, L. K. (1998). Happiness in stable marriages: The early years. In T. Bradbury (Ed.), *The developmental course of marital dysfunction* (pp. 152–179). Cambridge: Cambridge University Press.

Visher, E. B., & Visher, J. S. (1998). Stepparents: The forgotten family members. *Family & Conciliation Courts Review, 36*, 444–451.

Waite, L. J., & Gallagher, M. (2000). *The case for marriage.* New York: Broadway Books.

Waldron, V. R., & Kelley, D. L. (2005). Forgiveness as a response to relational transgression. *Journal of Personality and Social Psychology, 22*, 723–742.

Waldron, V. R., & Kelley, D. L. (2008). *Communicating forgiveness.* Thousand Oaks, CA: Sage.

Waldron, V. R., & Kelley, D. L. (2009). *Marriage at midlife.* New York: Springer-Verlag.

Walsh, F. (2003). Family resilience: Strengths forged through adversity. In F. Walsh (Ed.), *Normal family processes: Growing diversity and complexity* (3rd ed., pp. 399–423). New York: Guilford Press.

Walsh, F. (2005). Families in later life: Challenges and opportunities. In B. Carter & M. McGoldrick (Eds.), *The expanded family life cycle: Individual, family, and social perspectives* (3rd ed., pp. 307–326). Boston: Allyn and Bacon.

Walster, E., Berscheid, E., & Walster, G. W. (1973). New directions in equity research. *Journal of Personality and Social Psychology, 25*, 151–176.

Walster, E., & Walster, G. W. (1978). *A new look at love.* Reading, MA: Addison-Wesley.

Walster, E., Walster, G. W., & Berscheid, E. (1978). *Equity: Theory and research.* Boston: Allyn and Bacon.

Watzlawick, P., Beavin, J. H., & Jackson, D. D. (1967). *Pragmatics of human communication.* New York: Norton.

Weger, H. (2005). Disconfirming communication and self-verification in marriage: Associations among the demand/withdraw interaction pattern, feeling understood, and marital satisfaction. *Journal of Social and Personal Relationships, 22*, 19–31.

Weigel, D. J., & Ballard-Reisch, D. (2001). The impact of relational maintenance behaviors on marital satisfaction: A longitudinal analysis. *Journal of Family Communication, 1*, 265–279.

Weigel, D. J., & Ballard-Reisch, D. (2008). Relational maintenance, satisfaction, and commitment in marriages: An actor–partner analysis. *Journal of Family Communication, 8*, 212–229.

# References

White, L., & Edwards, J. N. (1990). Emptying the nest and parental well-being: An analysis of national panel data. *American Sociological Review*, 55, 235–242.

Whitton, S. W., Stanley, S. M., & Markman, H. J. (2007). If I help my partner will it hurt me? Perceptions of sacrifice in close relationships. *Journal of Social and Clinical Psychology*, 26, 64–92.

Wiederman, M. W. (1997). Extramarital sex: Prevalence and correlates in a national survey. *Journal of Sex Research*, 34, 167–174.

Wieselquist, J., Rusbult, C. E., Foster, C. A., & Agnew, C. R. (1999). Commitment, pro-relationship behavior, and trust in close relationships. *Journal of Personality and Social Psychology*, 77, 942–966.

Williams, K. (2003). Has the future of marriage arrived? A contemporary examination of gender, marriage, and psychological well-being. *Journal of Health and Social Behavior*, 44, 470–487.

Wilson, M., & Daly, M. (2001). The evolutionary psychology of couple conflict in registered versus de facto marital unions. In A. Booth, A. C. Crouter, & M. Clements (Eds.), *Couples in conflict* (pp. 3–26). Mahwah, NJ: Erlbaum.

Wolin, S. J., & Bennett, L. A. (1984). Family rituals. *Family Process*, 23, 401–420.

Worthington, E. L., Jr. (1998). *Dimensions of forgiveness: Psychological research & theological perspectives*. Philadelphia, PA: Templeton Foundation Press.

Worthington, E. L., Jr. (2001). Unforgiveness, forgiveness, and reconciliation and their implications for societal interventions. In R. G. Helmick, S. J. & R. L. Petersen (Eds.), *Forgiveness and reconciliation* (pp. 171–192). Philadelphia, PA: Templeton Foundation Press.

Worthington, E. L., Jr., & Drinkard, D. T. (2000). Promoting reconciliation through psychoeducational and therapeutic interventions. *Journal of Marital and Family Therapy*, 26, 93–101.

Worthington, E. L., Jr., Lerner, A. J., & Sharp, C. B. (2005). Repairing the emotional bond: Marriage research from 1997 through early 2005. *Journal of Psychology and Christianity*, 24, 259–262.

Wunderer, E., & Schneewind, K. A. (2008). The relationship between marital standards, dyadic coping and marital satisfaction. *European Journal of Social Psychology*, 38, 462–476.

Xiaohe, X., & Whyte, M. K. (1990). Love matches and arranged marriages: A Chinese replication. *Journal of Marriage and Family*, 52, 709–722.

Xu, X., Hudspeth, C. D., & Estes, S. (1997). The effects of husbands' involvement in child rearing activities and participation in household labor on marital quality: A racial comparison. *Journal of Gender, Culture, and Health*, 2, 187–210.

Yela, C. (2006). The evaluation of love: Simplified version of the scales for Yela's tetrangular model based on Sternberg's model. *European Journal of Psychological Assessment*, 22, 21–27.

# References

Yelsma, P. (1984). Functional conflict management in effective marital adjustment. *Communication Quarterly, 32,* 56–61.

Yerkes, R., & Dodson, J. (1908). The relation of strength of stimuli to rapidity of habit-information. *Journal of Comparative Neurology and Psychology, 18,* 459–482.

Zebrowitz, L. A., Brownlow, S., & Olson, K. (1992). Baby talk to the babyfaced. *Journal of Nonverbal Behavior, 16,* 143–158.

# Author index

Ainsworth, M. D. S., 80
Alberts, J. K., 114
Allan, G., 176–8, 185
Allemand, M., 186
Allred, K. G., 111
Altman, I., 71
Amberg, I., 186
Anderson, K. L., 174
Ansell, E., 163

Bachman, G. F., 186
Bailey, T. C., 30
Bakhtin, M. M., 40
Barnett, L. R., 32
Baucom, D. H., 179, 191
Baxter, L. A., 5, 39, 40, 43, 132, 155, 156, 167, 180, 181
Beach, S. R. H., 97, 182
Berscheid, E., 22, 79
Billingsley, J., 48, 50
Birditt, K. S., 47
Blacker, L., 150
Blehar, M. C., 80
Bochner, A. P., 32, 154
Bowlby, J., 80
Bradbury, T. N., 49, 56
Braithwaite, D. O., 5, 10, 132, 155, 156
Bruess, C. J. S., 72, 133

Buck, R., 118
Burgoon, J. K., 23, 24, 63, 66–8, 99, 163
Burleson, B. R., 103
Burpee, L. C., 17, 22

Cahn, D. D., 93
Canary, D. J., 33, 35, 38, 41, 43, 44, 53, 104, 124, 125, 183
Carstensen, L. L., 31, 72
Carter, B., 129, 131, 137, 144, 146, 154
Caughlin, J. P., 64, 95
Chmielewski, T. L., 32
Christopher, F. S., 173, 174
Cissna, K. N., 154
Clark, M. S., 144
Clements, M. L., 12, 85
Cobb, R. J., 140
Cohan, C. L., 49
Coleman, M., 155
Coleman, P. T., 112
Comstock, J., 75
Conville, R. L., 132, 134, 135
Cowan, C. P., 46, 48, 49, 143, 144, 153
Cowan, P. A., 46, 48, 49, 143, 153
Cox, D. E., 154
Cramer, D., 74

Author index

Crouter, A. C., 33
Cupach, W. R., 75, 166, 167, 175, 182

Dailey, R. M., 170
Dainton, M., 72
Davila, J., 185
Davis, J. L., 34
Davis, K. E., 81
Davis, M. S., 39
Denton, W. H., 103
Dickson, F. C., 151
Dindia, K., 39, 43, 180, 181
Dollahite, D. C., 119
Domschke, T. J., 36, 103
Dormor, D. J., 72
Doss, B. D., 140, 141, 153
Driver, J. L., 27, 120
Duck, S., 27

Evans, K., 163

Feeney, J. A., 81, 163, 164, 177
Fehr, B., 62, 68, 69, 77, 78, 84–6
Feldman, C. M., 171, 173, 174
Fincham, F. D., 77, 97, 182, 185, 186
Fingerman, K. L., 47, 147, 149
Finkel, E. J., 166
Fitzpatrick, M. A., 22, 42, 50, 51, 71,
   72, 105, 106, 107
Floyd, K., 74
Frankl, V. E., 27
Frieze, I. H., 80

Glenn, N. D., 30
Golish, T. D., 156
Gonso, J., 122
Gordon, K. C., 177, 179, 191, 192
Gottman, J. M., 18, 20, 21, 27, 28, 30,
   31, 36, 41, 42, 48, 50, 53, 56, 69,
   72, 76, 77, 98, 105, 107, 110, 113,
   114, 115, 116, 122, 124, 125, 172
Greeff, A. P., 36
Grote, N. K., 80, 144

Guerrero, L. K., 74, 113, 117, 124,
   186

Hale, J. L., 63, 99, 163
Hannon, P. A., 34, 166
Hanzal, A., 36, 103, 105
Hargrave, T. D., 192
Harvey, J., 97, 184
Harrison, K., 176–8, 185
Hatfield, E., 79
Hazan, C., 81
Hendrick, C., 79, 80
Hendrick, S. S., 79, 80
Hollander, E. P., 4
Holmes, E. K., 143–5
Holmes, J. G., 88
Horwitz, A. V., 13
Huston, T. L., 143–5

Imber-Black, E., 133, 134
Izquierdo, C., 56

Jacob, T., 33

Kachadourian, L. K., 185
Kantor, D., 51
Kaplan, R. E., 38
Karremans, J. C., 186
Keeley, M. P., 193
Kellermann, K., 15
Kelley, D. L., 4, 10, 32, 34, 52, 60,
   61, 63, 67, 85, 94, 99, 129, 146–8,
   151, 157, 167, 168, 181, 182,
   184–6, 189–91, 193–5
Kelley, H. H., 63
Kerber, K. B., 111
Klein, W., 56
Kluwer, E. S., 186
Krokoff, L. J., 50
Krueger, D. L., 32

La Valley, A. G., 113, 117, 124
Lakey, S. G., 104, 124, 125

232

Lambert, N. M., 119
Langan, C. J., 4
Langer, E. J., 14, 15, 17, 22
Laurenceau, J.-P., 12, 76
Lawrence, E., 140
Lazarus, R. S., 118
Leary, M. R., 163
Leder, S., 163
Lee, C. M., 170
Lee, J. A., 80, 81
Lee, Y. S., 54
Leeds-Hurwitz, W., 7
Lehr, W., 51
Levenson, R. W., 31, 41, 72
Levy, M. B., 81
Lewis, J. M., 181
Lewis, S. A., 4
Lloyd, S. A., 173, 174

Mace, D. R., 122
Mace, V. C., 122
Malherbe, H. L., 36
Mansfield, P., 72
Markman, H. J, 12, 85, 88, 97, 110
Marshall, L. L., 169, 171
McAllister, F. M., 72
McBride, M. C., 10
McCarthy, B., 75
McDonald, G. W., 111
McGoldrick, M., 129, 131, 137, 138, 144, 146, 154
Metts, S., 166, 167, 168, 182
Miller, R. B., 141
Montgomery, M. J., 80
Motley, M. T., 14

Navran, L., 31, 32
Naylor, K. E., 144
Negel, L., 163
Nicholson, J. H., 155
Nielsen, M. R., 54, 73
Nietzel, M. T., 32
Noller, P., 79, 81, 86, 88, 112, 118

Norton, R., 29
Notarius, C. I., 97, 110, 122
Nussbaum, J., 47
Nylen, K., 140

O'Hair, D., 193
Olsen, N., 34
Olson, D. H., 123, 135
Olson, L. N., 156
Ouwerkerk, J. W., 186

Paleari, F. G., 190
Papernow, P. L., 155
Parkman, A. M., 72
Parrott, R., 67
Pasupathi, M., 31
Patrick, S., 36
Patterson, B., 193
Pearson, J. C., 72, 133
Perlman, D., 62, 68, 69, 77
Perry-Jenkins, M., 33, 54
Petronio, S., 62, 64, 67, 68, 71, 76, 78
Pickering, J., 89
Pienta, A. M., 11
Poole, M. S., 48, 50
Prager, K. J., 62, 63, 68, 69, 76

Ragsdale, J. D., 43
Rempel, J. K., 88
Rhoades, G. K., 138
Ridley, C. A., 171, 173, 174
Rubin, Z., 79, 80
Rusbult, C. E., 34, 78, 166, 167, 182, 193

Sabatelli, R. M., 28
Sabourin, T. C., 172, 173
Sandberg, J. G., 141
Sanford, K., 77, 97, 112, 118, 119
Schrodt, P., 10
Segrin, C., 36, 103, 105
Shaver, P., 81

# Author index

Silberstein, L. R., 53, 55, 56, 73, 144, 145
Snyder, C. R., 30
Sorell, G. T., 80
Soukup, C., 156
Spanier, G. B., 29
Spitzberg, B. H., 95, 169, 170, 175, 176
Springer, C., 163
Stafford, L., 31, 33, 35, 38, 41, 43, 44, 53, 72, 183
Stamp, G. H., 4, 142, 172, 173
Stanley, S. M., 85, 88, 89, 123, 128, 138, 182
Stocker, S. L., 166

Taylor, D. A., 71
Turman, P., 156

Van Lange, P. A., 186
Vangelisti, A. L., 95, 163, 165

Waldron, V. R., 147, 148, 151, 157, 168, 179, 182, 184, 185, 186, 191, 194, 195
Wall, S., 80
Walsh, F., 158
Walster, E., 79
Waters, E., 80
White, M. B., 141
Worthington, E. L, Jr., 192, 194, 195

Yorgason, J. B., 141

Zimprich, D., 186

# Subject index

abuse, 169–74, 196
  and arousal, 171–2
  and communication, 172–3
  batterers, types of, 172, 174
  effects, 97, 174–5
  emotional abuse, 170
  physical abuse, 169, 171
  psychological abuse, 116, 170–1,
    174, 175
  substance abuse, 168, 172
  verbal aggression, 81, 168, 171,
    173
  violence, 37, 119, 169–75
  see also aggression, violence
Access and Affect Model of Intimacy,
    67–77, 91
  access, 65–77, 87–91, 178
  affect, 20, 31, 69–70, 77, 87, 91,
    99, 102, 104–5, 108, 114, 117,
    118, 121, 124
adaptability, 19, 56, 135, 145, 146,
    151, 157, 159
affair, 67, 98, 161, 176–9, 185, 192
  see also extramarital sex or
    relationship
aggression, 81, 82, 169, 171, 173,
    196
  common couple violence, 170
  communicative, 168, 170

expressive/instrumental, 170, 171
patriarchal terrorism, 170
  see also abuse, violence
aging, 146, 149, 150–2, 159
  see also centerstage couples
apology, 167, 188–90
approaches to marital communication
    research, 6
arousal, 21–2, 24, 25, 32, 78, 103,
    112–19, 120, 124, 126, 154,
    166, 171–2
  and mindlessness, 21–2, 113–19,
    154
  management, 120
  sex, 74
attachment, 74, 79, 80–2, 89, 91, 95,
    119, 164, 178
Attachment Theory, 78, 80, 164
attribution, 4, 110–11, 114, 171, 173
autonomy, 39–41, 51–8, 67–8, 107,
    142–3, 167

baby talk, 74
balance, 22, 40, 50, 59, 65, 69, 88,
    107–8, 125, 134–5, 139, 141,
    144, 159, 183
  balanced couples (Gottman), 107–8
  balanced couples (Olson;
    Circumplex Model), 135

# Subject index

betrayal, 34, 87, 168–9, 175–9, 196–7
blended families, 48, 154–7, 159
  adoptive families, 156–7, 159
  remarried couples, 48, 154–7, 159

centerstage couples, 147–50, 158–9
childcare, 53, 134, 139, 141, 143–5, 149, 185,
childless couples, 152–4, 157
children, 3, 9–10, 13, 25, 29, 32, 46–8, 53, 88, 96–8, 129–33, 135–57, 159, 177–8, 184
  adolescents, 130, 145–6, 159
  boomerang children, 47, 153
  couple communication effects, 141–5
cohabitation, 1, 31, 138
cohesion, 52, 63, 135
commitment, 4, 7–9, 25, 41–2, 52, 55, 82–92, 120, 122–3, 136, 139, 148, 151, 168, 178, 193, 197
  prototype model, 84–5
  public, 7–8, 136, 139
  and love
    Fehr (prototype model), 84–5
    Kelley (model of "Full" love), 85–9
    Sternberg (Triangular Theory of Love), 82–3
Communication Privacy Management, theory of, 64–6
conflict, 6–7, 10–11, 19–20, 25, 31, 36–7, 46, 51–3, 56, 58, 73, 77, 82, 93–127, 131, 137, 140–1, 143, 146, 149, 151, 153, 155–6, 158–60, 168, 170–1, 173, 181, 193
  arousal, 112–17, 120, 171–2
  Competence-Based Model of Interpersonal Conflict, 95–6

couple types, 105–8
  emotion, 117–19
  Four Horsemen of the Apocalypse, 114–17
  mindlessness, 19, 113–19, 121
  prescriptive approaches, 122–5
  religiosity, 119
  and satisfaction, 36–7
  sequences, 103–5
  styles, 101–3
  topics, 10–11, 97–8
  types of problems, 98–9
content level of meaning, 95, 99–101, 106, 126, 172
context, 3–11, 13, 15, 17, 20, 25, 33, 48, 63–4, 70, 73, 78, 89, 96, 99, 103, 119, 122, 129, 132, 134, 140, 163, 179, 182, 184–5, 196
  relational, 3–9, 182,
  social, 9–11, 129, 132, 140
control, 13, 15–16, 48–50, 53–4, 65–6, 97, 100, 106, 112, 114, 118, 123–4, 127, 142, 149, 169–70, 172, 174, 179, 192, 196
  abuse, 169–72
  mutual, 53–4
  uncontrollable, 15–16, 114, 142, 172, 179
couple types
  Fitzpatrick, 42, 51–2, 71, 106–7
  Gottman, 107–8
happy/unhappy, 20, 31–2, 58, 69–70, 89, 92, 98–9, 103–4, 109–11, 123–6

dark communication, 37, 84, 162
decision making, 44–50, 56, 58, 95, 97, 139, 143, 150, 185
demand–withdraw pattern, 20, 36, 77, 103–5, 118–19, 134–5, 158, 173–4

# Subject index

dialectical tensions, 39–41, 43, 58,
64–6, 68, 91, 133–5, 154
dual-income couples, 54–7, 73, 134,
144–5, 159

emotion(s), 3–4, 11–12, 27, 32, 36,
38, 39, 42–3, 47–9, 53–5, 58,
61–3, 66, 75–7, 79–84, 89, 91,
116–19, 124–6, 139, 146–50,
152, 159–60, 164–5, 167–72,
177–8, 181, 183, 188–92,
194–7
conflict, 117–19, 124
decision making, 45–9
expression, 4, 32, 38, 42, 61, 63,
75–7, 89, 117, 124, 141
flooding, 108, 113–14, 120
hard/soft/flat emotions, 77, 107,
112, 118
and love, 79–88
emotional bonding (connection),
76–7, 79, 84–92, 108, 138–9,
162, 184, 194
emotional distance, 32, 34, 40, 51,
108, 116–17, 146, 173, 175
emotional injury, 163, 176, 179
emotional support, 55, 82, 86, 146,
149, 152
equity, 34–5, 44, 53–4, 58–9, 76, 85,
95, 169, 183, 193
extramarital sex or relationship, 97,
162, 185
see also affair, infidelity
expectations, 4, 8, 30, 36, 46, 50, 52,
55, 58–9, 63, 65, 67, 84–5, 95,
105, 123, 135, 137, 139–40,
142, 148, 153, 155–6, 159–60,
166, 168, 176, 185
long-term, 4
relational behavior, 4, 30, 32, 36,
50, 52, 63, 166, 168
roles, 4, 32–3, 55
and satisfaction, 4, 32–3

forgiveness, 34, 120, 147–8, 162,
167–8, 176, 179–97
models of
Gordon & Baucom, 191–2
Waldron & Kelley, 182–4,
186–91
tasks, 186–91
Four Horsemen of the Apocalypse,
114–17, 126

gender, 11–12, 33, 43–4, 55–6, 72,
76, 95, 100, 111–12, 131, 140,
144, 155, 170, 177–8
goals, 4–5 , 9, 23–5, 37, 44, 77, 95–6,
111–12, 118, 123, 126, 158,
170, 191

health, 4, 8, 11–13, 43, 47, 85, 129,
146, 152, 159, 175, 185
household chores/tasks, 10, 33, 42,
47, 52–6, 58, 134, 141, 143–5,
150, 185
hurt, 70, 87, 92, 109, 118–19, 152,
163–6, 169–71, 175, 177,
179–81, 183–5, 188, 192,
195–7

identity, 7, 48, 56, 67, 132–3, 137,
143, 147–8, 155, 159, 163,
168–9, 177–8, 184–5, 196
infertility, 152, 157
infidelity, 141, 163–6, 168–9, 175–9,
184–5, 196–7
see also affair
in-laws, 3, 9, 11–12, 25, 97–8, 137,
146
intent, 15–17, 38, 100–1, 103, 110,
113, 165, 169–71, 173, 179,
181, 196
interaction history, 4–5
interdependence, 9, 34, 51, 55, 62,
71–2, 77–8, 81, 89, 92, 95,
106, 142–3, 172, 174, 184

# Subject index

Interdependence Theory, 22, 167–8
intimacy, 8–10, 28, 32, 34, 36–7, 44,
  49–50, 58, 60–4, 66–83, 85–7,
  89–92, 97, 99, 107, 122, 131,
  133, 139, 141, 148, 150, 162,
  178, 191
  behaviors, 133
  and love, 85–7, 89–92
  marital satisfaction, 28, 32, 34,
    36–7, 50
models of
  Access and Affect Model, 68–78
  Interpersonal Process Model of
    Intimacy, 62
  Prager, 62–5
  and privacy, 64–7

leisure, 73, 141–2, 153
life cycle, 29–31, 47–8, 67, 128–60
  limitations to life cycle research,
    131
  marital satisfaction, 29–31
love, 2, 4, 27–8, 42, 60–1, 68, 77–92,
  130, 145, 151, 164, 166, 168,
  177, 184, 190, 194
  and intimacy, 60–1, 68, 77–8,
    86–9
  models of 78–84
    attachment, 80–2
    Fehr's Prototype Approach, 84–5
    Kelley's Model of "Full" Love,
      85–6
    love styles, 80
    Sternberg's Triangular Theory of
      Love, 82–4
  as story, 90
  see also commitment, emotional
    bonding, self-sacrifice

marital quality, 13, 28–37, 53, 57, 72,
  92, 141, 144
  see also satisfaction
marriage, definition of, 3

marriage effects, see health
maintenance, 9, 33–5, 37–44, 47, 52,
  57–9, 65, 72–3, 158, 180
  dialectical tensions, 39–41
  equity, 35
  gender, 43–4
  models of, 38–43
  routine, 38, 40, 43, 73, 133, 150
  satisfaction, 33–5
  strategic, 38
mercy, 182–3
middle age, 47, 72, 131, 146, 149,
  152
  see also centerstage couples
mindfulness, 15, 18, 22–5, 121, 124,
  126
mindlessness, 14–22, 25, 113–21,
  154
  and arousal, 21–2, 113–20, 154
  benefits, 17–19
  costs, 19
  responsibility, 15–17
morality, 162, 166, 168–9, 176, 179,
  181–5, 187–8, 191, 194–6
motives, 101, 109, 189

negative reciprocity (negativity), 20,
  31, 36–7, 58, 69, 77, 82,
  103–5, 108, 110, 116–17,
  126–7, 152–3, 172–3
  see also Access and Affect Model of
    Intimacy: affect

openness, 14, 33, 39–41, 44, 48, 50,
  58–9, 64, 66–8, 91, 119, 176,
  194
optimism, 39, 158–60, 172

parenthood, 30, 46, 48–9, 130–1,
  135, 138–45, 153, 159
partnership (partners), 1, 3, 9–10, 44,
  142
patriarchal terrorism, 170

perception(s), 4, 15, 20, 33–4, 37, 43, 50, 53–4, 57–8, 62, 65, 69, 71, 76–7, 88, 92, 95, 97–8, 103, 109–12, 125–6, 134, 137, 163–4, 170, 176, 183, 185, 188, 193–4, 197

power, 54, 77, 97, 111–12, 118, 124, 126, 162, 165, 169–71, 177, 185, 196

pregnancy, 46, 133, 139, 141, 149, 153, 178

privacy, 40, 61, 64–8, 91, 168
  and intimacy, 64, 66–8, 91
  models of
    Burgoon, 66–7
    Petronio, 64–6

problem solving, 45, 49, 56, 82, 101, 122–3, 125–6, 134, 156, 158–60, 173–4

problems, 8, 10–11, 12, 24, 41, 49–50, 97–9, 119, 129, 131, 137, 148, 153, 157, 172
  sexual, 8
  solvable/perpetual, 98–9
  substance abuse, 12

prototype, 84, 86, 166

reconciliation, 119–20, 156, 162, 167–8, 182, 184, 192–5, 197

regulated/unregulated couples, 107–8, 116

relational culture, 4–5, 7, 137

Relational Dialectics Theory, 40–1, 64, 66, 68

relationship covenant, 2, 85, 168–9, 176, 184, 191, 196

relationship level of meaning, 95, 99–101, 106, 126, 172

religiosity, 119–20

repair, 37–9, 116, 120, 180–2, 184, 196–7

resilience, 157–8, 175

responsiveness, 31, 62, 64, 76, 89, 91–2, 164

restoration, 67, 108, 161–2, 167–8, 179–82, 189, 191–7

retirement, 11, 129, 133, 146, 151, 159, 187

ritual(s), 4, 7, 43, 72–3, 132–4, 136–7, 156, 159–60, 173, 180

roles, 10, 30, 33, 43–4, 50, 52–9, 62, 94–5, 111, 126, 132–5, 137, 139, 143–5, 147, 149, 151–2, 154–5, 159

romance (romantic), 3, 8–9, 25, 41, 74, 77, 80–4, 136, 140, 142, 152, 163, 165, 167

rules, 65–6, 78, 133, 144, 163, 166–9, 175–6, 179, 183–5, 188, 191, 193–7

runaway conflict, 113–16, 126, 171

satisfaction, 4, 11–2, 20, 28–37, 41, 43–4, 46, 49–50, 52–3, 55–6, 58–9, 63, 73–7, 80, 89, 96–8, 103–5, 110, 125–6, 130–1, 135, 138–41, 143–6, 150–2, 167, 174–5, 178, 185–6, 196
  across the life cycle, 29–31, 130–1, 135, 138–41, 143–6, 150–2
  assessment, 28–9
  conflict, 36–7, 56, 96–8, 103–5, 125–6
  daily interaction, 31–2
  expectations, 4, 32–3, 50, 63
  gender, 12, 44, 53
  relational maintenance, 33–5
  intimacy, 34, 36, 50, 63, 73–7
  *see also* couple types: happy/ unhappy

security, 8, 13, 79, 88, 135–6, 159, 164, 172

self-disclosure, 51–2, 61–4, 70–1, 75–6, 91

self-sacrifice, 84, 86, 89, 128

# Subject index

sense making, 179, 188–9, 192, 194, 196

sex (sexual, sexually), 8, 12, 33, 36, 54–5, 61, 64, 67, 74–5, 79, 82–3, 85–6, 89, 91, 97, 131, 138–9, 151–2, 164, 168, 176–8, 185, 196–7

skill deficit, 173–4

stress, 10–11, 54, 74–5, 95, 97–8, 106, 109, 111, 131, 133, 135, 139, 142, 145–6, 149–50, 152–3, 155–6, 168

trauma, 97, 135, 158, 168, 175, 177, 184, 192, 196

Theory of Communication Privacy Management, 64–6

collective boundaries, 66, 91

transgressions, 163–4, 166–9, 177, 179, 184–5, 190, 193, 196–7

transition

for couples, 30, 46, 49, 58, 129–36, 138–43, 146–9, 153–7, 159–60

forgiveness task, 188, 191, 195

Triangular Theory of Love, 78, 82, 84

*see also* love

trust, 1, 32, 36–7, 63, 88, 122, 128–9, 151, 176–7, 179, 185, 188, 191–3, 195, 197

violence, 37, 119, 141, 169–75, 196

*see also* abuse, aggression

wedding(s), 2, 4, 5, 7, 9, 132, 134, 136–7, 139, 185